Images of Animals

In the series

ANIMALS, CULTURE, AND SOCIETY,
edited by Clinton R. Sanders and Arnold Arluke

Images of Animals

Anthropomorphism and Animal Mind

EILEEN CRIST

TEMPLE UNIVERSITY PRESS
Philadelphia

Temple University Press, Philadelphia 19122
Copyright © 1999 by Eileen Crist.
All rights reserved
First Published 1999
Paperback edition published 2000
Printed in the United States of America

⊗ The paper used in this publication meets the requirements of
American National Standard for Information Sciences—Permanence
of Paper for Printed Library Materials, ANSI Z39.48-1984

Library of Congress Cataloging-in-Publication Data

Crist, Eileen, 1961–
    Images of animals : anthropomorphism and animal mind / Eileen
Crist.
        p.   cm. — (Animals, culture, and society)
    Includes bibliographical references (p.   ) and index.
    ISBN 1-56639-656-5 (cl)   ISBN 1-56639-788-X (pb)
    1. Animal behavior.   2. Animal intelligence.   3. Anthropomorphism.
I. Title.   II. Series.
QL751.C8824 1998
591.5—dc21   98-19425
                                                                   CIP

For my family, Despina Lala-Crist, Robert Crist, and Ray Crist
with gratitude and love

I have seen Swallows play a wonderfully graceful game of catching a feather. It was one August afternoon when I was sitting at the top of a steeply sloping farm field in the uplands of Devon, that I noticed more Swallows than usual were wheeling close together over one part of the field, presumably an abundance of flies on the hot, sunny day being the cause. Ducks and Geese roamed in this field and the grass was sprinkled with a few white breast feathers. I then saw a Swallow dip to the ground and sweep upwards with one of these feathers held in his beak and, circling above the other Swallows, he let it fall. As it floated down it was caught by one of the wheeling birds who then rose above the rest and again the feather was let loose, to float down through the many circling Swallows. This time it nearly reached the earth, then one bird swept down with graceful dip and flicker of wings, rising aloft with the feather, to drop it once more. Sometimes their wayward toy would fall uncaught, perhaps too worn for further use; then quickly a bird swooped to the grass, seized another feather while on the wing and the play continued as before. It was a beautiful game to watch in the setting of hills, with a background of wild moorland and far away the blue haze of distant sea meeting the deeper blue sky.

LEN HOWARD

Contents

List of Illustrations

Acknowledgments

I WOULD like to thank Arnold Arluke for inviting me to submit this work as part of the series Animals, Culture, and Society, published by Temple University Press. I also thank Marc Bekoff, whose careful, critical reading of the original version was invaluable for the process of rewriting. I thank Chip Burkhardt for bringing to my attention in a summer 1988 seminar at Woods Hole many of the writings I examine in this work. I'd like to express my appreciation to Donald Griffin for his bold books and for our conversations on the topic of animal mind.

The final version of this work was completed in the Department of Science and Technology Studies at Cornell University during my postdoctoral fellowship there. I would like to thank all my friends and colleagues at Cornell for providing a wonderful environment within which to work. In particular, I would like to thank John Carson, Charis Cussins, Adrian Cussins, Michael Dennis, Trevor Pinch, and Sheila Jasanoff for their close support. I would also like to express my gratitude to the Science Studies Program of the University of California at San Diego, where I began to rework my dissertation into this book as a postdoctoral fellow. In particular, I'd like to acknowledge the intellectual presence of Steven Shapin and Shirley Strum.

This book grew out of my dissertation work in the Sociology Department at Boston University. I thank my colleagues at Boston University during that period; their intellectual and personal support are the basis of this book. In particular, I'd like to thank David Bogen, Lynn Margulis, George Psathas, and Fred Tauber. Jeff Coulter's writings and seminars on ethnomethodology and the thought of Ludwig Wittgenstein opened new intellectual horizons for me; my indebtedness to his instruction is evident throughout this work. I would like to express my appreciation to Fred Wasserman, whose course on animal behavior was the inspiration for my dissertation topic. I must also acknowledge Tim Costelloe for our home in Boston and for his critical reading of many different drafts. Above all, I thank Michael Lynch, my advisor, mentor, and friend; without his unwavering support, in every way, this work would not have been possible.

Images of Animals

Introduction

The Significance of Language in Portraying Animals

A TENSION is built into the pursuit of knowledge about animal life, for it is heir to both the Cartesian verdict of an unbridgeable hiatus between humans and animals and the Darwinian affirmation of evolutionary continuity. The consequence of an intellectual and cultural heritage of opposed visions of the relationship between animals and humans is that the problematic of animal mind—whether affirmed or refuted, celebrated or doubted, qualified or sidestepped—is ever present, perhaps even the heart of the matter, in behavioral writings. Representations of animal life, whether intentionally or not, are always addressing what is for Western thought a most engrossing mystery—the contentious topic of animal mind or animal consciousness. In this book I address the theme of animal mind through a comparative study of representations of animals in behavioral works. Specifically, I examine the understanding of animal life in behavioral thought, from the writings of Charles Darwin and turn-of-the-century naturalists to works of classical ethology and contemporary sociobiology.

My focus is on the powerful role that language use plays in the portrayal of animals. Even a casual examination of different writings reveals that language, far from being simply a useful, neutral tool for inquiry, plays a formative part in how animals are depicted. While the different works I examine are kindred in their focus on naturally occurring animal behavior, they represent animal life in very discrepant ways.[1] My aim is to elucidate how different portraitures of animals are created. The works I study belong to the genre of behavioral science, in that the authors examined all share the ideal of discovering the realities of the natural lives of animals. It is paradoxical, then, that while they have this common goal of arriving at faithful representations of animals—documenting with great care their life histories, habits, and instincts—they nevertheless often reveal realities that are worlds apart. I approach this paradox of striking

1

discrepancies in the portrayal of animals by focusing on the effects of diverse linguistic mediums. In looking at different works of behavioral science, I set aside the ordinary connotation of "science" as a guarantee of "objectivity." The question of objectivity in the depiction of animal life is precisely what becomes a quandary upon comparative examination of representations that reflect divergent understandings of animals. Therefore I do not take for granted either the objectivity or the ostensible lack thereof of any particular form of reasoning, method, or theory, but instead, through a comparative approach, I make the very question of objectivity in the understanding of animals the central theme of this work.

A point of entry into the paradox of nonequivalent yet faithful representations is the observation that knowledge of animal life can be rendered in either ordinary or technical language. The ordinary language of action is largely the everyday language of human affairs, while technical language introduces a specially defined, often highly theoretical terminology. These linguistic mediums lead down very different paths of understanding animal life. In virtue of its affiliation with everyday reasoning about human action, the use of the ordinary language of action reflects a regard for animals as acting *subjects;* the immanent, experiential perspective of animals is treated as real, recoverable, and invaluable in the understanding of their actions and lives. Technical language, on the other hand, paves the way toward conceptualizing animals as natural *objects;* animals are constituted as objects in an epistemological sense, through conceptions that are extrinsic to their phenomenal world of experience. The epistemological constitution of animals as objects is agnostic and often inimical toward the idea that animals have an experiential perspective. Technical language construes such a perspective as irrelevant to scientific knowledge about animal behavior. Focus on the discrepant consequences of ordinary language vis-à-vis technical terminology opens a way to appreciate the powerful, formative role of language use in the portrayal of animal life. These mediums are affiliated with different epistemological conceptions of the inquiry into animal behavior.

The distinction between ordinary and technical mediums thus serves as a starting point for examining differences in imagery and knowledge of animals. It must be emphasized, however, that the two linguistic domains are neither insular nor discontinuous. Their juxtaposition is useful as a first approximation for addressing what is unique and intriguing about knowledge of animal life: that similar behaviors can be represented in ways that produce extremely different effects on the reader's understanding. To elucidate *how* dissonant portrayals of animals are produced, I focus on the work of language, such as uses of concepts and grammar, sentence construction, modes of description, logic of explanation, qualifying devices, and rhetorical strategies. The divergent uses of language of behavioral texts may be likened to maps with which the reader navigates through landscapes of animal life. Though the focus of my analysis is on language use, in spirit this work does not side with the so-called linguistic turn, or with the notion that "everything is text." The guiding interest is always in the places that the reader is taken with animal behavioral writings. For this reason, my emphasis throughout is on *seeing,* on how language is a medium of travel for the reader to look upon animal life.

The philosopher Peter Winch has drawn a useful distinction between "internal" and "external" depictions of phenomena. Winch argues that there is a sharp divergence between accounts of human behavior and natural phenomena: while conceptual formulations are internal to human action, they are external to natural phenomena. He points out, for example, that the concept of "war" is internal to human behavior, for persons act in ways that accord with, and are logically connected to, their knowledge that their country is at war. "The concept of war," he writes, "belongs *essentially* to . . . behavior" (1958: 128). Meaning, then, is internal to human conduct, being constitutive of the production, form, and reception of action in specific circumstances. As a contrast to the idea of "war," Winch gives the example of the physicist's concept of "gravity," which does not belong essentially to the behavior of a falling apple, but "belongs rather to the physicist's *explanation* of the apple's behavior" (ibid.).

Winch's point is that whereas concepts are internal to (or constitutive of) human action, the meaning of natural phenomena is supplied extrinsically, through the observer's framework of understanding. Concepts are part and parcel of human engagements, while they are contingently connected to the behavior of natural objects. To borrow Winch's example of war once again, the meaning of persons' actions is bound together with their understanding that their country is at war and with their evaluation of what that demands and signifies in terms of courses of action and moral obligations. This understanding of the internal connection between the concept "war" and how people act and think encompasses soldiers and pacifists, protesters and patriots, civilians, prisoners of war, and even children old enough to speak a language.

On the other hand, to say that the meaning of natural phenomena is supplied extrinsically is not to underestimate the explanatory or descriptive power of concepts of natural science. Winch's claim that such concepts do not "belong essentially" to their referents means that the sense of conceptual formulations derives from their place within theoretical frameworks and from the logical connections between statements and concepts within such frameworks. Thus "gravity" is external (or contingently related) to the behavior of falling objects in the following sense: it is conceivable that within the framework of a better theory—by whatever criteria of "better," for example, parsimony, general explanatory scope, affinity with other theories, or resonance with new knowledge—the concept of gravity may be superseded by a different (set of) notion(s) in the description of the behavior of falling objects.

Winch's distinction between internal and external conceptual formulations, between immanently meaningful and intrinsically meaningless phenomena, is useful in clarifying a fundamental starting point of this work: that knowledge of animal behavior can be formulated, through alternative uses of language, to fall on either side of this division. Grasped in the ordinary language of action, knowledge of animal behavior is oriented toward the behavior's intrinsic meaning, including the subjective experience in (and of) the world that the behavior expresses and embodies. Mediated through technical terms, on the other hand, the understanding of animal behavior becomes largely conceptually equivalent with knowledge of natural-type, intrinsically meaningless phenomena.

The vernacular of action is the everyday language of human action. In using this language in accounts of animal action, certain dimensions of its logic in regard to human action become assembled in the case of animals as well. Broadly speaking, the features assembled through ordinary concepts and reasoning are those of action as *meaningful, authored,* and *continuous,* which together deliver subjectivity to the world of animals. The idea of "meaningfulness" conveys that, within their world, actors experience objects and events, as well as actions and relations, as phenomena imbued with import and repercussions. "Authorship" imparts that actors have the power to bring about, or refrain from bringing about, events in their world, as a matter of agency and will. "Continuity" signifies that actions—whether of single or interacting animals—are coherently connected, dovetailing into one another in the stream of living. The inclusion of the dimensions of meaningfulness, authorship, and continuity is the gateway to a landscape that has the forms and ambiance of subjectivity, for to be a subject means to experience the world as a meaningful place, rather than merely existing in it; to accomplish actions, rather than sleepwalking through them; and to live in the flow of a temporally extended space rather than in disconnected pockets of time. Through close attention to particular writings, specifically those of Charles Darwin and certain naturalists, I argue that a diffuse background of subjectivity allows for the implicit or explicit emergence of animal mind. To put it somewhat simplistically but straightforwardly, in Darwin's and the naturalists' representation of animals subjectivity comes first, and then the tacit or direct ascription of mental predicates, *naturally*, supervenes.

The link, on the other hand, between the use of a technical idiom and the portrayal of animals as objects can be elucidated with Winch's notion of external representation. The terms employed derive their meanings from the observer's framework. Technical terms cannot be understood as connecting to the animals' phenomenal world, for they are alien to any possible experience or perspective of animals. While the ordinary language of action, in its common application to animals and humans, brings the two worlds into alignment, a technical language sustains distance between them, since extrinsic technical terms are semantically foreign to a lived experiential perspective on events and actions. Examples of technical terms are "stimulus-response," from behaviorism; "innate releasing mechanism," from classical ethology; and "maximizing fitness," from sociobiology. The meaning of such concepts is procured from theoretical frameworks that dictate their appropriate applications and logical interconnections with other concepts. Technical terms are not only alien to an experiential perspective, but causally implicated in the production of behavior. What I show through analysis of certain writings is that the deployment of a technical and causal language leads to the portrayal of animals as objects. A logical entailment of this language is that animals appear blind to the meaning and significance of their activities and interactions, and the production of their behaviors is depicted as determined by forces beyond their control and comprehension. Under the auspices of technical idioms, behavior comes through as something that happens to an animal, rather than an active accomplishment. Supervenient upon such a representation of behavior is the foreclosure of animal mind.

The deployment of the ordinary language of action or of technical terminologies has significant consequences for the overall view on animal life that is created. For preliminary purposes, the discrepancy of effect can be glossed by the contrast between animals as "acting subjects" and "natural objects." Animals as subjects emerge in virtue of their portrayal as actors initiating and directing action and living in a world where events and objects are meaningful and temporally continuous. Animals as objects emerge in virtue of their portrayal as entities through or upon which inexorable forces act, steering them to behave in certain ways. The disjointed imagery of animals as subjects and objects, affiliated with the diverse import of different language uses, is intimately connected with the problematic of animal mentality. In this investigation I endeavor to make explicit the relationship between the language of representing animals and the revelation or occlusion of animal mind. I propose that the divergent portrayals of animals as subjects, on the one hand, and as objects, on the other, form the conceptual foundations that, respectively, allow the emergence of animal mentality or prescind its very possibility. I substantiate this argument through close, comparative exegeses of various writings on animals.

The presentation of subjectivity emerges through, and rests upon, lexical elements, grammatical constructs, and patterns of reasoning that are *prior to* the ascription of mentality. Lexical elements are prior in the sense of forming a conceptual ecology within which the (direct or tacit) predication of mental phenomena can have realistic force—that is, be credible, visualizable, appropriate, or necessary. In other words, a fundamental consequence of the use of the vernacular of action is to render the animal world immanently meaningful; in turn, this affords the possibility of assigning, or creates an atmosphere that can carry within it, the compelling presentation of inner life. Analogously, the picture of animals as objects is composed through lexical elements, grammatical constructs, and patterns of reasoning that are logically *prior to* a suspicious or inimical stance toward animal mind. These elements create the conceptual milieu within which the (direct or tacit) negation or doubt of animal mind can take the form of a rational or judicious stance. I explore this by examining the forms of discourse that acknowledge or deny the witnessability of inner life. Given that from a human vantage point only a subject can experience feelings, have thoughts, and act on the basis of intentions, when the methods of representation deliver animals as subjects, then inner life can surface as a natural facet of the behavioral scenery, that is, as a viewable aspect. On the other hand, when the methods of representation portray animals as objects, a view of inner life becomes blocked.

The necessity of establishing a conceptual home that is prior to affirming or denying the existence of animal mind is entailed by the fact that mentality is not something that can simply be either attributed or denied to animals. Instead, extensive groundwork must be in place before animal mind can be disclosed in a compelling fashion, or be foreclosed, not by fiat, but again in a way that appears credible and nondogmatic. In short, the status of mental life can be neither legislated by simple proclamations nor settled by appeal to indisputable evidence. Conceptual environments need to be created and elaborated within which mental ascriptions can have a realistic grip, or within which the success of such ascriptions is defeated, again in some reasonable manner.

In Chapters 1 and 2, I focus on Charles Darwin and the naturalists George and Elizabeth Peckham and Jean Henri Fabre. Their language of representation embodies a way of knowing animals that affirms a most powerful alignment between human and animal worlds. The tropes of this alignment have often incited the label "anthropomorphism." The idea of anthropomorphism has no precise definition; its meaning is tied almost strictly to its aspersive connotations, for it suggests a manner of representation entailing the figurative, erroneous, or naive attribution of human experiences to animals. The label of anthropomorphism is used to undermine the credibility, or realist force, of accounts that in some way picture animal life and human affairs as permeable to one another. In this work I set aside evaluative overtones, for my interest is to disclose the methods of reasoning that underpin the perceptual and epistemic effects of what is called anthropomorphism. Far from dismissing or humoring certain accounts as anthropomorphic, I argue that in the hands of impeccable observers of animals the anthropomorphic perspective deserves serious attention, for it discloses the nature of animal life with the power and internal cohesion that real worlds possess.

I begin with Charles Darwin, for his evolutionary thought marks the inception of the contemporary era of behavioral science. A separate treatment of Darwin is called for, given the momentous significance of his contribution to behavioral studies and the landmark status of his thinking for biological science as well as the broader culture. Darwin's representation of animals also serves as the foundational, comparative backdrop against which to examine classical ethology and neo-Darwinian sociobiology in Chapters 3 and 4. While these behavioral schools champion evolutionary thinking, they are reticent to partake of Darwin's predilection for depicting animal action in complete conceptual continuity with human action. With his consistent use of the ordinary language of action and mind in depicting animal life, Darwin's approach is unabashedly anthropomorphic. Based on the consistency of his style and explicit arguments, I argue that Darwin's anthropomorphism cannot be dismissed as metaphorical, erroneous, or trivial, but merits serious attention in its own right. Nor can anthropomorphism be deemed careless or naive in the hands of Darwin, a sterling observer and a thinker who revamped our worldview with his conception of the genealogical kinship between humans and animals. I argue that his anthropomorphic portrayal of animals reflects his understanding of the scope of evolutionary continuity and submits a commanding form of witnessing animal life.

In Chapter 2, I turn to the naturalist genre, focusing on the turn-of-the-century naturalists George and Elizabeth Peckham and Jean Henri Fabre. Naturalists aim to give accounts of animal life that are faithful representations; they record behaviors after close, long-term observation of animals in their natural surroundings; and they relate their observations and findings in nontechnical language. I argue that naturalists bring to the study of animals what social scientists have called the *Verstehen* approach, which seeks to understand the meaning of action from the point of view of the actors themselves. Naturalists apply the *Verstehen* perspective, for they regard animal action as evidencing a subjective dimension. As a consequence, their aim is to understand and deliver the meaning that is immanent in animal life. I argue that the effect of naturalists' forms of reasoning about animals is the unveiling of a lifeworld—an everyday, meaningful world that constitutes a plenum of action and experience for its inhabitants.

In Chapter 3, I take up the school of classical ethology, established between the 1930s and 1950s. Specifically, I look at the behavioral writings of Konrad Lorenz and Nikolaas Tinbergen, who instituted the study of naturally occurring behavior as a legitimate subfield of biological science. Classical ethologists took as their inspiration naturalists, with their methodology of long-term, close observation, and their interest in the natural lives of animals, yet naturalists remained largely peripheral to the academy, and their work was often not regarded as "proper science." The founders of ethology preserved much of the methodology and focus of naturalists, but introduced a theoretical framework and an accompanying technical vocabulary modeled on the physical sciences.

My interest, however, is not in the motives or institutional consequences of the ethologists' construction of a technical language. Rather, I attend to the ramifications of their idiom, namely, the objectification, and ultimately the mechanomorphic portrayal, of animals. In contrast to anthropomorphic depictions, which create an alignment between human and animal worlds, mechanomorphic depictions maintain a distance between them. I analyze how the distance between animal life and human affairs is created and sustained through ethological language use, and I argue that ethological language ends up representing animals as blind to the upshot of their behaviors, and without command over their expression. Thus animals' behaviors emerge as involuntary—not in the sense of being forcefully coerced or more subtly obliged, but rather compulsively steered by (interior-physiological and/or exterior-environmental) stimuli beyond their control and comprehension.

In Chapter 4, I turn to the present-day neo-Darwinian approach to animal behavior, with specific attention to the sociobiological view of animal life. In the same vein as the previous chapters, my interest is in the import of the sociobiological portraiture of animals, the world of animal being that it creates. I focus especially on two predominant aspects of the conceptual structure of sociobiology. First, I look at the ramifications of the pervasive application of an economic language, as depictions of animal behavior are mediated by ideas of success and failure, competition, costs and benefits, investment, advertising, and the like. The economic idiom forms the central network of sociobiological thinking—all hypotheses, descriptions, and emphases tend to flow from or connect back to its grid. Next, I explore the consequences of applying categories of social structure and action, such as class, suicide, kinship, nepotism, harem, selfishness, altruism, cooperation, dominance, and the like, to the animal world. I examine the ways in which sociobiology takes economic and social-category concepts from ordinary language and transforms them into either technical terms or natural-kind terms, thereby creating an encompassing view of animal life that excludes its understanding as a lifeworld.

The analyses in this book are informed by a comparative interest. The different effects of naturalist, ethological, and sociobiological writings on how animals are pictured are made visible and vivid by considering them in connection and contrast to one another. Chapter 5 focuses explicitly on the comparative epistemology of different representations, examining divergent portrayals of animal courtship. The purpose of this chapter is to drive home the central argument that in the depiction of animals language is never a neutral medium. Whatever language is chosen or constructed has unavoidable imagistic and conceptual effects on the reader's understanding of the nature of animal life. These effects are closely linked with the theme of animal mind, for alternative linguistic maps invite readers to witness the scenery of animal life as experientially meaningful or, conversely, as devoid of intrinsic meaning.

The connection between language use and mind culminates in the examination of the distinction drawn between "action" and "behavior," ideas that have been sharply distinguished in behavioral and philosophical thought. Their division is conceived as that between two essentially different species of conduct, one originating in or connected with the mind, the other deriving purely from physical operations upon and/or states of the body. The artificiality of the distinction between action and behavior, as two ostensibly natural species of conduct, is visible in its perennially controversial character in behavioral science, as well as in the ultimate inability to "purify" a language of behavior from mental contaminants. What I argue implicitly throughout this whole work, and explicitly in the final chapter, is that the construction of this distinction requires elaborate discursive groundwork—that is, marshaling background assumptions, conceptual and argumentative resources, grammatical patterns, stylistic techniques, and rhetorical tropes.

1 Darwin's Anthropomorphism

CHARLES DARWIN'S work was of pivotal significance for the biological study of behavior. His arguments for evolution established the phylogenetic continuity between humans and animals, thereby irreparably undermining the credibility of the religious doctrines of the fixity of species, of special creation, and of the unique status of human beings. The link between human and animal worlds made possible by the notion of common ancestry, accepted widely as an incontestable fact shortly after the publication of Darwin's *On the Origin of Species,* opened the twin conceptual possibilities of naturalist approaches to human behavior and of inquiry into phenomena of mind, will, and language in the animal world. After Darwin, the domains of humans and animals were no longer separated by the barrier of a metaphysical-religious doctrine of essential difference (Mayr 1982). Besides the shift in worldview concurrent with the discovery of evolutionary continuity, Darwin's evolutionary perspective provided the study of animal behavior with its most fundamental theoretical framework. The adaptive role of different behaviors could now be conceived under the auspices of the theory of natural selection: like morphological features or physiological processes, behavioral patterns could be appreciated as vital for the survival and reproduction of animals. The final seminal contribution of Charles Darwin to behavioral science was his virtual inception of the field of the biological study of natural behavior (which came to be called "ethology") with his 1872 work *The Expression of Emotions in Man and Animals.* In this work Darwin inaugurated the scientific study of human and animal behavior and mind in light of an evolutionary viewpoint (Lorenz 1965; Burkhardt 1985).

Despite his crucial contribution to the study of behavior, there is a profound discrepancy between Darwin's depictions of animal life and those of much twentieth-century behavioral inquiry. From a contemporary perspective, Darwin's language has been evaluated as "anthropomorphic." The ethologist Samuel Barnett, for example, criticizes Darwin's depiction of animal life as anthropomorphic, and thereby in need of correction

11

(1958). Michael Ghiselin, a Darwinian scholar, attempts to downplay Darwin's anthropomorphic style by claiming that his language was largely intended as metaphorical rather than literal representation (1969). For the most part, however, Darwin's representation of animals has been greeted with silence. According to the historian Richard Burkhardt, at least one reason for the relative neglect of Darwin's work on animal behavior has been "the anthropomorphic cast of many of [his] discussions of behaviour" (1985: 328). Overall, Darwin's predilection for rendering animal life in what have been widely regarded as "human" terms is dismissed as a quaint relic of a past epoch, reappraised as metaphorical, or ignored as irrelevant next to his major contributions.

However, Darwin intended his anthropomorphic portraiture of animals as a realistic, veridical appraisal. Rather than assessing his anthropomorphism as either error, metaphor, or undeserving of serious attention, I argue that his understanding of animal life reflects his view of evolutionary continuity. I show that Darwin's language embodies a coherent and powerful understanding of animal life, one that is at odds with mechanomorphic and skeptical views widespread in behavioral thought during the twentieth century.

First I survey Darwin's characterizations of animals, so as to give a flavor of his anthropomorphic language. To show that his portrayal of animal life was aligned with his understanding of evolution, I then discuss his explicit standpoint on the continuity among all animals with respect to behavioral traits and mental qualities. In the section that follows, I focus on Darwin's understanding of animal mentality, examining his work *The Expression of Emotions in Man and Animals*. Then, in contrast to the idea that Darwin's anthropomorphic style is either erroneous or metaphorical, I show that his representational language reflects his perception of subjectivity in the animal world; his premise is that living is experientially meaningful for animals and that their actions are authored. Finally, I investigate the anecdotal method in Darwin's behavioral writings in order to assess what kind of knowledge anecdotes about animals can foster. Darwin's representation of animals, deeply rooted in evolutionary reasoning, calls for the suspension of the sweeping indictment of anthropomorphism as a distorted perspective on the reality of animal being. Setting aside the deep-seated, a priori suspicion of so-called anthropomorphic language allows an appreciation of the knowledge that Darwin's perspective on animal life embodies.

Darwin's Language of Continuity

Darwin's language for representing animals is a resounding affirmation of the evolutionary continuity between animals and humans. His argument for continuity takes shape through a generous, unabashed use of the commonplace terms of (human) mind and action as resources through which to witness and understand animal life. As Carl Degler argues, "underlying Darwin's anthropomorphism was his determination to demonstrate as often and as thoroughly as possible the continuity between the so-called lower animals and human beings" (1991: 8). In the same vein, Ghiselin admits that for Darwin "to attribute 'higher' mental processes to 'lower' animals was one way of arguing for evolution" (1969: 202).

Darwin's aversion to a mechanistic view of animals—a legacy of Descartes' philosophy—is evident in his portrayals.[1] A mechanistic rendering of behavior is not necessarily incompatible with either evolutionary theory or a mental continuity between animals and humans, as is clear in the views of Darwin's close ally, T. H. Huxley, who regarded animals, including human beings, as "conscious automata" (1874), but Darwin did not share Huxley's ideas. In his last letter to his friend, with tenderness and not without irony, Darwin wrote, "I wish to God there were more automata in the world like you" (1958: 347). Though Darwin rarely discussed philosophical issues explicitly, he was not unfamiliar with the philosophical debates of his day, and his disinclination from a mechanistic perspective may also be seen in his favorable citation of Humboldt in *The Descent of Man:* "The muleteers in S. America say, 'I will not give you the mule whose step is easiest, but Las mas racional,—the one that reasons best;' and Humboldt adds, 'this popular expression, dictated by long experience, combats the system of animated machines better perhaps than all the arguments of speculative philosophy'" (1981, 1: 48).

Ghiselin wants to defend Darwin against the charge of anthropomorphism by arguing that there "has been a confusion of his language with his real meaning: there is a world of difference between his metaphorical use of anthropomorphic terms and the propositions which he actually asserts" (1969: 188). But Ghiselin also acknowledges that Darwin "lapses into anecdotal evidence and genuine anthropomorphism" (1969: 203). Yet the ubiquity and consistency of Darwin's depiction of animal life do not support the reading of an occasional lapse into anthropomorphism. His view is not simply at odds with a mechanistic conception of animal behavior, but advances an alternative understanding of animal life. Darwin did not doubt that animals have rich mental lives, and throughout his writings animals emerge as subjects—agents who experience the world and author their actions. I provide a brief sampling from Darwin's writings as a snapshot of his language of continuity—a language commonly denigrated with the label "anthropomorphic."[2]

Contemporary behavioral writings rarely refer to "love" and "attachment" among animals. Darwin, however, uses these terms even in reference to animals that among contemporary behavioral scientists are sometimes regarded as "mindless automata"—invertebrates, for example.[3] Darwin writes that among Lamellicorn beetles "some live in pairs and show mutual affection." Regarding crustaceans, he cites an anecdote from a naturalist about a male and female of a pair that were separated. When "the male was again put into the same vessel he dashed into the crowd, and without any fighting at once took away his wife"; Darwin concludes from this that "the males and females recognize each other, and are mutually attached." Recounting that "in many parts of the world fishes are known to make peculiar noises," he conjectures that fishes may possibly use sounds "as a love-call or as a love-charm." With respect to birds, Darwin writes of males and females "exciting each other's love," and says that parrots "become so deeply attached to each other that when one dies the other for a long time pines." Noting that dogs and monkeys show jealousy, he comments that "this shews that animals not only love, but have the desire to be loved." Just as "we long to clasp in our arms those whom we tenderly love," so "with the lower animals we see the same principle of pleasure derived from contact in association with love." Cats express affection by rubbing themselves on objects, which perhaps originated from "the young themselves loving each other." And in "the deep love of the dog for his master," Darwin discerns an evolutionary echo of "the feeling of religious devotion."

Regarding intense and passionate emotions, Darwin states that "even insects express anger, terror, jealousy, and love by their stridulation." The beetle Chiasognathus produces this shrill, grating noise "in anger or defiance," while others do so "from distress or fear." Darwin cites Wallace on certain male beetles fighting "apparently in the greatest rage." The male Ateuchus beetle "stridulates to encourage the female in her work and from distress when she is removed"; the male of a certain species of locust, "whilst coupled with the female, stridulates from anger or jealousy when approached by another male"; and it is probable, according to Darwin, that female cicadas, "like birds, are excited and allured by the male with the most attractive voice." "Bees express certain emotions, as of anger, by the tone of their humming, as do some dipterous insects"; and again, "everyone who has attended to bees knows that their humming changes when they are angry." Further, "with birds the voice serves to express various emotions, such as distress, fear, anger, triumph, or mere happiness"; male macaws use their loud voices "when they are excited by strong passions of love, jealousy and rage." Hummingbirds are characterized as "quarrelsome," and one hybrid goldfinch as having an "irascible disposition." With respect to frogs and toads, Darwin writes that "though cold-blooded, their passions are strong"; "chameleons and some other lizards inflate themselves when angry," and snakes "have some reasoning power and strong passions." Darwin also writes of "the intense grief of the female monkeys for the loss of their young." Cats express "terror combined with anger," as well as "rage or anger." "Porcupines rattle their quills and vibrate their tails when angered"; rabbits "stamp loudly on the ground as a signal to their comrades" and "when made angry." Male stags use their voice "under the strong excitement of love, jealousy and rage."

With respect to notions encompassing what are often referred to as higher mental qualities, Darwin argues that animals have powers of imitation, attention, memory, imagination (seen in animals' dreaming), and reason. He observes that where fur-bearing animals have been pursued with traps "they exhibit, according to the unanimous testimony of all observers, an almost incredible amount of sagacity, caution and cunning"; and, quoting the naturalist Swinhoe, Darwin suggests that "the victory of the common rat over the large Mus coninga [is due] to its superior cunning." He comments that "the mental powers of Crustacea are probably higher than expected," as "anyone who has tried to catch shore-crabs will have perceived how wary and alert they are." Darwin notes that spiders "exhibit much intelligence." He finds in the worm "attention and some mental power," as well as "some degree of intelligence." "There can be no doubt," he writes, "that birds closely attend to each other's song." Dogs have five different kinds of barks, expressing eagerness, anger, despair, joy, and demand. Darwin implicates a capacity for judgment in the dog when he notes that "a young shepherd-dog delights in driving and running round a flock of sheep, but not in worrying them"; "dogs," he writes, "possess something very like a conscience." Porcupines are "so fully conscious of the power of their weapons, that when enraged they will charge backwards with their spines erected, yet still inclined backwards." Citing another naturalist, Darwin writes that when hyenas fight "they are mutually conscious of the wonderful power of each other's jaws, and are extremely cautious. They well know that if one of their legs were seized, the bone would instantly be crushed." With regard to monkeys and other animals, Darwin notes that "many anecdotes, probably true, have been published on [their] long-delayed and artful revenge." He says that "one horse shows another where he wants to be scratched, and they then nibble each other." Generally, among social animals "gestures and expressions are to a certain extent mutually intelligible. Anyone who has watched monkeys will not doubt that they perfectly understand each other's gestures and expression."

Darwin makes frequent reference to animals' showing feelings of satisfaction and pleasure. He writes of "the deep grunt of satisfaction uttered by a pig, when pleased with its food." He notes that "even cows when they frisk about from pleasure, throw up their tails in a ridiculous fashion." Horses show eagerness to start on a journey by "pawing the ground [which] is universally recognized as a sign of eagerness." A foxhound "delights in hunting a fox"; a dog can be "cheerful" and in the "highest spirits." When ewes and lambs reunite, "their mutual pleasure at coming together is manifest." In general, "under a transport of Joy or vivid Pleasure," there is a tendency to "purposeless movements," as seen in young children, dogs, and horses. Among birds, the bowerbirds create "curious structures" (bowers), "solely as halls of assemblages, where both sexes amuse themselves and pay their court." Darwin observes that "we can plainly perceive, with some of the lower animals, that the males employ their voices to please the females, and that they themselves take pleasure in their own vocal utterances." Later I discuss the epistemic consequences of Darwin's understanding of animals acting for the sake of pleasure.

As these examples show, Darwin's anthropomorphic vocabulary of animal action and mind is characteristic of his writing. It exemplifies a use of language that differs profoundly from that of more recent behavioral writing. For instance, in contrast to writings in the wake of the twentieth-century schools of behaviorism and ethology, Darwin never places quotation marks around any concepts, even though much of his vocabulary refers to phenomena widely assessed as "human" or "subjective." The practice of enclosing mental predicates (such as love, anger, jealousy, grief, understanding, pretending, knowing, and so forth) in "scare-quotes," which function as markers of skepticism, is corollary to the assumption that such terms refer to processes or states that are either off-limits to animals or ostensibly unavailable for observation. As I will discuss in connection with classical ethology (Chapter 3), however, scare-quotes also function as devices that, while exonerating the writer from a full commitment to the language, allow her or him to make use of certain (anthropomorphic or otherwise controversial) concepts. The reader grasps the meaning of particular behaviors under the auspices of these concepts whether or not they are enveloped in quotation marks.

The practice of placing quotation marks around terms referring to mental processes assumes that such terms stand for invisible, and hence unverifiable, phenomena. However, the absence of quotation marks, and of other skeptical qualifications, in Darwin's works does not indicate that he is making unfounded inferences about what goes on inside animals. Instead, he is concerned with the observable behavioral and physiological manifestations that support the ascription of subjective phenomena. For Darwin, evolutionary common descent entails the probability that subjective phenomena are not the sole province of human beings. This approach is most fully developed in his *The Expression of Emotions in Man and Animals,* where Darwin provides detailed observations of emotions and sensations such as terror, pain, pleasure, joy, anger, love, jealousy, dejection, affection, and so on, showing their universality and perceivability in expression and physiological manifestation.

DARWIN'S VIEW OF EVOLUTIONARY CONTINUITY

Regarding Darwin's anthropomorphism, Ghiselin writes that "one reason . . . Darwin's psychology has not been understood is his tendency to express himself in anthropomorphic terms. A natural inference would be that he really believed in a close correspondence between animal and human mentality. There is some truth in this interpretation, but it has many pitfalls as well" (1969: 188). To say that this interpretation holds "some truth" is something of an understatement, for there is abundant evidence that Darwin held such a view. His lack of skepticism regarding the attribution of ostensibly human qualities to animals originated from his commitment to the entailments of common descent. The evolutionary perspective compelled him to acknowledge continuity not only at the level of physiological and morphological traits, but with respect to behavioral and mental attributes as well.[4]

The first chapter of *The Descent of Man* presents physiological evidence for the common descent of humans and animals. The remainder of this work is devoted to "mental faculties" such as moral sense, aesthetic sensibility, reasoning, imagination, and self-consciousness. The argument permeating the discussion of these topics is that "there is no fundamental difference between man and the higher mammals in their mental faculties" (1981, 1: 35). In agreement with his gradualist view of evolutionary change—that "natura non facit saltum" (nature makes no leaps)—Darwin regards "mental powers" as represented in "numberless gradations" in the animal world (1981, 1: 35): "The difference in mind between man and the higher animals, great as it is, is certainly one of degree and not of kind" (1981, 1: 105). For Darwin, the inexorable implication of evolutionary continuity is that "as man possesses the same senses with the lower animals, his fundamental intuitions must be the same" (1981, 1: 36).

In his *Selection in Relation to Sex,* Darwin makes an explicit and strong link between mental faculties and sexual selection.[5] Commenting on sexual selection in general, Darwin characterizes it as "an extremely complex affair, depending as it does, on ardour in love, courage, and the rivalry of the males, and on the powers of perception, taste, and will of the female" (1981, 1: 296). In the same vein, with respect to birds in particular, he states that "their courtship is often a prolonged, delicate and troublesome affair" (1981, 2: 103). Relying on this connection between mental qualities and sexual selection, Darwin argues that secondary sexual characters do not appear in the "lowest" classes of animals (such as protozoans, coelenterates, jellyfish, and so on), since they have "too imperfect senses and much too low mental powers to feel mutual rivalry, or to appreciate each other's beauty or other attractions" (1981, 1: 321). In this context, he reiterates that the acquisition of secondary sexual characters "depends on the will, desires, and choice of either sex" (ibid.).

For Darwin, then, evolutionary relatedness signifies an unbroken continuum between humans and animals in all respects, including behavioral patterns and mental faculties. In standing by this momentous entailment of evolutionary continuity, he went well beyond what his contemporaries were willing or able to accept. As the Darwinian scholar Robert Richards writes, "By detailing the intellectual heritage man shared with the lower animals Darwin set out on the final stretch of an evolutionary path, along which not even some of his strongest supporters . . . could travel" (1987: 195–96).

Ernst Mayr has cogently argued that Darwin's evolutionary perspective is inimical to essentialist and typological forms of thought and argumentation (1982, 1984). In contrast to regarding "core" qualities as real and important, and "variations" as inconsequential fluctuations around stable essences, evolutionary thinking stresses the paramount significance of inconstancies, gradations, and permutations. The shift from essentialist to evolutionary thinking hinges precisely on the recognition of the importance of variation, which is the very basis of species transformations over geological time. Darwin notes that "individual differences are highly important for us, as they afford materials for natural selection to accumulate" (1964: 45). This antiessentialist thrust carries forward into Darwin's behavioral thought. Overtly or tacitly, he rejects polarities traditionally summoned to draw a sharp boundary between human and animal life. Specifically, he did not accept that distinctions between instinct and reason, instinct and intelligence, invariability and plasticity of behaviors, or involuntary and willful action support a saltus between animal and human nature. While he did not develop a full-scale critique of these bifurcations, Darwin rarely treated them as contrastive or mutually exclusive. Because Darwin did not think in terms of typologies, but emphasized variation, he did not reify categories, that is, he did not conceive them as essential properties of phenomena.

Richards notes that "Darwin never hesitated to predicate of animals an ability to adjust their innate behavior" (1987: 130; see also 108–9). In this vein, Darwin did not treat reason and instinct as discontinuous or mutually exclusive bases of action. For instance, he writes that "the anthropomorphous apes, guided probably by instinct, build for themselves temporary platforms; but as many instincts are largely controlled by reason, the simpler ones, such as this of building a platform, might easily pass into a voluntary and conscious act" (1981, 1: 53). He also objected to a typological, contrastive treatment of intelligence and instinct, writing that "those insects which possess the most wonderful instincts are certainly the most intelligent. In the vertebrate series, the least intelligent members, namely fish and amphibians, do not possess complex instincts" (1981, 1: 37). To some extent Darwin accepted the distinction between "learned" and "instinctual" behaviors, considering them characteristic of the human and animal realms, respectively (see 1964: 207). He maintains that "man cannot on his first trial, make, for instance, a stone hatchet or a canoe, through the power of imitation. He has to learn by practice; a beaver, on the other hand, can make its dam or canal . . . as well, or nearly as well, the first time it tries, as when old and experienced" (1981, 1: 39). At the same time, Darwin did not regard the capacity to learn as the sole criterion for intelligence, as he observes that "amongst mammals the animal most remarkable for its instincts, namely the beaver, is highly intelligent" (1981, 1: 37). Anticipating what ethologists would later call "imprinting" (Lorenz 1957a), Darwin recognized that certain behaviors combine inextricable instinctive and learned components. He writes that "man has an instinctive tendency to speak as we see in the babble of our young children. . . . Young male [birds] continue practicing, or, as bird-catchers say, recording [their future song] for ten or eleven months. Their first essays show hardly a rudiment of the future song; but as they grow older we can perceive what they are aiming at; and at last they are said 'to sing their song round'" (1981, 1: 55). He concludes that "an instinctive tendency to acquire an art is not a peculiarity confined to man" (1981, 1: 56).

Cognitive ethologist Donald Griffin has observed that in twentieth-century behavioral science the "absence of learning is . . . taken, almost universally, as proof that the animal has no conscious awareness of its instinctive behavior" (1984: 42). Darwin did not hold this a priori assumption of an incompatibility between innate behavior and conscious awareness. So, for instance, he writes that "when we behold two males fighting for the possession of the female, or several male birds displaying their gorgeous plumage, and performing the strangest antics before an assembled body of females, we cannot doubt that, though led by instinct, they know what they are about, and consciously exert their mental and bodily powers" (1981, 1: 258). As this passage (among many others) shows, Darwin did not regard the notion of "conscious instinct" as oxymoronic.[6] In affinity with the evolutionary emphasis on variation and inconstancy, neither did Darwin advance a monolithic picture of animal behavior; thus he did not hold that animal behavior is always "consciously exerted" (for example, see 1981, 1: 39).

In addition to not treating instinctual behaviors as contrastive to or incompatible with reason, learning, or conscious awareness, Darwin also objected to a polarization between voluntary and involuntary action. In particular, he opposed the idea that animal behavior is involuntary while human behavior is voluntary, arguing instead that behavioral responses combine involuntary and willful components. Thus, countering Sir C. Bell's wish "to draw as broad a distinction as possible between man and the lower animals," and in disagreement with Bell's claim that animals can express little beyond rage and fear, Darwin draws the following analogy between man and dog:

> But man himself cannot express love and humility by external signs, so plainly as does a dog, when with drooping ears, hanging lips, flexuous body, and wagging tail, he meets his beloved master. Nor can these movements in the dog be explained by acts of volition or necessary instincts, any more than the beaming eyes and smiling cheeks of a man when he meets an old friend. (1965: 10–11)

With this comparison Darwin makes his point compellingly, as it is clear that "the beaming eyes and smiling cheeks of a man when he meets an old friend" are not responses that can be neatly classified as either willful or involuntary. Implicitly criticizing a typological view of human and animal action, Darwin suggests that not only do the responses of dog and man resist classification in terms of "involuntary" or "voluntary," but they afford a common conceptualization of action and feeling—in this case descriptions employing the terms *love* and *humility*.

Mayr's characterization of Darwin as an antiessentialist thinker is valid, then, in that Darwin's behavioral writings resist typological oppositions and treat mentality as intractable to inventories of essential, monolithic types. Indeed, Darwin criticized thinkers who deployed such distinctions so as to "preserve the conventional distinction between animals and men" (Richards 1987: 108).

DARWIN'S THE EXPRESSION OF EMOTIONS IN MAN AND ANIMALS

Nowhere is Darwin's understanding of mental continuity clearer than in his 1872 work on emotion. In *The Expression of Emotions in Man and Animals,* Darwin establishes shared genealogical descent as the background against which to inspect expressions and gestures of animal and human emotion. He claims that "he who admits on general grounds that the structure and habits of all animals have been gradually evolved, will look at the whole subject of Expression in a new and interesting light" (1965: 12). Further on, he describes his methodological approach in even more explicit terms, proposing that the test of the soundness of an explanation of "the cause or origin of the several expressions" of emotion is "whether the same general principles can be applied with satisfactory results, both to man and the lower animals" (1965: 18). Throughout this

work, Darwin points out that the convergence of behavioral and physiological expressions of emotions between animals (including humans) is
intelligible and explainable under the auspices of evolutionary common
descent.

In an essay critical of Darwin's generous ascription of mental qualities,
particularly emotions, to animals, Barnett voices the skeptical perspective
on animal mind in its typical twentieth-century form. Barnett treats Darwin's use of language with a certain degree of condescension, as though it
were a quaint relic of a naïveté that has been superseded in more recent
behavioral inquiry.

> Darwin . . . took it for granted that terms like *love, fear* and *desire* can
> usefully be employed to describe the behaviour of animals—or at least of
> mammals—generally.[7] He accepted the colloquial use of the word emotion.
> In doing so he assumed (by implication) that other species have feelings like
> our own. . . . Since his time it has gradually been found more convenient to
> describe animal behaviour, not in terms of feelings of which we are directly
> aware only in ourselves, but in terms of the activities which can be seen and
> recorded by any observer; we may also try to describe the internal processes
> which bring these activities about. Thus today it is unusual for ethologists
> to speak of emotions, though they continue to study the various types of
> behaviour which Darwin described as expressive of emotion. If the word
> emotion were to be used in the scientific study of animal behaviour, its
> meaning would have to be shifted from the familiar, subjective one: it would
> have to be used to refer, not to feelings, but to internal changes which could
> be studied physiologically. (1958: 210)

Barnett regards the colloquial use of mental terms as problematic, since it
implies that animals "have feelings like our own." He invokes an opposition between feelings and activities in terms of "subjective" and "objective." For Barnett, there is insufficient evidence to attribute love, fear, or
desire to animals, as these are feelings that "we are directly aware of only
in ourselves." Activities, on the other hand, "can be seen and recorded by
any observer."

In contrast to Barnett's evaluation, however, Darwin bases his ascription of emotions such as love, fear, and desire to animals on observational
evidence and evolutionary unity. It is important to note that he does not
share Barnett's skeptical premise, namely, the severing of "subjective" feelings from "objective" activities. In *The Expression of Emotions*, Darwin
discusses the various emotions in humans and animals, documenting their
countenance—that is, the entire complex of facial, gestural, and postural

forms that is the grounds of recognition and ascription of different frames of mind. His approach to emotions is scientific in the twofold sense of the naturalist's attentiveness to the countenance of emotion and the evolutionist's interest in the occurrence of similar (and hence possibly homologous) expressive forms in different species. Darwin details the expressiveness that is part and parcel of different frames of mind and systematically points out the intimate connections between "body" and "mind," drawing attention to the ties between behavioral-physiological expressions and the recognition of states of mind. He notes that "when our minds are much affected, so are the movements of our bodies" (1965: 32); "so strongly are our intentions and movements associated together, that if we wish an object to move in any direction we can hardly avoid moving our bodies" (1965: 64); and again, "most of our emotions are so closely connected with their expression, that they hardly exist if the body remains passive—the nature of the expression depending in chief part on the nature of the actions which have been habitually performed under this particular state of mind" (1965: 237–38).

While these passages appear to endorse a split between mind and body, Darwin repeatedly draws attention to the instantaneous and preanalytical character of recognizing emotions, emphasizing the connection between bodily expressiveness and the perception of mental modalities, and thereby ultimately undermining dualism. Regarding, for example, the expression of grief in a human face, he writes that "when observed, [it] is universally and instantly recognized as that of grief or anxiety, yet not one person out of a thousand who has never studied the subject, is able to say precisely what change passes over the sufferer's face" (1965: 182). He reiterates the same idea in broader terms: "We may actually behold the expression changing in an unmistakable manner in a man or animal, and yet be quite unable, as I know from experience, to analyze the nature of the change. . . . It has often struck me as a curious fact that so many shades of expression are instantly recognized without any conscious process of analysis on our part" (1965: 58–59). Darwin's monistic view of body and mind does not reduce mind to physical movements of, or events in, the body. Rather, through his observational acumen he demonstrates that behavior and mental states are a single, fused totality. The unity of body and mind is evidenced in the instantaneous, often precise recognition of the emotional states of others—both humans and animals.

Darwin discusses the entire gamut of emotions describing expressive forms closely. In the case of intense sensations and emotions—pain, rage, joy, and terror—he notes how vivid their manifestations are in both behavior and physiological changes. He describes pain as expressed in "writhing with frightful contortions" and in "piercing cries and groans," observing that with pain every muscle of the body is brought into action and the teeth may be clenched or gnashed; moreover, "perspiration bathes the entire body," and "circulation and respiration are much affected" (1965: 69–70). About joy, Darwin writes that "under a transport of Joy or of vivid Pleasure, there is a strong tendency to various purposeless movements, and to the utterance of various sounds. We see this in our young children, in their loud laughter, clapping of hands, and jumping for joy; in the bounding and barking of a dog when going out to walk with his master; and in the frisking of a horse when turned out into an open field" (1965: 76). Regarding experiences of lesser intensity than pain or joy, Darwin retains his empirically robust method of close observation and detailed description: the manifestations of pleasure, hostile intention, discomfort, attention, affection, impatience, listlessness, and dejection are also available in facial and bodily countenance, in obvious or subtle physiological and behavioral expressions.

As Barnett notes, Darwin unproblematically uses the colloquial term *emotion* in relation to animals. While relying on ordinary language and common knowledge to illustrate the emotional life of animals, Darwin provides the perspective of the naturalist in detailing specific aspects of behavior and the insights of the evolutionist regarding the origin and unity of expressions. In his description of a cheerful dog, for example, Darwin depicts an illustrative scene from everyday life: "A dog in cheerful spirits, and trotting before his master with high elastic steps, generally carries his tail aloft, though it is not held nearly so stiffly as when he is angered" (1965: 116). His concern is to identify the expressive form of cheerfulness in the dog. As the example continues, his naturalist's vision discriminates degrees of stiffness of the tail, while his interest in evolutionary unity leads him to note that the same pattern of holding the tail aloft is encountered in other animals, such as horses and cows, in similar states of mind. He marks the crucial difference between the expressions of cheerfulness and anger—a difference that may easily go unobserved by the lay person, particularly if the circumstances implicating the appropriateness of cheerfulness or anger are not obvious.

The science of the naturalist involves creating inventories of the details of expression and posture. Darwin's work is rich with observations about the position and movement of ears, the bristling or smoothness of hair or feathers, the holding of the tail at different heights and in different degrees of rigidity, the baring of teeth, the eyes' expression and their relative brightness or dullness. At the same time, evolutionary concerns lead him to seek the recurrence of patterns: the pricking and directing forward of the ears is an expression of attention in numerous animals; the pawing of the ground, seen in creatures as diverse as wasps and horses, expresses impatience or eagerness; the raising of the eyebrows in dogs, apes, monkeys, and humans shows astonishment; the drawing back of the ears in cats, seals, dogs, and horses, among others, expresses hostile intention or savage disposition; and dullness of the eyes often manifests dejection or ill health.

In Darwin's work on the emotions, naturalist and evolutionary sensibilities merge in sustained sets of observations. This is illustrated by the following passage, where he discusses the expressive character of the position of the ears in mammals:

> The ears through their movements are highly expressive in many animals.
> . . . A slight difference in position serves to express in the plainest manner a
> different state of mind, as we may daily see in the dog. . . . All the Carnivora
> fight with their canine teeth, and all, as far as I have observed, draw their
> ears back when feeling savage. This may continually be seen with dogs when
> fighting in earnest, and with puppies fighting in play. The movement is dif-
> ferent from the falling down and slight drawing back of the ears, when a
> dog feels pleased and is caressed. . . . The lynx has remarkably long ears;
> and their retraction . . . is very conspicuous, and is eminently expressive of
> its savage disposition. Even one of the Eared Seals . . . which has very small
> ears, draws them backwards, when it makes a savage rush at the legs of its
> keeper. . . . Every one recognizes the vicious appearance which the drawing
> back of the ears gives to a horse. (1965: 110–12)

The familiarity and wide recurrence of similar expressions form the basis for the recognition of mental phenomena—even in cases where knowledge and experience are limited. Thus the recognition of "the vicious appearance which the drawing back of the ears gives to a horse" is indeed likely even for those unfamiliar with horses, and despite the absence of other giveaway signs such as growling and the baring of teeth. Yet while many of his examples are drawn from daily life and are thus easily available to his readers, his detailed knowledge of the countenance of emotion is the province of the naturalist. Moreover, Darwin's general survey of the expressive appearance of the ears in carnivores, and animals in general, is the province of the evolutionist, and he points out that the retraction of

Figure 1　Photograph of smiling man

ears is an adaptation that protects them from the opponent's teeth during a fight (1965: 111).

Darwin consistently relies on the common capacity to recognize the expressions of emotions. He then analyzes and discloses the empirical basis of this tacit knowledge. For example, Darwin experimented with showing people two different photographs of a man smiling, asking for their reactions.

The image on the left "was instantly recognized by everyone to whom it was shown as true to nature," while the other was "an example of an unnatural or false smile" (1965: 201). He writes of the second one: "That the expression is not natural is clear, for I showed this photograph to twenty-four persons, of whom three could not in the least tell what was meant, whilst the others, though they perceived that the expression was of the nature of a smile, answered in such words as 'a wicked joke,' 'trying to laugh,' 'grinning laughter,' 'half-amazed laughter,' etc." (1965: 201–2). After establishing the shared understanding of the difference between a true smile and a false one, Darwin proceeds to dissect closely the elements of this tacit knowledge through a consideration of the different muscles of the face that come into play in each of the smiles. The shared recognition of expressions is thus the starting point for Darwin's subsequent biological inquiry into the connection of body and mind.

Darwin's method of identifying the emotions consists largely in descriptions that remind the reader of their countenance. He often argues from the basis of commonsense knowledge. In describing, for instance, the countenance of "a man in high spirits," Darwin writes: "I heard a child, a little under four years old, when asked what was meant by being in good spirits, answer, 'It is laughing, talking, and kissing.' It would be difficult to give a truer and more practical definition" (1965: 210). Similarly, Darwin identifies the feeling of affection by describing a mundane scene of a cat's postures and behaviors: "She now stands upright, with slightly arched back, tail perpendicularly raised, and ears erected; and she rubs her cheeks and flanks against her master or mistress. The desire to rub

Figure 2 Affectionate cat

something is so strong in cats under this state of mind, that they may often be seen rubbing themselves against the legs of chairs or tables, or against door posts" (1965: 126–27).

Relying on the shared knowledge of a cat's expressions, and using descriptive and visual elucidations, he recalls the demeanor of a "cat in an affectionate state of mind." Darwin conveys that the emotion embodied in the cat's expressive forms is perceptually transparent, and the mental concept of "affection" delivers that perception fully.

The divergence between Darwin's understanding and skeptical reasoning is striking. The power of mental language to assemble what is perceived—in the moment or in memory—is lost to the skeptical perspective, for the latter begins with the premise that mind is unobservable. In Darwin's analyses, on the other hand, mental concepts condense constellations of (subtle or vivid) expressions—of face, eyes, body, and movement. Emotion is incarnate for Darwin. His work on emotions can be read as a philosophical treatise on the availability of mind, a detailed document of the "face" of emotion throughout the animal kingdom. For the skeptic, mental concepts are taken to refer to something hidden and therefore perennially out of empirical reach. Barnett is a quintessential representative of a skeptical critic of Darwin's use of mental concepts for animals. His skepticism is so deep-seated that he objects to Darwin's phrase "cat in an affectionate frame of mind," stating that "today this behaviour might be described in terms of 'cutaneous stimulation'" (1958: 225).

That Barnett proposes "cutaneous stimulation" as something that could come to replace the authenticity and recallability of Darwin's "cat in an affectionate frame of mind" is a measure of how deeply doubt about animal mentality can capture the imagination. Indeed Barnett's wonderfully disingenuous formulation crystallizes certain issues that arise in connection to the problem of animal mind in the behavioral literature. It exemplifies the move of displacing a mental concept with a technical term under the auspices of achieving ostensibly greater objectivity. The assumption that fuels this move is that mind and body are separate realms, such that the cat's behavior might be rendered completely in terms of body—for example, "cutaneous stimulation." The consequence, however, of this game of words—of displacing ordinary description with a technical idiom—is that in the reader's mind the very image of the cat's "body" is transfigured. What in Darwin's hands are expressive gestures become in Barnett's description nonsignifying movements; from an experiencing subject, the cat is transformed into a vacant object.

In contrast to Barnett's fears, however, Darwin's anthropomorphism does not naively conflate human and animal qualities, but instead reveals his distance from the skeptical premises that Barnett takes for granted. Darwin's use of language embodies a deliberate and powerful alternative perspective that is based on close observation of expressive form and evolutionary common descent. His anthropomorphic language (as well as that of the naturalists I examine in the next chapter) works at a deeper layer than a mere transposition of human attributes to animals: Darwin's language of representation reflects his understanding of animals as subjects.

DARWIN'S NATURALIST VIEW OF ANIMALS AS SUBJECTS: ACTION AS MEANINGFUL AND AUTHORED

Beyond providing an appreciation of Darwin's portrayals of animal life in their own right, the examination of his language use also allows closer scrutiny into the nature of anthropomorphism, an idea often loosely identified as an unwarranted attribution of human mental experiences to animals. Yet anthropomorphism clearly involves a broader territory than the use of mental concepts alone. More comprehensively, it encompasses the description and explanation of animal life in the ordinary language of objects and events, relations and community, action and mind (cf. Asquith 1984: 143). The effect of the sustained use of this broad spectrum of vocabulary and reasoning is the emergence of animals as subjects. This effect has been synoptically labeled, hitherto pejoratively, "anthropomorphism."

Far from being fuzzy or impressionistic, the idea of subjectivity encompasses two dimensions: it refers to the *meaningfulness* of experience and action of sentient life and it implicates the *authorship* of action (Schutz 1962; Davidson 1980). Darwin's vision of animal life as meaningful and authored extends to the entire animal kingdom, as may be seen in his beautiful description of ant life:

> To describe the habits and powers of a female ant, would require, as Pierre Huber has shewn, a large volume; I may, however, briefly specify a few points. Ants communicate information to each other, and several unite for the same work, or games of play. They recognize their fellow ants after months of absence. They build great edifices, keep them clean, close the doors in the evening, and post sentries. They make roads, and even tunnels under rivers. They collect food for the community, and when an object, too large for entrance is brought to the nest, they enlarge the door, and afterwards build it up again. They go out to battle in regular bands, and freely

sacrifice their lives for the common weal. They emigrate in accordance with a preconcerted plan. They capture slaves. They keep Aphides as milch-cows. They move the eggs of their aphides, as well as their own eggs and cocoons, into warm parts of the nest, in order that they may be quickly hatched; and endless similar facts could be given. (1981, 1: 186–87)

This description of an ant community is quite literally anthropomorphic, as ant life is portrayed in terms equivalent to human life: substitute a human community for the ants and, with only a few alterations, the intelligibility of the passage would be preserved intact.

Darwin's language is the vernacular of objects, action, communal life, and mind. Certain philosophers of the human sciences have compellingly argued that the conceptual structure of this language is internal to, or constitutive of, the life it portrays (Coulter 1979; Winch 1958). What this means may best be illustrated with an example. In observing construction workers carrying out certain activities, the characterization that they are "making a road" expresses both the intelligibility, for the observer, of what they are doing, and the coherence of how the workers themselves plan and concert their undertakings. As Peter Winch would put it, the *idea* of making a road is *embodied* in the workers' activities (1958: 128). The relationship, then, between the idea of "making a road" and the activities so characterized is a constitutive relationship, in the sense that the conceptual rendering of the activity cannot be disentangled from the way in which the activity is witnessed; a constitutive or internal concept thus cancels any distance between the way action is witnessed and how it is linguistically represented. Moreover, the idea of "making a road"—and similarly for the other descriptions in the passage about ants—is a linguistic representation that expresses how the observer sees the activity and, at the same time, describes what the activity is for the actors themselves. In other words, description in the ordinary language of action does not accommodate a dichotomous conception of the observer's "objective" comprehension, on one hand, and the actor's "subjective" orientation, on the other. The first- and third-person perspectives of witness and actor converge and imbricate in that what the witness sees and reports is congruous with what the actor experiences. The two perspectives are subject to rupture, but only for contingent reasons, and not as a perennial possibility.

Keeping the analysis of the example of "making a road" in mind, we can see the effects of Darwin's representation of ant life. Writing that ants unite for work, build edifices, keep them clean, close doors, post sentries, make roads and tunnels, and so forth invites the understanding that these ideas are constitutive of the ants' engagements, or internal to their experiential world. As in the case of human workers, to propose that the ants "make roads" is to disclose what they are doing and why they are doing it. The coherence, purpose, systematics, and coordination of their actions centers purely on this: *that they are making a road*. In Winch's terminology, the overall picture of the ants' activities is consilient with the view that those activities "embody ideas." The perspectives of the actor and the witness—in this case, the ants and the human observer—are brought into alignment because action is captured as embodying ideas that are both experienced from within and witnessed from without. Darwin's description does not allow for a separation between the actor's subjective orientation and the observer's objective comprehension. The first- and third-person perspectives of witness and actor are confluent, in that what the witness sees and reports from "Here" is essentially on a par with what the actor experiences "over There" (see Schutz 1962: 315). The ordinary language of living—with its objects, events, relations, action, sentiment, and mind—embeds the actors' *subjective* orientation, not as some inferred private dimension, but as the glow that lights up the surface designs of action and being.

It is noteworthy that there is very little overt reference to mental experience in Darwin's passage; he writes that the ants "recognize their fellow ants after a long period of absence" and "emigrate according to a preconcerted plan." I propose that beyond the contestable question of whether such mental attributions are reasonable assessments or unwarranted conjectures, they nonetheless have their home within a conceptual environment that is constructed of humbler building blocks: ascriptions such as making roads and tunnels, collecting food, enlarging the door, closing the door, posting sentries, and so forth. In this sense, the ordinary language of action and mind discloses subjective orientation not as a private, inner spring of action, but as an acknowledgment that the very *raison d'être* and sensual form of action cannot be extricated from the perception of action as experientially meaningful.

The life of ants is thus delivered by Darwin as an active embodiment of ideas. As a consequence, the reader perceives the ants' communal life as an experientially and subjectively meaningful world. This supervenient impact on the reader's understanding is a significant facet of anthropomorphism; thus the reason that "anthropomorphism" is not crisply defin-able or identifiable is that it is an *effect* of language, rather than a set of circumscribable features of its use. Indeed, a recalcitrant problem in iden-tifying anthropomorphism in behavioral writings is that of drawing a clear line between terms that are purportedly off-limits to animals and those that are not. Pamela Asquith makes this point succinctly, stating that "the selection of appropriate terms [by behavioral scientists] is based on little more than a vague apprehension of 'anthropomorphic license'" (1984: 142). As an example of the ad hoc, rule-of-thumb criteria applied in avoiding anthropomorphism, Asquith mentions the preference for the term *bond* over *friendship* with respect to primate relations. She explains that "'bond' is deemed more acceptable in that it need not imply such a complex arrangement of emotions as does 'friendship'" (ibid.).

Generalizing Asquith's example, terms referring to sensations, such as *pleasure* and *pain,* are not always shunned in behavioral literature, though the cognate terms *happiness* and *misery* are distinctly absent. They are avoided, as Asquith puts it, on the vague apprehension that they are an-thropomorphic. Like *happiness* and *misery,* so terms such as *enjoyment, joy, excitement,* or *ennui* are rarely encountered. Yet Darwin does not de-mur to use such concepts in his descriptions, writing, for instance, that "happiness is never better exhibited than by young animals, such as pup-pies, kittens, lambs, etc., when playing together, like our own children." He then goes on to note that "even insects play together, as has been de-scribed by that excellent observer, P. Huber, who saw ants chasing and pretending to bite each other, like so many puppies" (1981, 1: 39). In general for Darwin, "the lower animals, like man, manifestly feel pleasure and pain, happiness and misery" (ibid.), and he observes that "animals manifestly enjoy excitement and suffer from ennui, as may be seen with dogs, and, according to Rengger, with monkeys. All animals feel Wonder, and many exhibit Curiosity" (1981, 1: 42). Darwin also conjectures that "migratory birds are miserable if prevented from migrating, and perhaps they enjoy starting on their long flight" (1981, 1: 79). Moreover, "under the expectation of any great pleasure, dogs bound and jump about in an extravagant manner, and bark for joy" (1965: 120).

What is peculiar about terms such as *happiness, misery, joy, ennui, wonder,* and *curiosity* is that, unlike *pleasure* and *pain,* which are often directly connected with the senses (for example, with taste or touch), they rather allude to "states of being" that need not correlate with imme-diate or specific sensory experiences. States of being are thus not witnessed through obvious or stable expressive responses. Happiness, for example, is not attributable on the basis of a single (or a few) behavioral manifestation(s) that can be pinpointed in a brief time span. For while one feels pleasure at specific moments, happiness is a compound state of being that is both temporally more extended and sensually more subtle. The same applies to the conceptual pair of pain and misery (or pain and suffering). With the ascription of states of being such as happiness and misery, Darwin acknowledges the relevance, in animal life, of the subtleties and complexities of experience that these concepts imply. The effect of evidencing happiness and misery, as well as joy, ennui, wonder, triumph, grief, and so forth, in animal conduct is the tacit admission of a fullness, complexity, and temporal extendedness of being.

The view that Darwin's references to happiness, misery, joy, and so forth might be a metaphorical way of speaking (see Ghiselin 1969) derives from the assumption that such terms designate mental phenomena unavailable to direct observation; hence, the logic runs, Darwin could not have been proposing them as literally applicable to animals. There are two counterresponses to this interpretation. First, as I argued, Darwin's generous use of mental terminology is far too pervasive to be considered metaphorical; moreover, he rarely qualifies his language with caveats or quotation marks. Second, he does not present states of being in animal life on the basis of inferences from "observable" behavior to "unobservable" mind, for he does not reason on the skeptical assumption that body and mind are separate domains, nor on the dualist thesis that "inner" subjectivity is something invisible that can be at best tenuously deduced from "outer" behavior.

Close attention to Darwin's forms of reasoning reveals that he does not speculate about mental (or subjective) states from behavioral expressions, but rather witnesses such states in behavioral expressions. This form of reasoning can be seen quite clearly when Darwin uses mental concepts as a way to *describe* a behavioral scene. Darwin's description of a horse's comportment is a case in point:

> Animals which live in society often call to each other when separated, and *evidently* feel much joy at meeting; as *we see* with a horse, on the return of his companion, for whom he has been neighing. (1965: 84–85, emphasis added)

The perceptual terms *evidently* and *we see* convey "feel[ing] much joy at meeting" as a descriptive statement, rather than an indirect inference or speculation. By descriptively bonding subjective states of being with behaviors, Darwin guides his readers to perceive the scenery described in alignment with his own direct perception of behaviors in light of the understanding and atmosphere that subjective language makes witnessable. The reader is invited to *see* the reunion of the horses as joyful. The expression "joy at meeting" delivers an icon of the horse's manner of response upon "the return of his companion for whom he has been neighing," even though the physical movements of that response are not provided. The joy of reunion, delivered in a language of perception, solicits ways to imagine the behavioral-physical comportment of the horses.

Darwin presents subjectivity as directly witnessable in animal life. His descriptions of the "dancing-party" of the birds of paradise and of the "great magpie marriage" illustrate the perceptual appreciation of subjective life that characterizes Darwin's thought:

> With Birds of Paradise a dozen or more full-plumaged males congregate in a tree to hold a dancing-party, as it is called by the natives; and here flying about, raising their wings, elevating their exquisite plumes, and making them vibrate, the whole tree seems, as Mr. Wallace remarks, to be filled with waving plumes. When thus engaged, *they become so absorbed,* that a skilful archer may shoot nearly the whole party. (1981, 2: 89, emphasis added)

> The common magpie (Corvus pica, Linn.), as I have been informed by the Rev. W. Darwin Fox, used to assemble from all parts of Delamere Forest, in order to celebrate the "great magpie marriage." . . . [The birds] had the habit very early in the spring of assembling at particular spots, where they could be seen in flocks, chattering, sometimes fighting, bustling and flying about the trees. *The whole affair was evidently considered by the birds as of the highest importance.* (1981, 2: 102, emphasis added)[8]

The propositions that the birds consider the courtship affair absorbing and important clearly incorporate the idea that the actions involved are meaningful from the birds' point of view. The effect of this intimation is that the reader pictures the birds' activities in light of the understanding and feeling that subjective meaningfulness invokes.

For Darwin, the fervor of the engagement among the birds of paradise, coupled with an archer's ability to shoot them down without being noticed, is the basis for perceiving that the birds are absorbed by their courtship activities. As for the magpies, their wealth of behaviors—the chattering, bustling, fighting, and so on—and the prolongedness of the affair are apprehended as evidencing that the affair "is considered by the birds as of the highest importance." Darwin is focusing on the birds' expressive largesse: when an affair is absorbing and of the highest importance, *this* is what it looks like in action. This is not to say, however, that his descriptions are exact or incontestable representations of the birds' experience. Nowhere in the birds' activities can it be documented, *specifically*, that they consider the courtship affair important, or that they are absorbed. While Darwin's wording is warranted by the intensity of the birds' involvement and their obliviousness to other events, at the same time it recommends a particular perceptual angle on the birds' activities. The evidence for his characterizations is obliquely, rather than blatantly, available on the surface of behaviors. The characterizations themselves thus contribute a way of witnessing the birds' conduct.

The idea that action embodies an experiential point of view is a powerful current in Darwin's accounts of animal life. A division between "inner life" and "outer behavior" is abrogated in the presentation of subjective experience as directly witnessable rather than speculatively deduced. He sees birds "flying easily, obviously for pleasure," or the magpies' courtship as "evidently of the highest importance." With the evidentiary force of such recurrent expressions as *obviously*, *evidently*, and *manifestly*, Darwin intimates that his proposals are not deductions but observations. He thereby invites his co-observer, the reader, to witness visually the expressiveness of the described scene. The language of his report—"how often do we *see* birds which fly easily, gliding and sailing through the air *obviously* for pleasure"—enjoins the reader to assemble flying as something birds perform and experience. How actions are put into words can thus work as a gateway to seeing actions in particular ways, for, more than sense, words impart imagery and atmosphere to their referents.

Animals' orientation toward the pleasures of life embeds authorship, for Darwin presents this orientation as a *cause* of action, rather than an epiphenomenal or ancillary aspect of it. Just as attributions of states of being, discussed previously, are rare in contemporary behavioral writings, so is providing accounts for animal activities in terms of the pleasure they afford. In contemporary behavioral thought the idea of "acting for the sake of pleasure" is treated as either epiphenomenal or irrelevant and, instead, paramount emphasis is placed on the function and adaptive value of behaviors. To give an example, Joan Silk discusses grooming—a visibly sensual affair—among primates in the economic terms of "costs and benefits" (1987: 325). The pleasure that primates may take in the activity of grooming is not denied, but it is tacitly treated as irrelevant next to the proper functional, adaptive account.

The avoidance of alluding to acting for pleasure reflects a persistent vigilance against the charge of anthropomorphism. "Anthropomorphophobia," as Donald Griffin has called it (personal communication), is entirely absent in Darwin's behavioral writings, where acting for the sake of pleasure or amusement is a recurring theme. In his *Selection in Relation to Sex*, for example, Darwin makes an extended argument that male birds sing in order "to excite or charm" female birds. After considering a counterargument, he concludes:

> It has . . . been argued that the song of the male cannot serve as a charm, because the males of certain species . . . sing during the autumn. But nothing is more common than for animals to take pleasure in practicing whatever instinct they follow at other times for some real good. How often do we see birds which fly easily, gliding and sailing through the air obviously for pleasure . . . Hence it is not at all surprising that male birds should continue singing for their own amusement after the season for courtship is over. (1981, 2: 54, 55)

Acting for pleasure or amusement embeds an experiential viewpoint. As in the case of states of being—such as happiness, joy, misery, wonder, or grief—acting for pleasure is inclusive not only of what animals do, but of what they experience as well. It is precisely this level of inclusion that allows Darwin to report something as mundane as "birds which fly": "How often do we see birds which fly easily, gliding and sailing through the air {obviously for pleasure}." If the bracketed portion of the sentence were eliminated, the statement would be too trivial to state. With the qualification "obviously for pleasure," however, the act of flying becomes subjectively expressive and hence worth reporting. The simple qualification "obviously for pleasure" transforms an unremarkable behavior, "flying," into an intentional action, "sailing through the air *for pleasure*."

While the idea of animals acting for pleasure or amusement appears, at first glance, a trivial matter, when considered in comparative perspective its significant ramifications may be appreciated. Darwin's ideas that birds "fly for pleasure" and "sing for their own amusement" are at odds with the adaptationist proclivity of much contemporary neo-Darwinian thinking.[9] Darwin draws a distinction between an instinct followed "for some real good" and one "practiced for pleasure," thereby implicitly opposing the adaptationist view that all behaviors must be accounted for in terms of an ultimate, functional explanation (see Burkhardt 1985).

When compared, moreover, with the classical ethological proclivity to define behavioral patterns in terms of underlying mechanisms, the divergent effects of Darwin's reasoning about animals pursuing pleasure come into stark relief. For example, Darwin remarks that "the weaver bird . . . when confined in a cage, amuses itself by neatly weaving blades of grass between the wires of its cage" (1981, 2: 54). A similar type of "nonutilitarian" behavior is discussed by one of the founders of ethology, Konrad Lorenz, who recounts a captive starling's hunting, capturing, and eating a (nonexistent) insect, in the complete absence of any insects in the room.

> The starling flew up onto the head of a bronze statue in our living room and steadily searched the "sky" for flying insects, although there were none on the ceiling. Suddenly its whole behavior showed that it had sighted a flying prey. With head and eyes the bird made a motion as though following a flying insect with its gaze; its posture tautened; it took off, snapped, returned to its perch, and with its bill performed the sideways lashing, tossing motions with which many insectivorous birds slay their prey against whatever they happen to be sitting upon. Then the starling swallowed several times, whereupon its closely laid plumage loosened up somewhat, and there often ensued a quivering reflex, exactly as it does after real satiation. The bird's entire behavior . . . was so convincing, so deceptively like a normal process with survival value, that I climbed a chair not once, but many times, to check if some tiny insects had not after all escaped me. But there really were none. (1957b: 143)

Lorenz reports the starling's behavioral sequence for the theoretical purposes of illustrating what ethologists have called "vacuum behaviors." His interpretation of the starling's behaviors is given extensively in another paper:

> It is hardly possible to point out a more impressive feature of instinctive actions than their property to "go off in vacuo" when the specific releasing stimuli are lacking. If an innate behavior pattern, for want of adequate stimulation, is never released in captivity, the threshold for this stimulation, strange to say, is lowered. This can go so far that the activity in question finally breaks through and "goes off" without any detectable releasing stimulus. It is as though the latent behavior pattern itself finally became an internal stimulus. Let me recall the instance of the starling who performed the full motor sequence of a fly-hunt without a fly. . . . As . . . this observation proves clearly . . . the bird . . . follows no purpose, however obscure, but the "blind plan" . . . of its instincts. (1957a: 101)

Lorenz's portrayal of the starling as compelled to perform a series of behaviors differs profoundly from Darwin's understanding of the weaver bird's weaving for amusement. For Lorenz the starling's fly hunt is exemplary of a vacuum behavior. The idea of vacuum behavior is conceived as an innate behavioral pattern whose corresponding "action-specific energy" has accumulated to such a degree that the behavior finally "breaks through" in the absence of the appropriate external circumstances, which ethologists call "releasing stimuli" (see Tinbergen 1989). On Lorenz's interpretation, the full pattern of the starling's fly hunting "goes off" in the absence of insects because the necessary "threshold" of external "stimulation" has reached its theoretically possible limit of zero and the accumulated energy corresponding to the behavioral pattern has become an "internal stimulus" sufficient to "trigger" the expression of the pattern (see Lorenz 1950: 246–47). The mechanical imagery evoked in the account of the starling is made metaphorically explicit elsewhere, where Lorenz characterizes vacuum behaviors as having "an effect somewhat suggestive of the explosion of a boiler whose safety valve fails to function" (1950: 247).

What is of interest in the context of this comparative discussion is that Lorenz's interpretation *precludes* the possibility that the starling's mock fly hunt is a form of amusement—akin to a game—even as the bird is aware that there are no flies in the room. The explanation of the starling's hunt as a vacuum behavior is conceptually wedded to the proposition, as Lorenz puts it, that "the bird follows no purpose but the blind plan of its instincts." In other words, the notion of a vacuum behavior is not only confluent with, but logically hinges upon, the condition that the bird's actions be disconnected from its awareness. Conversely, Darwin's account of an animal engaging in meaningless activity, like weaving grass on the wires of its cage, for the sake of amusement is consilient with the understanding of action as subjectively expressive and authored. While Darwin's weaver bird is present to the import of its own engagements, Lorenz's starling is an unwitting executor of the blind plan of its instincts. To articulate the contrast more starkly, while weaving grass or hunting nonexistent insects for amusement are voluntary actions, these same activities qua "vacuum behaviors" are determined, that is, they are physiologically caused. The difference of the two accounts lies in their incompatible conceptions of the causation of actions.

The philosopher Alan White has noted that to author action means that the actor is the cause of what is brought about through his or her actions; on the other hand, unauthored action is extrinsically caused (1968). What this means is clarified by picturing the logical difference between jumping and falling: a "jump" is authored, a "fall" is not; a brief suspension of a human being or an animal in the air is the consequence of either a jump or fall, but not both. To draw out the analogy with the examples under consideration, while a bird's mock fly hunt as a vacuum behavior is equivalent to a fall, the same action for the sake of amusement is akin to a jump. The conception of action as authored tacitly precludes other causal (as opposed to simply enabling) factors, such as physiological states or environmental stimuli. While bodily states and contextual features are obviously part and parcel of action, they cannot be advanced as causes of authored actions. The understanding of the author as the cause of action radically shrinks the conceptual space for deterministic causation.

In distinguishing between something one does and something that happens to one, and using the example of "falling" and "jumping," White points out that "actions are events or occurrences that it makes sense to qualify in certain ways. We can, for instance, intend, try, choose, decide, be ordered, resolve or refuse to *jump*, but not to *fall*" (1968: 7). It is not, then, that "human actions must [always] be voluntary, intentional, purposive, conscious, etc.; but only that they must be the sorts of occurrences of which it makes sense to ask whether they are any or all of these" (1968: 8). On the other hand, once animal behavior is portrayed as extrinsically caused, it becomes something that happens to animals, and then it is logically barred from being qualified in the ways that White describes, namely, as potentially voluntary, intentional, purposive, conscious, and the like.

Darwin's description of a dog's treatment of a biscuit, which would be considered a vacuum behavior from a classical ethological perspective, again reveals the contrast between the two perspectives in terms of their discrepant conceptions of causation:

> When a piece of brown biscuit is offered to a terrier of mine and she is not hungry (and I have heard of similar instances), she first tosses it about and worries it, as if it were a rat or other prey; she then repeatedly rolls on it precisely as if it were a piece of carrion, and at last eats it. It would appear that an imaginary relish has to be given to the distasteful morsel; and to effect this the dog acts in this habitual manner, as if the biscuit was a live animal or smelt of carrion, though *he knows better than we do* that this is not the case. (1965: 45, emphasis added)

There is conceptual kinship between "the dog worrying the biscuit as if it were prey and the assessment that "he knows better than we do that this is not the case." If, on the other hand, the dog's treatment of the biscuit is conceived as a vacuum behavior, any implication of "knowledge" on the dog's part is foreclosed; the behavior is seen as the blind execution of an innate pattern. The action and its object are connected only from the observer's perspective, via the technical concept of vacuum behavior, and there is no meaningful fit between action and external circumstances. Conversely, the concept of knowledge implies a meaningful connection between a subject's execution of an action and the occasion or object that is targeted by the action. On Darwin's view, the dog's rolling on the biscuit is akin to, or expressive of, an act of the imagination. Reference to knowledge is germane in that the "as if" trope ("as if it were prey") is understood as belonging to the dog's point of reference (as well as to the human observer's). The action of rolling and the object of the action, the biscuit, are grasped as meaningfully connected from the dog's vantage point. The dog's knowing guarantees she is the author, and hence the cause, of her action.

Darwin's view of animals acting for pleasure, amusement, or with imagination thus leads down a profoundly different path of understanding than does the subsumption of such activities under the technical conception of vacuum behavior. The idea that "the weaver bird amuses itself by neatly weaving blades of grass between the wires of its cage" conveys a very different sense and image than a vacuum behavior released under the pressure of internal stimulation. I have explored the contrast in order to draw out the effects of Darwin's understanding of animal behavior. Simple ideas—like a bird weaving for pleasure or singing for its own amusement—embody assumptions and consequences that are far from simple, namely, that animals' actions are experientially meaningful and actively authored. Darwin's accounts systematically foster the witnessing of subjectivity in animal life by representing action as performed by, rather than happening to, animals. His loyalty to this perspective, reflected in the consistency of his language use, engages the imagination of the reader to regard the landscape of animal life as lit from within.

THE SIGNIFICANCE OF ANECDOTAL EVIDENCE

Anecdotes are narratives of singular instances of animal behavior. They are rarely reports of commonplace behaviors, but rather narrate striking, extraordinary, or rare events. In contemporary science, as Daniel Dennett puts it, anecdotes have been "officially unusable" (1987: 250). The rejection of anecdotal evidence rests on the assessment that such uncorroborated evidence is unverifiable and hence unreliable. While the "official unusability" of anecdotal data weeds out the occasional tall tale with respect to animal capacities, it also excludes exceptional or unique information (ibid.). Further, in connection to the question of animal mind, Griffin has noted that because of the disparagement of anecdotal data, "field observers often fail to report evidence suggestive of conscious thinking even when they obtain it, and editors of scientific journals are reluctant to publish it" (1984: 14, 15).

Darwin did not rely on anecdotes of animal life as massively as his disciple George Romanes (1882), yet he uses the anecdotal method consistently.[10] By examining the range of behaviors that anecdotal evidence makes admissible in Darwin's works, the *kind of knowledge* advanced with anecdotes may be brought to light. Darwin's use of anecdotes brings two important aspects to the foreground. First, the inclusion of singular events as behavioral evidence implicitly admits a wider ambit of variation within a species (or population). The use of such data reflects the assumption of, and evidences, considerable individual variation in behaviors. Conversely, the exclusion of anecdotes cloaks the range of variability and heterogeneity of behaviors among individual members of a species. The view, therefore, of certain behavioral repertoires as homogeneously distributed and fixed may partially be an artifact of the scientific orthodoxy that has excluded the singular event as a legitimate or useful datum. The second aspect of anecdotal evidence is that it brings into view certain types of phenomena that are too complex to present in a generalized format. This is especially the case with phenomena of ratiocination. Conversely, the inadmissibility of singular behavioral instances as "good data" may exclude the assessment of capacities (for example, of "thinking") that on account of their complexity require recounting specific instances in order to be convincingly documented. These points will become clearer with the consideration of examples from Darwin's writings. I turn first to the connection between anecdotes and individual variability.

Darwin placed paramount importance on variability, which was the mainspring of his devastating attack on the idea of the fixity of species. In his work *On the Origin of Species* he shows that variation is not a matter of insignificant deviations from some fixed type, but the material basis of evolution. He argues compellingly that differences found between individuals, lesser varieties, well-marked varieties, subspecies, and species "blend into each other in an insensible series; and a series impresses the mind with the idea of an actual passage" (1964: 51). Darwin remained consistent in emphasizing individual variation with respect to mental and behavioral characteristics as well: "The variability of the faculties in the individuals of the same species is an important point for us. . . . I have found on frequent enquiry, that it is the unanimous opinion of all those who have long attended to animals of many kinds, including birds, that the individuals differ greatly in every mental characteristic" (1981, 1: 36).

The most conspicuous contrast to this view has been the classical ethological conception of innate behaviors as "fixed action patterns" (Lorenz and Tinbergen 1957; Thorpe 1973: 10–11; Grier 1984: 36). Especially early in the development of the field, ethologists emphasized the stereotypy and invariance of innate behaviors. For Lorenz, "individual variability can be neglected when giving a general biological description of a species. This conception is not incompatible with the fact that certain instinctive actions can have a high regulative 'plasticity.' So do many organs" (1957a: 121). Lorenz did not regard "plasticity" (or variability) as a significant aspect of innate behaviors, but rather as incidental modularity around a fixed type or essence. Elsewhere Lorenz articulates his conception of innate behavior in the following terms: "Behaviour patterns are not something which animals may do or not do, or do in different ways, according to the requirements of the occasion, but something which animals of a given species 'have got,' exactly in the same manner as they 'have got' claws or teeth of a definite morphological structure" (1950: 237–38). The representation of behaviors as fixed is closely connected with the ethological proclivity for generic description. As I will argue in Chapter 3, ethologists' predilection for the abstract description of typified behavior conjures a mechanomorphic portrait of animals, for in the human imagination, absence of variation is connected with a mechanical icon of behavior. Hence the neglect of individual variation of behaviors and the disparagement of anecdotal evidence, coupled with generic description as a method of writing, contributed to the impression that the ethological theoretical *construct* of fixed action patterns was an ontological *property* of animal behavior in general.

The neglect or underestimation of variability goes hand in hand with the devaluation of anecdotal evidence, for there is a powerful link between recognizing the existence of individual variation in behaviors and capacities and valuing the collection and recounting of individual instances.[11] While some anecdotes related by Darwin may be unreliable testimonies, the great majority are probably veridical descriptions of unique or rare events. The veridicality of an anecdote does not guarantee that the occurrence it narrates is typical of the particular species. What such veracity may attest to, however, is a wider scope of individual variation in behavioral repertoires and capacities than might otherwise be assumed.

> Many animals . . . certainly sympathise with each other's distress or danger. . . . Mr. Blyth, as he informs me, saw Indian crows feeding two or three of their companions which were blind; and I have heard of an analogous case with the domestic cock. We may, if we choose, call these actions instinctive; but such cases are much too rare for the development of any special instinct. I have myself seen a dog, who never passed a great friend of his, a cat which lay sick in a basket, without giving her a few licks with his tongue, the surest sign of a kind feeling in a dog. (1981, 1: 77)

Darwin's reliance on anecdotes to demonstrate the capacity of animals to express sympathy is implicitly connected with his admission that "individuals differ greatly in every mental characteristic," as well as with his appreciation of actions that are "rare." Thus he does not react to extraordinary stories about animals with skepticism, but rather is willing to consider them as potentially unusual behaviors, instantiating individual variability.[12] He regards the individual case as a valuable datum, even if it does not represent what happens on average. He appreciates the dog's show of sympathy for the cat ("a great friend of his"), without reservation, as sound evidence of the capacity of sympathy in dogs.

One significant facet of anecdotal evidence, then, relates to the admission of a wide spread of individual variation. As I mentioned, the other involves the discernment of phenomena whose conceptual and ascriptional complexities require overcoming what may be referred to as "limits of evidence." The attribution of ratiocination to animals is difficult to document or justify in abstract, general terms. In the predication of a mental process such as thinking (or of closely related phenomena, such as reasoning, considering, deliberating, and planning), behavioral anecdotes are a most effective form of evidence.

Local evidence is the most convincing type of evidence for thinking, because there are no consistent or conspicuous behavioral expressions on the basis of which to perceive and maintain that an animal is thinking.

The difficulties are twofold: first, the concept of thinking does not have a simple and uniform meaning, and second, its ascription cannot be stably paired with particular behaviors or expressions. There is one sense of thinking—namely, private soliloquy—that can be entirely divorced from behavioral expression.[13] This type of thinking presents perhaps insuperable difficulties, as there are no ratifiable grounds for ascribing to animals thinking that has no (obvious or necessary) connection with some action or expression. Yet it is worth underscoring Darwin's distance from skepticism even in this connection, as he was willing to speculate that animals may think in this purely inward and imperceptible fashion. With his characteristic candor and largesse, he writes, "no one supposes that one of the lower animals reflects whence he comes or whither he goes,—what is death or what is life, and so forth. But can we feel sure that an old dog with an excellent memory and some power of imagination, as shewn by his dreams, never reflects on his past pleasures in the chase? and this would be a form of self-consciousness" (1981, 1 :62).

Thinking that is divorced from overt or perceptible expression is, however, only one type of thinking, and only one of the senses in which the concept is used. Another sense of thinking is internally and locally connected with (some course of) action. By "internally," I mean to emphasize the cogency of ascribing thinking, under the particular circumstances; and by "locally," I emphasize the concrete behaviors and events that occasion such an ascription. Yet the phenomena of thinking are so complex and heteromorphous that neither is this sense of thinking uniform, as there are various degrees of certainty in discerning thinking synchronously with (and in) a course of action. On one end, thinking is visibly, and always contextually, linked with action. Hesitating just prior to action can be witnessed as the expressive indication of this kind of thinking. Darwin identifies hesitation before action as a sign of reasoning, writing that "few persons any longer dispute that animals possess some power of reasoning. Animals may constantly be seen to pause, deliberate, and resolve" (1981, 1: 46).[14]

Darwin proceeds to make his case for animals' possession of some form of reason by giving particular examples. Recounting an anecdote from Rengger, Darwin writes that "when he first gave eggs to his monkeys, they smashed them and thus lost much of their contents; afterwards they gently hit one end against some hard body, and picked off the bits of shell with their fingers" (1981, 1: 47). Darwin also recounts two anecdotes about retrievers as evidence that dogs are capable of dealing with contingencies by apparently reasoning out the situation:

> Mr. Colquhoun winged two wild-ducks, which fell on the opposite side of a stream; his retriever tried to bring over both at once, but could not succeed; she then, though never before known to ruffle a feather, deliberately killed one, brought over the other, and returned for the dead bird. Col. Hutchinson relates that two partridges were shot at once, one being killed, the other wounded; the latter ran away, and was caught by the retriever, who on her return came across the dead bird; "she stopped, evidently greatly puzzled, and after one or two trials, finding she could not take it up without permitting the escape of the winged bird, she considered a moment, then deliberately murdered it by giving it a severe crunch, and afterwards brought away both together. This was the only known instance of her ever having wilfully injured any game."

Darwin concludes this anecdote with the comment:

> Here we have reason, though not quite perfect, for the retriever might have brought the wounded bird first and then returned for the dead one, as in the case of the two wild-ducks. (1981, 1: 48)

The evidence for reasoning is adduced in the "deliberate killing" of the wounded birds by the retrievers to solve the practical problem of securing two game birds that have fallen at once. The use of the anecdote here is crucial, because the evidence for reasoning is quite literally circumstantial. What is notable in this example is how many different aspects must jointly converge to furnish evidence for reasoning. For the killing to be seen as deliberate action, first there is the exceptional or unusual circumstance of two birds having fallen at once—one dead, the other wounded. The deliberateness is then corroborated by the background information that neither of these dogs had previously ever "ruffled a feather" or "wilfully injured game," and in the case of one dog it is given further support by the brief hesitation prior to action (namely, "she considered for a moment," which can only be visualized by the reader as a pause before action). The assessment of *deliberate* killing is linked with the pressing necessity of resolving the problem at hand. The solution provided by the dogs evidences reasoning, since it meets the end requirement of securing all game with method and efficacy. So with these anecdotes, reasoning (and related phenomena, such as considering and deliberating) becomes transparent in the specific dogs' course of action, with some reference to their background history, and under concrete and peculiar circumstances. Returning to the theme under discussion—the complexity of the phenomena of thinking and their evidencing through anecdotes—the story of these dogs instantiates a case of thinking that is scenically available, given local circumstances and prior history.

Darwin's examples disclose that phenomena of ratiocination are evidenced most effectively in concrete instances of actions that require, warrant, or strongly suggest that such phenomena are indeed at work. On a case-by-case basis, through the offering of specific instantiations (with all the necessary details of expressive-behavioral form, transpiring events, and relevant historical material), the existence of ratiocinating capacities in the animal world is made *generally* perspicuous. To wit, local and concrete evidence is the best (if not the only) evidence for the global and abstract claim that thinking and reasoning do exist in the animal world.

In addition, there is also the case of ratiocination that may be locally but not visibly—that is, not *evidently*—connected with action. In his discussion of reason, Darwin writes that "it is often difficult to distinguish between the power of reason and that of instinct" (1981, 1: 46). To show the difficulty, he relates, after Hayes, that dogs generally draw sledges as a "compact body," but "they diverged and separated when they came to thin ice, so that their weight might be more evenly distributed. This was often the first warning and notice which the travellers received that the ice was becoming thin and dangerous" (1981, 1: 46-47). Darwin goes on to state that it is "most difficult" to assess the dogs' actions: their spreading apart over thin ice may be a consequence of the "experience of each individual," of "the example of the older and wiser dogs," or of "instinct" selected for when the dogs' progenitors, the Arctic wolves, were impelled "not to attack their prey in a close pack when on thin ice" (ibid.). Here, coming up against limits of evidence means that the dogs' action of parting on thin ice could be attributed to their reasoning out what needs to be done, yet such reasoning is neither necessarily nor visibly connected with the course of action they take. This shortage of evidence—coupled with the fact that there are alternative accounts for their action—warrants that, in this particular instance, there is no foolproof basis for ascribing reasoning to the dogs.

So on one end of a continuum, thinking may be visible in a course of action, while on the other, thinking may be plausibly inferred but not obvious. Yet another twist in the complexity of the phenomena of thinking are cases that are intermediate to these extremes. Darwin relates another anecdote after Gardner, "a trustworthy naturalist" who, while watching a shore crab making its burrow, threw some shells toward its hole:

> One rolled in, and three other shells remained within a few inches of the mouth. In about five minutes the crab brought out the shell which had fallen in, and carried it away to the distance of a foot; *it then saw* the three other shells lying near, and *evidently thinking that* they might likewise roll in, carried them to the spot where it had laid the first. It would I think be difficult to distinguish this act from one performed by man by the aid of reason. (1981, 1: 334–35, emphasis added)

This case, again, reveals the connection between unusual events and the discernment of thinking, illustrating the role of anecdotal data in presenting evidence of thinking among crabs. While attesting to Darwin's distance from a skeptical standpoint, this case exemplifies another difficulty in evidencing reasoning in the animal world: namely, that the grounds for accepting an action as manifesting reasoning are taken to corrode the more distant the animal is in relation to human beings, even if the behavioral evidence remains compelling. Thus, in his discussion of the capacity of individual recognition among shrimp, Griffin points out that "because mantis shrimp are crustaceans a few centimeters in length, it is assumed a priori that they cannot possibly be conscious" (1992: 200). Darwin appears to be alluding to this sort of parti pris when he explicitly underlines that the crab's action has the character of "one performed by a man by the aid of reason."

Overall, then, an abstract or comprehensive argument for the case that animals are capable of thinking is unconvincing, since there are no firm or invariant expressions by which to descry thinking. The concept of "thinking" does not refer to a single type of phenomenon, and there are no context-free criteria (such as stable behavioral patterns) on the basis of which to attribute thinking. However, Darwin and other naturalists he cites do not take the complexities of thinking and the lack of transcontextual standards as grounds for endorsing an in-principle skepticism, but instead advance evidence of thinking by providing local examples. Testimony for phenomena of ratiocination in the animal world is thus grounded in *inductive* reasoning and argumentation. Arguably, therefore, anecdotes document the phenomena of thinking in animal life no more, but also no less, than they can possibly be documented. After recounting a number of examples, as though to underscore the inductive nature of the argument, Darwin remarks that "anyone who is not convinced by such facts as these, and by what he may observe with his own dogs, that animals can reason, would not be convinced by anything" (1981, 1: 47). In this way, Darwin explicitly ties the narration of anecdotes (and drawing on personal knowledge, which is a special case of anecdotal evidence) with the admission that animals can reason. This is a connection that other naturalists make as well. For example, L. H. Morgan writes that "anecdotes of the intelligent conduct of animals are innumerable. They are not only constantly appearing, and arresting attention, but a sufficient number of instances to illustrate the subject are within personal knowledge of every individual" (1965: 260).

The anecdotal method's implied recognition of the wide scope of individual variability and its ability to provide concrete cases of complex or subtle qualities often go hand in hand. For example, Darwin cites E. Layard, "an excellent observer," on a cobra's solution to capturing a toad:

> A Cobra thrust its head through a narrow hole and swallow[ed] a toad. "With this incumbrance he could not withdraw himself; finding this, he reluctantly disgorged the precious morsel, which began to move off; this was too much for snake philosophy to bear, and the toad was again seized, and again was the snake, after violent efforts to escape, compelled to part with its prey. This time, however, a lesson had been learnt, and the toad was seized by one leg, withdrawn, and then swallowed in triumph." (1981, 2: 30–31)

Showing a unique, rare event and evidencing that "a lesson had been learnt" by the cobra, this observation highlights the two features of behavior, uniqueness and adaptability, that the anecdotal method documents especially well. The junction of these features has been described by Griffin as "versatility"—the provision of "enterprising solutions to newly arisen problems" (1984: 209), or "cop[ing] with novel and unpredictable challenges in simple but apparently rational ways" (1992: 27). Griffin proposes that versatility can be considered "a widely applicable, if not all-inclusive, criterion of conscious awareness in animals" (1984: 37).

An example of versatile behavior related by Griffin is the contemporary discovery that green herons sometimes use bait to capture fish. In one pond studied, only about 10 percent of the bird population practiced baiting, in which the heron will "pick up small pieces of bread, drop them onto the water, and then capture fish . . . attracted to this bait" (Griffin 1984: 123). With contemporary technology this behavior can be documented, even though it is exceedingly rare, whereas previously the gathering of anecdotal evidence was the method for recording what Griffin calls "enterprising behavior." With the disparagement of the anecdotal method in twentieth-century behavioral science, this central method of documenting versatility, which Darwin utilized when necessary, was largely excluded from the outset. If Griffin's conception of versatility is indeed a robust criterion for conscious awareness, then clearly the devaluation of the method of anecdotal evidence has both accompanied and reinforced the skeptical attitude of twentieth-century behaviorists and ethologists toward the existence of conscious awareness in animals.

Conclusion

Based on the pervasiveness of his style and on his explicit statements, in this chapter I have argued that Darwin's anthropomorphism is not a metaphorical extension of language from the human to the animal case. Darwin intends his descriptions, including those replete with a vocabulary of mental activity, as realistic representations of animal life. His realistic approach to the transparency of animal subjectivity differs profoundly from mechanomorphic imagery, and implicitly stands in opposition to skepticism about animal mind. In contrast to critics who either downplay or condemn his anthropomorphism, I have argued that Darwin's language reflects his view of animal life as meaningful and authored. Finally, in letting Darwin's words speak for themselves, I have endeavored to show that, far from being naive or the consequence of conflating human and animal qualities, his vision of animal life is lastingly powerful.

Darwin's anthropomorphic language emanates from a commitment to evolutionary continuity that, for him, inexorably includes behavioral and mental continuity. He defends this view explicitly in providing numerous instantiations of a wide gamut of behavioral continuities and cognate mental faculties in many different species, from insects to primates and birds, with examples ranging from the commonplace to the rare and anecdotal. The breadth and character of his understanding of behavioral and mental continuity, as well as its strong empirical support, come to center stage in *The Expression of Emotions in Man and Animals*.

While Darwin openly advocates continuity between all animals, his use of the ordinary language of living makes the same argument in an even more resounding manner. In affinity with the genre of naturalist writing, which I investigate in the next chapter, the anthropomorphic language of Darwin, the naturalist, reflects an understanding of subjectivity in animal life in terms of animals as authors of action, and of action as transparently embodying an experientially meaningful dimension. As a final illustration of the features of authorship and experience, I conclude with a most memorable passage from Darwin's writing.

> I formerly possessed a large dog, who, like every other dog, was much pleased to go out walking. He showed his pleasure by trotting gravely before me with high steps, head much raised, moderately erected ears, and tail carried aloft but not stiffly. Not far from my house a path branches off to the right, leading to the hot-house, which I used often to visit for a few moments, to look at my experimental plants. This was always a great disappointment to the dog, as he did not know whether I should continue my' walk; and the instantaneous and complete change of expression which came over him as soon as my body swerved in the least towards the path (and I sometimes tried this as an experiment) was laughable. His look of dejection was known to every member of the family, and was called his *hot-house face*. This consisted in the head drooping much, the whole body sinking a little and remaining motionless; the ears and tail falling suddenly down, but the tail was by no means wagged. With the falling of the ears and of his great chaps, the eyes became much changed in appearance, and I fancied that they looked less bright. His aspect was that of piteous, hopeless dejection; and it was, as I have said, laughable, as the cause was so slight. Every detail in his attitude was in complete opposition to his former joyful yet dignified bearing. (1965: 57–60)

The description of the dog's expressions, as well as of the circumstances that occasioned those expressions, assembles the attentive reader's perceptual focus. Along with Darwin, the reader does not *infer* joy and dejection *from* the dog's bearing, but rather, by imbricating visual memories onto the described scene, *sees* joy and dejection *in* the dog's bearing. Darwin's understanding, without a moment's pause, skirts past the idea of mind as a private domain, and in this unassuming fashion delivers a serious blow to the skeptical disjunction between observable body and unobservable mind.

2   Lifeworld and Subjectivity
Naturalists' Portraits of Animals

IN THIS chapter I turn to naturalists' portrayal of animal life. In the naturalist genre, I argue, the understanding of animals is coextensive with the approach to human action that social scientists have called "*Verstehen*" (Weber 1947; Schutz 1962). *Verstehen* involves the understanding of action from the actor's point of view; it pursues the subjective import of action. Applying the *Verstehen* approach to animals has striking epistemic and visual effects on their portrayal. Here I elucidate these effects by examining the writings of the renowned turn-of-the-century naturalists George and Elizabeth Peckham and Jean Henri Fabre.

Naturalist writing about animals may be regarded as an extension of the *Verstehen* approach, for animal life is treated as immanently meaningful. In his discussion of *Verstehen*, phenomenologist Alfred Schutz writes that the human social world "is experienced from the outset as a meaningful one. The Other's body is not experienced as an organism but as a fellow-man" (1962: 55). Similarly for naturalists, what animals do is "experienced from the outset as meaningful," and the animal's body "is not experienced as an organism," but as a subject's body. While naturalists do not presume that an unambiguous understanding of animal behavior is always available, they nevertheless take it that such an understanding is generally achievable with close and patient observation. Before turning to focus on naturalists' understanding of animals, I briefly clarify the idea of *Verstehen* in connection to human life.

Schutz points out that in everyday reasoning we take for granted the knowledge of the meaning of human actions we participate in or encounter (1962: 56). Even though this knowledge is not formal and may be open-ended and fragmentary, nevertheless it is both sufficient and powerful in coming to grips with situations of everyday reality. While *Verstehen* is often regarded as a method of social science, Schutz points out that it is not, in the first place, a scientific method. Rather, it is "the particular experiential form in which common-sense thinking takes cognizance of the

51

social cultural world" (1962: 56). The *Verstehen* approach to the meaning of actions and events does not originate in social science, but rather derives from everyday forms of practical perceiving and reasoning through which the subjective meaning of others' responses is understood.

In everyday life, in Schutz's words, "we normally 'know' what the Other does, for what reason he does it, why he does it at this particular time and in these particular circumstances" (1962: 55). This knowledge of the meaning of the action *for* the actor embeds a potential contradiction: it refers to *public* knowledge and procedures for understanding the *subjective* meaning of actions. The simultaneous character of *Verstehen* as public and subjective, however, appears as a contradiction only when subjective meaning is identified with insight into the private world of another. In the *Verstehen* attitude of everyday life, persons do in fact routinely assign or wager private motives (reasons, justifications, concerns, or whatever) in understanding the meaning of action for another. This sense of private, then, is publicly shared. Ethnomethodologist Harold Garfinkel comments on the thoroughly intersubjective nature of this sense of "private," stating that human actors regularly assume "that there is a characteristic disparity between the publicly acknowledged determinations and the personal, withheld determinations of events, and this private knowledge is held in reserve, i.e., that the event means for both the witness and the other more than the witness can say" (1967: 56).

Two senses of "private" can be confused when pondering the idea of subjective meaning as "private." One is the vernacular, shared meaning—a personal matter, an aspect kept hidden, or a secret jealously guarded. The other sense of "private"—the skeptical—denotes something ineffable, inscrutable except to the owner, in principle unobtainable, or always incompletely known. While the first sense of private is an integral aspect of human (inter)action, the second sense appears blatantly spurious in the face of the largesse of subjective transparency in human life.[1] The *Verstehen* approach is interested simply in the meaning action has for the actor her- or himself. The *Verstehen* idea of "subjective meaning" denotes not only that action has meaning from the actor's perspective, but also, more powerfully, that the actor's meaning is internally linked with the production of action. The first feature alone, namely, the presence of a subjective perspective, does not deliver the essential insight of the *Verstehen* approach. The strong claim of *Verstehen* asserts not only the existence but above all the *significance* of subjective meaning, in that the latter is constitutive of, and therefore inseparable from, action itself.

The link between subjective meaning and action is fastened in diverse ways by human actors and with various degrees of transparency and opacity, availability and secrecy, conventionality and eccentricity. What *Verstehen* underscores is that beyond the multifarious links that subjects contrive between meaning and acting, from the perspective of the witness the meaning of a subject's actions is routinely and massively—though not infallibly—visible, available, or at least obtainable with some detective work of practical action or of the imagination. Because understanding the meaning of others' actions is a situated and motley affair, it is not amenable to the closure of a single epistemological standpoint (for example, of a philosophical school or a social theory). The intelligibility of action from another's perspective can range from being directly perceivable to tenuously inferred, on the basis of knowledge that ranges from thoroughly commonsensical or universal to particular and private.

In the *Verstehen* approach of the naturalists discussed here, understanding the activities of animals traverses a parallel though not isomorphic gamut to understanding human action. Even as the meaning of animals' actions ranges from directly perceivable to thoroughly opaque or indeterminate, it is always assumed that actions *are* meaningful, and that their meanings are largely available. In naturalist writing, the meaningfulness of animal life and action is conveyed not as an imputation from an external vantage point, but as internally constitutive of the behaviors and events depicted. Naturalists thus acknowledge an experiential perspective in animal life and tacitly reject the skeptical conception of subjectivity as a hopelessly inaccessible realm.

Naturalists' *Verstehen* approach to the subjective meaning of animal action relies upon the ordinary language of action and mind, that is, the everyday language of human life. Implicitly yet resolutely, naturalists deny that the ideas and reasoning of this language are exclusive possessions of human life. In deploying this language, they both discover and create an alignment between animal action and human action. It is precisely the forms of this alignment that have been pejoratively labeled "anthropomorphic." As discussed in connection to Darwin, this label insinuates that the use of the language of human affairs for animal life creates distortions—hence implying that such language should be either tolerated as metaphorical and quaint or rejected as a category mistake. In contrast, however, to this evaluation of anthropomorphic language as figurative or erroneous, I argue that it is clear that the naturalists discussed here intend their analyses as *realistic* depictions of animal life. In this chapter, as in the investigation of Darwin's behavioral thought, the aspersive evaluation of naturalists' anthropomorphic portrayals is suspended, for in order to see the landscape of animal life that naturalists create, their bid for realism must be taken seriously.

The Animal's World as a Lifeworld

Perhaps the most encompassing way to characterize the portraiture of naturalist writing is to say that it composes lifeworlds. A *lifeworld* is an everyday world where things, activities, relations, and events have experiential significance. The idea of lifeworld denotes that the world of a subject is, first and foremost, a world filled with action—filled with things that have been, are being, and will be done. Subjects are always already ceaselessly engaged in meaningful activity in the lifeworld, with no reprieve.[2] Although actions in the lifeworld vary in modality and intensity, and in degree of routinization and improvisation, they tend to recur in cycles, such as temporal cycles of day and night, of times of day, or of the seasons, and they are directed expectably and habitually with respect to others, objects, and places. In their recurrence and expectability the actions themselves are anonymous, that is, they are ordinary, recognizable, and shared both in signification and form. However, in a lifeworld the agents of actions are always existentially eponymous, that is, they are specific, singular, and irreplaceable.

George and Elizabeth Peckham in their work *Wasps: Solitary and Social* (1905) make an observation consonant with this view of the animal as an inhabitant of a lifeworld:

> In reading much popular natural history one might suppose that the insects seen flying about on a summer's day were a part of some great throng which is ever moving onward, those that are here today being replaced by a new set on the morrow. Except during certain seasons the exact opposite of this is true. The flying things about us abide in the same locality and are the inhabitants of a fairly restricted area. The garden in which we worked was, to a large extent, the home of a limited number of certain species of wasps that had resided there from birth, or having found the place accidentally, had settled there permanently. (1905: 280)

The Peckhams indicate that from a cursory perspective (which they identify as "much popular natural history," although it could belong to any nonspecialist) there appears to be no everyday life, no existential permanence in the world of insects. After careful observation this view is redressed by the naturalists, in that anonymous and indefinite "flying things" are seen to be "permanent inhabitants" of a restricted area, such as the garden. A fundamental step in the disclosure of a lifeworld is that the animal's world is no longer faceless. The world of a garden, for instance, takes form as a world of everyday life, filled with specific actors engaged in anonymous, and for the most part unremarkable, actions.

The lifeworld, pictured as a meaningful space replete with actions with no time-out, might be regarded as a spatial metaphor for the fullness of life. Every instance of action, however trivial it may appear, bears testimony to this plenum. The Peckhams see the wasps as being in constant action. They observe, for instance, that "the wasps love the heat of noontide, and with every rise of temperature they fly faster, hum louder, and rejoice more and more in the fullness of life" (1905: 2–3). This, then, is a salient angle of the naturalist outlook on the animal world: because that world is meaningful, action is not strictly identified with energetic engagement but equally can be passive or inconsequential. In accordance with the *Verstehen* view of action, the naturalist sees action as exhibiting— patently, or after close attention—a subjectively meaningful orientation to the world. Since the animal's world is always already meaningful, as long as animals are alive they are in action.

The passage that follows illustrates this point. Describing the natural history of the wasp *Bembex spinolae*, the Peckhams observe that when the weather is overcast or rainy the wasps do not work at excavating and provisioning their nests. The Peckhams report an observation made on such a day:

> On going over to the island one cloudy morning to spend some hours in watching the Bembex activities, we found the spot quiet and lifeless. No one seeing it for the first time would have dreamed of the multitudes of living creatures beneath his feet. The nests seemed to be all closed, but on peering curiously about we found one on sloping ground, in the suburbs of the colony, of which the door was open. Just within was the proprietor gazing out on the landscape, as she is shown in the illustration. She seemed to be leaning on her elbows, and her face, enlivened by two great goggle eyes, had an irresistibly comic aspect. (1905: 130–31)

Once again the Peckhams juxtapose a superficial perspective on animal life to knowledge after close observation. Just as the view of insects as "ever-passing throngs" is an illusion, so the appearance of the location as "life-

Figure 3   Gazing wasp

less" is an illusion. Beneath the quiet surface, the ground is full of wasps in their closed nests. The naturalist's knowledge is unique, for it eludes strict classification as either "commonsense" knowledge or "specialized" knowledge. It may be characterized as "uncommon-sense knowledge" (see Garfinkel 1967: 118), in being simultaneously esoteric and nontechnical. The naturalist's knowledge is uncommon, or extraordinary, not in the sense of being highly technical, but in deriving from practices of observation and learning that are not widely implemented. Naturalists' knowledge may also be characterized, after Michael Polanyi, as "personal knowledge," transcending the split between subjective and objective: while their pursuit of knowledge is guided by personal passion, they are intent upon revealing the reality of the natural world within which they become immersed (cf. Polanyi 1962: 300ff.).

The location of the wasps' nests is sequestered from its surroundings through notions that are lifeworld-derived. At first the Peckhams refer to it as "the spot." However, the boundaries of the spot are not purely physical. They are circumscribed through the idea of a colony that has suburbs.

Like a city, the spot becomes a centrally populated location, which is more sparsely inhabited in the outskirts. The colony is made of nests, which have doors, and these nests are owned by the proprietors who built them. The location is thus configured as the physical manifestation of a lifeworld, one created by the activities of the wasps.

Just as the quietness of the spot conveys an illusion of lifelessness, so the wasp at the door of her nest, if noticed at all—though this requires "peering curiously about," that is, a nonordinary engagement of perceptual action—might be seen as "doing nothing." There is nothing remarkable about a wasp sitting motionless at the foot of her burrow. In the world that the Peckhams are disclosing, however, this wasp is "gazing out on the landscape." The wasp's action is grasped as "gazing," for the location of the nest on sloping ground indicates that there is something to gaze *at*. The wasp's sitting position discloses a diachronous, stable, and comfortable quality in her comportment: she was in the position of "leaning on her elbows" when discovered and, if not disturbed, will remain in this position until she stops gazing. The disclosure of the wasp as gazing out on the landscape is an example of the naturalist's simultaneous interpretation and perception of animals as always already engaged in meaningful action. This outlook is all the more conspicuous in the portrayal of inactivity—of passive or quiet action. For the Peckhams, nonaction simply does not exist in the wasps' world. This ceaseless, always meaningful activity contributes crucially to the portraiture of the animal world as a lifeworld, a world filled to the brim.

The lifeworld is not only the world of the stream of everyday actions, but one that is also a world-in-common. For Schutz, it is "the one unitary life-world of myself, of you, of us all" (1962: 120). The understanding of the animal world as a shared world of everyday life is illustrated beautifully by the Peckhams in another description of the early period of the life history of the wasp *Philanthus punctatus*:

> When the wasps emerge from the cocoon they find themselves in the company of their nearest relatives and in possession of a dwelling-place, and they live together for a time before starting out independently to seek their fortunes. On the fifth of August we discovered on the island a happy family of this kind, consisting of three brothers and four sisters, the females with their bright yellow faces and mandibles, being handsomer than the males. They seemed to be on the most amicable terms with each other, their only trouble being that while they were all fond of looking out, the doorway was too small to hold more than one at a time. The nest was opened in the morn-

ing at about nine o'clock, and during the next thirty or forty minutes their comical little faces would appear, one after another, each wasp enjoying the view for a few minutes with many twitchings of the head, and then retreating to make way for another, perhaps in response to some hint from behind. Then one by one they would come out, circle about the spot, and depart, sometimes leaving one of their number to keep house all day alone. (1905: 154–55)

In a few brushstrokes, this passage encompasses the canvas of a complete lifeworld—"of myself, of you, of us all." The burrow does not simply hold organisms in physical proximity. It is a "dwelling-place," a "house" in which "nearest relatives" ("brothers and sisters") live "in the company" of each other "on the most amicable terms." There is multiple interplay in this description of intersubjective mirroring of what Schutz calls the Here and the There, crystallizing in the perception that the world as a common place-of-action is at once perspectival and shared. The Peckhams witness the There of the wasps as an experienced Here from the wasps' point of view. As subjects, *and only as subjects,* can wasps be "in company," "a happy family," and "amicable with each other"; "live together," "keep house," "enjoy a view," or "retreat to make way for another." None of these conceptions of understanding, with their rich fields of meaning— denoting feeling and awareness—is applicable to "mere" organisms.

THE HERE AND THE THERE: THE WORLD AS BOTH PERSPECTIVAL AND SHARED

In the description of the brother and sister wasps there is, first, the mirroring between the Here of the human observers and the There of the wasps, accomplished with the use of terms and ideas common to both worlds, yet indexically distinct.[3] "Indexically distinct" means that the senses of the shared concepts of wasp and human worlds resound within one another, rather than collapse into each other. The common terms refer to objects and actions that are similar in certain ways, but at the same time nonidentical. For example, while in appearance the openings of wasp burrows have little in common with the doorways of human houses, the common grounds of construction through work and functional usage to enter an abode admit reference to a wasp "doorway."

The effect of common conceptions of wasp and human life, especially of domestic life—"possessing a dwelling-place," "being a family," "looking out the doorway," or "keeping house"—is to form a connecting line between the wasps' There and the human Here. Inhabited spaces cast non-identical reflections onto one another as spaces produced through work, embodying the abstract intention of being lived in, and charged with the ways of companionship and affection. The connecting link between wasps and humans does not remain a single thread, but becomes a resilient cable as it is spun over and over by a plethora of vernacular terms of life, action, and feeling. The compelling effect is that the wasps' potentially anonymous and insignificant world is transformed into an eponymous and signifying lifeworld.

There is, second, an interplay of the Here and There of the wasps themselves, in their daily routine of taking turns looking out the doorway. The There of the wasp looking out is the upcoming Here for the wasp waiting to look out. The There at the foot of the doorway, with its coveted view, is seen by the Peckhams as experienced by each wasp as the Here that is either upcoming or to be relinquished. Under the auspices of this view, "some hint from behind" urging retreat from the spot—while not seeable—is appresented to the observer's imagination. In the lifeworld, actions are abstract, while actors are concrete. No matter who is performing it, the anonymous action of "looking out" the doorway abstractly encompasses the same intention, expresses the same desire, and is achieved by the same movements, namely, standing at the doorway and turning the head about. At the same time, each wasp is a singular and concrete subject, being *one of* the three brothers and four sisters, each "fond of looking out," that is, both desiring and intending.

In this passage about the seven sibling wasps, reciprocity and kinship between humans and wasps is revealed and created in a language deploying terms that share territories of common meaning even while referring to different objects and situations. The interplay of Here and There is seen in another episode related by George and Elizabeth Peckham, concerning a wasp (*Ammophila urnaria*) carrying her prey, a caterpillar, to her nest.

For sixty feet she kept to open ground, passing between two rows of bushes; but at the end of this division of the garden, she plunged, very much to our dismay, into a field of standing corn. Here we had great difficulty in following her, since, far from keeping to her former orderly course, she zigzagged among the plants in the most bewildering fashion, although keeping a general direction of northeast. It seemed quite impossible that she could know where she was going. The corn rose to a height of six feet all around us; the ground was uniform in appearance, and, to our eyes, each group of corn-stalks was just like every other group, and yet, without pause or hesitation, the little creature passed quickly along, as we might through the familiar streets of our native town.

At last she paused and laid her burden down. Ah! the power that had led her is not a blind, mechanically perfect instinct, for she has traveled a little too far. She must go back one row into the open space that she has already crossed, although not just at this point. Nothing like a nest is visible to us; the surface of the ground looks all alike, and it is with exclamations of wonder that we see our little guide lift two pellets of earth which have served as a covering to a small opening running down into the ground.

The way being thus prepared, she hurries back with her wings quivering and her whole manner betokening joyful triumph at the completion of her task. We, in the mean time, have become as much excited over the matter as she is herself. She picks up the caterpillar, brings it to the mouth of the bur-row, and lays it down. Then, backing in herself, she catches it in her man-dibles and drags it out of sight, leaving us full of admiration and delight. (1905: 19–21)

The reciprocity of the Here of the observers and There of the wasp is vivid in this episode. While the perspectives of the Here and There coexist in the same physical location, they look out onto different worlds. In the Peck-hams' Here of the cornfield, each row of cornstalks is the same as every other and the ground is uniform. The There of the wasp, then, is not the Here of the Peckhams from a different physical angle; for in such a case it is "quite impossible that she could know where she was going." As it be-comes clear that "she does know where she is going," the wasp's Here cannot be the uniform Here of the Peckhams. Rather, in that the wasp's rows of cornstalks are equivalent to the human's familiar streets of a town, the wasp's Here is the not-present Here of the Peckhams.

Schutz presents the idea of the "reciprocity of perspectives" that exists in the human world with the notions of the Here and the There. He ob-serves, "I take it for granted, and I assume my fellow-man does the same, that I and my fellow-man would have typically the same experiences of the common world if we changed places, thus transforming my Here into his, and his—now to me a There—into mine" (1962: 316). This taken-for-granted assumption of reciprocity forms one of the pillars of the Ver-stehen attitude of everyday life—the understanding of others as "alter subjects." In the case of the Peckhams and the wasp, the interplay of per-ceptual perspectives both is and is not reciprocal. It is *not* reciprocal in that this cornfield will always be a different place for the Peckhams and for the wasp; and it *is* reciprocal in that what the rows of cornstalks are to the wasp is what the familiar streets of their native town are to the Peckhams.

A final point about the connection between the Here and the There is that in the naturalist's genre there is no such thing as "disinterestedness." The science of the naturalist is, in that sense, quite distinct from the understanding of science that identifies objectivity with emotional and intellectual aloofness.[4] The Peckhams put themselves into the writing; their presence is a feature of the scenes and episodes they recount. Their "admiration and delight" expresses an unembarrassed exhilaration in pursuing knowledge about the wasps. This interested participation is integral to the perception of the wasp as an alter subject and is a point I will revisit further on.

On the Decidability of Meaning of Animal Action

Thus far I have indicated that the Peckhams' portrayals entangle a background presupposition and a local perception of the animal's world as inherently meaningful, and that this perspective is primarily displayed in grasping animals' conduct as ceaselessly oriented to things and events in the world. To circumvent the opposition between constructivist and realist epistemologies, this simultaneity of seeing and assuming that actions are meaningful may be referred to as the naturalist's "assembling a way to witness" animal behavior.[5] Insofar as naturalists *construct* the understanding of animal action, this does not license hazarding a possibly meaningful interpretation at any cost, for their clear commitment is fidelity to the phenomena under study. At the same time, insofar as naturalists *witness* the meaning of animal action, this does not guarantee that its sense will always be transparent. Indeed, when adequate criteria or evidence for understanding what an animal is doing is absent, then the observer meets an interpretive impasse. As will be seen in the next chapter, on classical ethology, the fact that the meaning of animal action is sometimes intractably opaque from a human perspective can play a key part in the construal of animal behavior as a "natural-type" phenomenon, which is intrinsically meaningless and experientially empty.

Our facility with accounts of both animal and human actions in the ordinary language of living reveals that the scenery of those actions, by and large, is generous with evidence of their sense. Yet this contiguity of interpretive transparency of the two worlds fails at certain moments, for the intimate familiarity of human action is incomparable with the more removed way we bear witness to animal action. One dimension of "undecidability" of the meaning of animal behaviors relates to the necessity in certain cases to witness the final outcome of a series of actions in order to decide the meaning of the act as a whole. A second relates to the equivocality of certain actions that cannot be resolved via the communicative option that Garfinkel and Sacks call "formulating" (1970). I clarify these points with examples.

With respect to interpreting human action, Garfinkel writes that "it frequently happens that in order for the investigator to decide what he is now looking at he must wait for future developments, only to find that these futures in turn are informed by their history and future. By waiting to see what will have happened he learns what it was that he previously saw. Either that, or he takes imputed history and prospects for granted. Motivated actions, for example, have exactly these troublesome properties" (1967: 77). As Garfinkel notes, the routine taking-for-granted of the meaning of others' courses of action is backed by the force of our practical knowledge of human affairs. More often than not, we understand a course of action presently witnessed without having to wait for its future outcome or development, thereby "taking imputed history and prospects for granted." This imputation is far from arbitrary, as it is based, often without a second thought, on "what is known" (1967: 78). To give a mundane example, a person at a bus stop is seen to be waiting for the bus; there is no need to see the person getting on the bus to ascertain that they were, in fact, all along waiting for the bus. The meaning of human action is massively available that way—at a glance. What is known allows for the sense of actions, in their full temporal extensions into an unseen past and an unseen future, to be visible without having to see what will have happened.

With respect to actions in the animal world, however, and especially with actions witnessed for a first time and with no available precedent as an interpretive resource, the observer sometimes has to see what will have happened in order to learn what she or he previously saw (or is seeing). If nothing determinate happens, then the sense of the action may well remain undecidable. A passage from the Peckhams illustrates this undecidability of meaning. In the course of reading the episode recounted, the reader can feel, along with the authors, the anticipation for what will happen, in order to decipher what is being witnessed. The background to this passage is that a particular species of wasp—*Aphilanthops frigidus*—specializes in hunting queen ants. When a wasp captures a queen ant, she stores it in her burrow and lays her egg on it, like all hunting wasps. The Peckhams, however, have never seen an actual capture of a queen ant. This event is particularly intriguing since even though queen ants come out of their nests only once, during their nuptial flight, the wasps somehow manage to capture and store thousands of them. The question, then, is how the wasps do it. The Peckhams describe an event that, in the course of its unfolding, they hoped might result in the observation of the capture of a queen:

> Much interested in the matter [of how the wasp captures the queen ant], we carefully examined the ant-hills of the neighborhood. Those on top of the hills had openings too small to admit frigidus [the wasp], supposing she had wanted to enter, but down on the roadside below we found some larger doorways and sat down beside them. We had scarcely arrived when a frigidus appeared on the scene, alighting six feet away. That she should have come hunting so soon seemed almost too good to be true, but she certainly was not doing anything else. She did not dig, nor feed on the clover, nor circle about as though looking for her nest, but began to clean and brush herself assiduously. Then she climbed a tall grass blade, and swinging at the top went through some curious gymnastic performances. Then she brushed herself again, drawing her third legs over the sides of her abdomen. This went on from moment to moment, until half an hour had passed, and more than once the painful suspicion crossed our minds that this was some trifling male putting in the hours between breakfast and luncheon. One encouraging fact cheered us: aimless as the wasp appeared she was slowly drawing nearer and nearer to the nest; and at last, alighting on the top of a weed close by, she crouched there in a most peculiar attitude, and gazed intently at the opening. Absorbed and tense, she looked about to leap upon her prey; but after a time she relaxed and moved about a little. Presently she came close to the entrance and seemed on the point of going in; but the ants were swarming up and down, and we thought that perhaps that step required more courage than she possessed. At any rate she did not enter, but hung about for some minutes and then flew away. (1905: 174–75)

This passage illustrates the occasional undecidability of the meaning of animal action. Not only is it unclear what the wasp is doing, but the Peckhams are uncertain whether the wasp is male or female, which is intrinsically connected to what it might be doing. Each action of the wasp is graspable as an action, namely, "cleaning," "brushing," "climbing," "slowly drawing nearer," "crouching," "gazing," and so forth. But in the absence of a final outcome, the actions fail to acquire sequential cohesion, that is, they cannot be witnessed as linked pieces of an unfolding single act—potentially the act of hunting. The climax of the episode arrives when the wasp "crouches" and "gazes intently," "absorbed and tense," and "looking about to leap"; at this moment she can almost be seen as perhaps stalking her prey. But neither do these actions have a decidable import. This episode, then, is an example of a series of behaviors whose ultimate meaning remains opaque in the absence both of some kind of outcome and of previous knowledge about the hunting behavior of this particular species.

The role of previous knowledge is important, since understanding animal action does not always require witnessing a final outcome; nor does the decidability of meaning always depend exclusively upon scenic evidence. These points are elucidated in a series of events describing the activities of *Sphex ichneumonea*, a wasp also known as the great golden digger. Over the course of a couple of days, the Peckhams follow the work of a particular wasp in building and provisioning her nest. Their observations commence with her digging her nest for several hours. Eventually

> she came out and walked slowly about in front of her nest and all around it. Then she rose and circled just above it, gradually widening her flight, now going further afield and now flying in and out among the plants and bushes in the immediate vicinity. The detailed survey of every little object near her nest was remarkable; and not until her tour of observation had carried her five times entirely around the spot did she appear satisfied and fly away. All her actions showed that she was studying the locality and getting her bearings before departure. (1905: 58)

The thoroughness, systematicity, and reiteration of the golden digger's flight around her nest just prior to departing are the evidence that the flight pattern, far from being random or meaningless, is a "detailed survey." The Peckhams remark that her "studying the locality" (i.e., a single act) is "shown" (i.e., evidenced) in "all her actions." While the flight is seen as a locality study partly on the basis of its design alone, the Peckhams corroborate this assessment with the previous knowledge, from an independent source, that a wasp fails, or finds it difficult, to locate her nest when the surrounding landscape is altered, sometimes even in small details. Therefore what is known (in this case, by experiment) confirms that the wasp's flight is to be seen, legitimately, as a survey. The intricacy of the

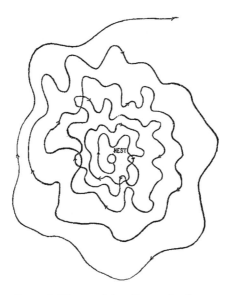

Figure 4   Thorough locality study of wasp

flight designs is witnessed as the method by which the wasp surveys, and so memorizes, the location of her nest. This same form of documentation—of combining local evidence with established knowledge—holds in understanding human action: "Not only is the underlying pattern derived from its individual documentary evidences, but the individual documentary evidences, in their turn, are interpreted on the basis of 'what is known' about the underlying pattern. Each is used to elaborate the other" (Garfinkel 1967: 78).

The Peckhams continue their observations of this particular wasp:

When she flew away we naturally supposed that she had gone in search of her prey, and we were on the *qui vive* to observe every step in her actions when she came home. Alas! when she came back half an hour later, she was empty-handed. She dug for four minutes, then flew off and was gone two minutes, then returned and worked for thirty-five minutes. Another two minutes' excursion, and then she settled down to work in good earnest and brought up load after load of earth until the shadows grew long. We noticed that on these later trips she flew directly away, depending upon her first careful study of the surroundings to find her way back. At fifteen minutes after five the patient worker came to the surface, and made a second study, this time not so detailed, of the environment. She flew this way and that, in and out among the plants, high and low, far and near, and at last, satisfied,

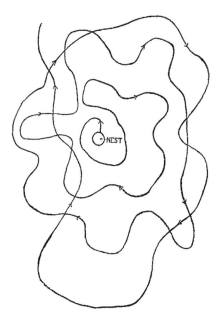

Figure 5 Hasty locality study

rose in circles, higher and higher, and disappeared from view. We waited for her return with all the patience at our command, from fifteen minutes after five until fifteen minutes before seven. We felt sure that when she came back she would bring her victim with her, and when we saw her approaching we threw ourselves prone on the ground, eagerly expecting to see the end of the drama; but her search had been unsuccessful,—she carried nothing. In the realms of wasp-life, disappointments are not uncommon, and this time she had us to share her chagrin, for we felt as tired and discouraged as she perhaps did herself. (1905: 60–62)

In assessing the meaning of an animal's action, a verifying outcome is not always necessary. Twice in the course of this observation the Peckhams conjecture that the wasp has gone hunting, though both times the wasp returns without prey. Instead of taking the wasp's empty-handedness as grounds to doubt the correctness of their original judgment, the Peckhams understand it as indicating that she failed to capture prey. The basis of their assessment that she has been hunting unsuccessfully is that the next logical step, after the wasp has dug and worked on her nest, is to provision it with captured prey. The Peckhams' reasoning, then, preserves the logical connection of actions, revealing that a tacit commitment to the meaningfulness of the wasp's actions imbues how they witness her activities, even in the absence of solid evidence. In affinity with *Verstehen* reasoning, even while there is no direct access to the wasp's whereabouts or activities when she is away, the intrinsic meaningfulness of actions is preserved by maintaining the view that they are organized in logical sequence. While there is plainly no guarantee, or proof, that the Peckhams' interpretation is correct, the effect of their reasoning on the basis of the wasp's orientation to the sequential logic of her actions is to sustain a cohesive picture of subjective presence and coherent agency.

Indeed, there is method and logic to all the actions of the wasp in this episode. When she flies off for short periods of time, she makes no study of the nest's location; when she flies away to be gone for an extended period of time, she makes another study, which is, however, less detailed than the very first one. It is noteworthy that while the Peckhams do not explicitly attribute intent and knowledge to the wasp, both are tacitly embedded in the apprehension of the wasp's actions. As she makes no study of the location before leaving for short periods, it is intimated that she *intends* to be gone briefly. When she is about to leave for a longer period, she makes a second study, indicating her intention to be gone for an extended time; her second study, however, is "hasty," as she already *knows* the locality from her first "thorough" study (compare Figures 4 and 5). Maintaining the logical link of the wasp's activities is thus entangled with their embodiment of knowledge and intention. The Peckhams do not directly ascribe mental processes or states to the wasp. Rather, the relevance of intention and knowledge in the wasp's world emerges as an effect of, rather than an attribution in, their writing. By presenting, and when necessary preserving, the sequential logic of the wasp's actions, mental predicates are implicitly made applicable and pertinent.

Returning for a final time to this particular episode with the golden digger, the Peckhams write that the next day the wasp was finally successful in bringing

> a light green meadow-grasshopper which was held in the mouth and supported by the fore-legs, which were folded under. On arriving, the prey was placed, head first, near the entrance, while the wasp went in, probably to reassure herself that all was right. Soon she appeared at the door of the nest and remained motionless for some moments, gazing intently at her treasure. Then seizing it (we thought by an antenna) she dragged it head first into the tunnel. (1905: 65–66)

Throughout the entire episode with this wasp, the nuances of her actions are conveyed, as are their modifications relative to what happened before and what is about to happen, and their reiterations in slightly different versions. For instance, in this particular passage, the Peckhams narrate the small detail that the wasp "gazes intently" at her prey for some moments before dragging it into her burrow.

Relating this type of detail has a significant impact on the reader. Even if it does not embed intention and knowledge with the same directness as did the wasp's modifications of her locality study, the detail that the wasp was "gazing intently" at her prey conveys the local modularity of action, and thus its subjective expressiveness. Though the Peckhams do not take an explicit position on the question of animal mind, this type of detail subverts the portrayal of wasps, or any other animal, in accordance with a mechanistic perspective.[6] Animals emerge as mindful through the naturalists' method of episodic, detailed description of their behaviors. As I discuss in the next chapter, the inverse also holds: animal behavior can appear automated as a consequence of descriptions that are generic and thin. When the focus is on concrete animals, subjective peculiarities are inevitably described. When the generic individual, or the typical case, is presented, then behavioral patterns can appear uniform and even mechanical.

In the final set of events surrounding this golden digger, after she laid her egg in the nest and flew off, the Peckhams dug up her nest in order to retrieve and study the caterpillar and the attached egg. The Peckhams then describe the remarkable events that followed:

> We had not supposed that the digging up of her nest would much disturb our Sphex, since her connection with it was so nearly at an end; but in this we were mistaken. When we returned to the garden about half an hour after we had done the deed, we heard her loud and anxious humming from the distance. She was searching far and near for her treasure house, returning every few minutes to the right spot, although the upturned earth had entirely changed its appearance. She seemed unable to believe her eyes, and her persistent refusal to accept the fact that her nest had been destroyed was pathetic. She lingered about the garden all through the day, and made so many visits to us, getting under our umbrellas and thrusting her tremendous personality into our very faces, that we wondered if she were trying to question us as to the whereabouts of her property. Later we learned that we had wronged her more deeply than we knew. Had we not interfered she would have excavated several cells to the side of the main tunnel, storing a grasshopper in each. Who knows but perhaps our Golden Digger, standing

among the ruins of her home, or peering under our umbrella, said to herself: "Men are poor things; I don't know why the world thinks so much of them." (1905: 68)

This passage reveals a dimension of undecidability of the meaning of animal behavior that sets it apart from the occasional undecidability of the meaning of the human behavior. So far I have endeavored to show how naturalists engage *Verstehen* practices of commonsense perception and reasoning in order to grasp the subjective meaning of animal action. Interpretation and understanding are achieved on the basis of both the scenic qualities of activities or events and what is known about them (through others' studies, repeated observations, or experimentation) in their full temporal extensions. In the course of *human* (inter)action, when *Verstehen* fails remedial action may be taken in what Garfinkel and Sacks call "formulating," which is "saying-in-so-many-words-what-we-are-doing." Formulating can be used to dispel equivocality or unclarity in communication. In the course of conversing, for example, a problematic feature of the conversation can be isolated and itself turned into the topic of conversation. Participants are then not only "doing" but "saying-in-so-many-words-what-they-are-doing" (Garfinkel and Sacks 1970).

Obviously it is not possible to ascertain the meaning of an animal's behavior by this means, and the story of the wasp's intense response to the destruction of her nest makes visible the absence of this option. The wasp's actions appear almost as a plea or a demand for an account. In her bewilderment—her "inability to believe her eyes"—there is an intractable unclarity about how, specifically, to understand her reaction: is it distressed, saddened, angered, uncomprehending, shocked? Her "thrusting her immense personality" in the Peckhams' faces invokes an irreparable deficit of knowledge about what she is doing: is she accusing, questioning, suspecting, attempting to communicate? Her response appears intelligent and charged, yet, at the same time, it is almost a testimony to the absence of what, for the human form of life, involves the "precision" of words. While this want of a stable sense to her actions appears irremediable, so is the feeling that there is sense to them: her actions are overflowing with meaning, but her words are missing. It is not coincidental, then, that the observers "put words in her mouth." It is also clear, though, that these words—"Men are poor things; I don't know why the world thinks so much of them"—are not given by the Peckhams as a serious possibility of the wasp's thoughts. It is rather a literary solution to their inability to understand the wasp's response, as well as an indirect admission of regret for destroying her "treasure house."

While the absence of the option of "formulating," as a way to clarify the meaning of the wasp's response, reveals a distance between human observer and animal subject, at the same time an affinity between them is suggested in this passage with respect to the common significance of work. "Working," writes Schutz, "is irrevocable. My work has changed the outer world. . . . I cannot make undone what I have done. . . . Having realized my work or at least portions of it, I chose once for all what has been done and have now to bear the consequences. I cannot choose what I want to have done" (1962: 217). The indelibleness and irrevocability of having worked on the world is the background against which the wasp is "unable to believe her eyes" as she "stands among the ruins of her home." Through work, she has acted upon and changed her physical and experiential world in a definite way. What is conveyed in her response is that the inexorability of this fact—that once an aspect of the world has been physically altered, this cannot be revoked—keeps her "searching" and "returning" over and over to the location of her nest.

Despite the inability to characterize the wasp's intense response with the kind of conceptual precision that we regard as emanating from words, a fundamental alignment between certain aspects of human and wasp "natural attitudes" is forged in this episode. The "natural attitude" is the field of being and practicalities within which actors are always essentially encountering what Schutz characterizes as the "taken-for-granted." He defines the taken-for-granted as "always that particular level of experience which presents itself as not in need of further analysis" (1967: 74) Discussing the knowledge at hand of the human natural attitude, Schutz clarifies that "to this stock of knowledge at hand belongs our knowledge that the world we live in is a world of well circumscribed objects with definite qualities, objects among which we move, which resist us and upon which we act" (1962: 208). This fundamental knowledge—about objects that have unforgettable significance, about the physical contours of lived-in landscapes, with their existential permanence and alterability by, and resistance to, work—is called forth as the background of the wasp's response to the destruction of her work. The nest's undoing undermines the hitherto dependable knowledge of the existential stability of objects, especially objects of work. What is, then, conveyed in the wasp's "inability to believe her eyes" is that this knowledge is so deeply rooted and taken for granted that clear sensuous evidence of the nest's destruction is refused, "pathetically," driving the wasp into a state of crisis.

THE NATURALIST'S DEPICTION OF THE TROPE OF WORK IN THE ANIMAL WORLD

The common significations of work make the human and wasp worlds pervious to one another, without the two worlds ever becoming confounded. One shared signification is the aspect of work just discussed, that of leaving a relatively permanent mark on the world. Another signification of work, tacitly conveyed as shared by humans and animals, is that of a practical orientation. Schutz remarks that "we work and operate not only within but upon the world . . . modifying or changing its objects and their mutual relationships. On the other hand, these objects offer resistance to our acts which we have either to overcome or to which we have to yield. Thus, it may be correctly said that a pragmatic motive governs our natural attitude toward the world of daily life" (1962: 209). The methodical character of work, the continual adjustments of the action of work to meet the contingencies that arise, and the use-value of the products of work all embody and signify a practical orientation and rationality.

This signification is an integral aspect of work, regardless of whether it is animal or human work. An example of practical rationality in the work of a wasp is perspicuous in another story of a "most fastidious and perfect little worker."

Just here must be told the story of one little wasp whose individuality stands out in our minds more distinctly than that of any of the others. We remember her as the most fastidious and perfect little worker of the whole season, so nice was she in her adaptation of means to ends, so busy and contented in her labor of love, and so pretty in her pride over the completed work. In filling up her nest she put her head down into it and bit away the loose earth from the sides, letting it fall to the bottom of the burrow, and then, after a quantity had accumulated, jammed it down with her head. Earth was then brought from outside and pressed in, and then more was bitten from the sides. When, at last, the filling was level with the ground, she brought a quantity of fine grains of dirt to the spot, and picking up a small pebble in her mandibles, used it as a hammer in pounding them down with rapid strokes, thus making this spot as hard and firm as the surrounding surface. Before we could recover from our astonishment at this performance she had dropped her stone and was bringing more earth. We then threw ourselves

Figure 6 *Ammophila* wasp using a pebble as a hammer

down on the ground that not a motion might be lost, and in a moment we saw her pick up the pebble and again pound the earth into place with it, hammering now here now there until all again was level. Once more the whole process was repeated, and then the little creature, all unconscious of the commotion that she had aroused in our minds,—unconscious, indeed, of our very existence and intent only on doing her work and doing it well,— gave one final, comprehensive glance around and flew away. (1905: 38–39)

A practical, rational bent is discernible in the methodical character of the sequence of actions, the fastidiousness of "doing her work and doing it well," and the appropriate modulations of action with the unfolding progress of the work. The work of the wasp—especially as it is recounted in its concrete instantiation, and is thus an image of an actual here and now, or what I call "episodic description"—is not accomplished by passive or mechanical "motion in space," but is witnessed as intentional movement that "generates space."[7] This work, then, denotes action that is attentive and aware; it signifies what Schutz calls the attitude of "wide-awakeness." "By the term *'wide-awakeness,'*" he writes, "we want to denote a plane of consciousness of highest tension originating in an attitude of full attention to life and its requirements. Only the performing and especially the working self is fully interested in life and, hence, wide awake. It lives within its acts and its attention is exclusively directed to carrying its project into effect, to executing its plan. This attention is an active not a passive one" (1962: 213).

The intimated condition of wide-awakeness underlies the arresting quality of work in the animal world; the Peckhams are astonished to witness the wasp's hammering actions. The methodical action of work, in molding and transforming some aspect of the world in a useful manner, gives the ineluctable indication of aware presence.[8] Hence a wasp's use of a pebble as a hammer may be unsettling, because the rationality of the hammer's use, its assiduous directedness to the end of packing the ground, and its internal intentionality of configuring the disturbed earth to match the undisturbed surroundings all disclose the hammer's agent to be wide-awake. If the effect is uncanny, it is because it collides with what Griffin aptly calls the image of "ganglion on legs" that "dominates our view of invertebrate animals" (1976: 48).

EPISODIC DESCRIPTION IN NATURALIST WRITING

A central theme of this investigation of behavioral studies is that language use is not a neutral instrument in the depiction or interpretation of animal life. Neither are modes of description neutral with respect to how animals are portrayed. Naturalists' attention to the detailed nuances and variations of actions is connected with their focus on *episodes* of animal life. In documenting animal life, they choose to narrate concrete behavioral events, episodes actually witnessed. This method of depicting animal behavior, which the Peckhams deploy extensively in their work and which is also Jean Henri Fabre's chief method of inscription, may be called "episodic description." An episode is an actual and specific sequence of observed behaviors of notable though varying duration. With their consistent reliance on episodic description, naturalists give prominent position to the activities in the here and now of specific animal(s). Episodic description preserves both the uniqueness and the holistic character of action. Focus on concrete episodes reveals the unique character of even thoroughly mundane behaviors, and the narration of events in their specific sequential integrity assembles a set of actions as a complete, self-contained "act" (see Harré 1984: 94ff.).

These features of episodic description have important ramifications in the portrayal of animals. The narration of commonplace, specific episodes creates a world of everyday life in which ordinary activities are accomplishments of real individuals. Activities acquire significance not in being exceptional or brilliant, but in virtue of the simple fact of having to be achieved. This view of action as achievement delivers animals as the authors of their actions. With episodic description, therefore, the fact that actions may be routine and anonymous does not obfuscate the remarkability of their accomplishment in the here and now by a real and singular actor.

A second consequence of episodic description relates to reconstructing the set of actions observed in a given episode. In episodic description the actions composing an event do not merely form a series, in the sense of occurring one after another, but are a sequence, in the sense that adjacent actions—whether of one individual or of interacting individuals—are meaningfully interconnected. A sequence indicates that contiguous parts of an unfolding act are organizationally connected.[9] The sequential link between actions guarantees an episode's coherence as a self-contained event, as somehow *one* thing that happened. The significance of portraying actions sequentially is that they are thereby seen as forming a unified and meaningful act. The holistic character of the act, then, emerges with the preservation of the organizational continuity of the actions that comprise it. For example, an animal may be said to be "hunting prey" or "building a nest" only if the continuity of actions—in their sequential tightness—is descriptively preserved.

The method of episodic description, then, safeguards authorship and meaning in the animal's world. On the other hand, a significant departure of the classical ethologists from their naturalist predecessors is that their accounts of behavioral patterns are generic, that is, they are accounts of the "typical" case, not the singular instance. The portrayal of animals through generic description tends to support, if not advance, a mechanistic picture of the animal, because "generic description" carries the implication that the typical description of an action maps onto all its specific instantiations, and this, in turn, calls forth a rigid image of animal behavior. Generic description elides the modulations and permutations of concrete expressions, which, in episodic description, precisely derail an automatonlike image of animals. What format of description is chosen, therefore, is highly consequential for the understanding of animal life. The method of description generates the bulk of the writing, and thus constitutes the groundwork of the overall view of the nature of animal life educed by the reader. As a consequence, whether a portrayal of animals is "mindful" or "mindless" may hinge less on the writer's specific opinions or positions than on the manner in which behaviors are recorded—as concrete instantiations or through a format of typification.

A passage from Fabre's *The Hunting Wasps* (1915), where he describes a predatory encounter between a wasp and a cricket, is useful in highlighting seminal features and effects of episodic description:

> The terrified Cricket takes to flight, hopping as fast as he can; the Sphex pursues him hot-foot, reaches him, rushes upon him. There follows, amid the dust, a confused encounter, wherein each champion, now victor, now vanquished, by turns is at the top or at the bottom. Success, for a moment undecided, at last crowns the aggressor's efforts. Despite his vigorous kicks, despite the snaps of his pincer-like mandibles, the Cricket is laid low and stretched upon his back.
>
> The murderess soon makes her arrangements. She places herself belly to belly with her adversary, but in the opposite direction, grasps one of the threads at the tip of the Cricket's abdomen with her mandibles and masters with her fore-legs the convulsive efforts of his thick hinder thighs. At the same time, her middle-legs hug the heaving sides of the beaten insect; and her hind-legs, pressing like two levers on the front of the head, force the joint of the neck to open wide. The Sphex then curves her abdomen vertically, so as to offer only an unattackable convex surface to the Cricket's mandibles; and we see, not without emotion, its poisoned lancet drive once into the victim's neck, next into the joint of the front two segments of the thorax and lastly toward the abdomen. In less time than it takes to relate, the murder is consummated; and the Sphex, after adjusting the disorder of her toilet, makes ready to haul home the victim, whose limbs are still quivering in the throes of death. (1915: 82)

If it is imagined that language works like a camera, then metaphorically Fabre's account might be said to magnify the depicted scene with two lenses. The first magnification creates a bridge between human and wasp: the detailed description is given entirely in the vernacular of action, and because this is prototypically the language of human affairs—that is to say, the language of intersubjectivity—its immediate effect is to bridge the first- and third-person perspectives. Fabre's description embeds the suggestion that just as the events are being described from the observer's perspective, so they are unfolding for, and experienced by, the wasp (and cricket). The wasp's endeavors and the subsequent events are, through this lens of the vernacular, brought close to the reader. The second magnifica-

tion derives from the relentless visual quality of the scene. The visual availability of the episode is an effect of the attention to concrete individuals
involved in a singular course of events. The use of the ordinary language
of action in concert with the description of a specific course of events—
episodic description—magnifies the scenery by a conceptual-visual bridg-
ing between reader and wasp. The overall effect is that this description of
the wasp's activities presents her as inhabiting a world of meaningful objects, signs, and events, and as authoring her actions. Consequently she
comes through as mindfully responsive to what transpires, even though
there is little explicit ascription of mental experience in the passage.

The indelible characteristic of this portrayal is its concreteness. It is
about *this* wasp and *this* cricket. While this description may recount the
typical predatory behavior of the species, as a representation it pictures
only this specific encounter. It constitutes a single and coherent act of
hunting, with the wasp's methods being meaningful as a sequence of logically connected steps. The quality of the encounter as a matter of life and
death is owed no less to the "terrified" cricket, who "takes to flight,"
"hops as fast as he can," and (in vain) defends his life with "kicks" and
"snaps of his mandibles." The actions of the wasp's final "arrangements"
emerge as abstractly rational in the methodical, deliberate, and efficient
way that she pins the cricket by his limbs, abdomen, and neck, while keeping her own body out of the reach of his mandibles. Fabre's filigreed portrayal submits that the wasp's success in overcoming the cricket is guaranteed only as an outcome of her course of actions. The visual quality of
the description intimates that the wasp's subdual of the cricket—no matter how many times it occurs in a season, and no matter how similar it is
every time—has always to be accomplished locally and in the face of the
contingencies of "another first time" (Garfinkel 1967: 9–10). In this sense,
the same act of hunting is episodically never the same.

The encounter of wasp and cricket is action-packed, communicated
through a slow-motion representation of the episode with a plethora of
action verbs. Such verbs are not, perhaps, as immediately noticeable as the
morally loaded and strikingly anthropomorphic conceptions of "murder"
and "terror." Yet in their ubiquity and cumulative effects, these action
verbs guide the reader to see the wasp as a coherent agent who performs
her actions and is present to their import: she pursues, reaches, rushes
upon the cricket; the cricket is stretched upon his back; the wasp grasps
one of the threads, masters with her forelegs, hugs the beaten insect, forces

the neck open, adjusts her toilet, and so forth. Not only are most verbs in the *active* voice—with the wasp as grammatical subject—they are also largely *intentional,* in the sense of indicating the specific attitude of a subject toward some feature of, or event in, the world. Here the intentional verbs are describing the active attitude of the huntress toward her victim in a moment-to-moment unfolding of a predatory encounter. The effect of the sustained usage of action verbs is to charge the interaction with a sense of awareness, for such verbs are semantic alloys of physical action and mental attitude; thus, for example, the meaning of the verb *pursue* is conceptually composite, referring to a form of physical action that imbricates motion, intention, and affect.

Fabre's narrative owes its power to the effects of the fine-grained detail of the temporal unfolding of a real event. The compelling picture the reader receives is not simply guaranteed by the intrinsically dramatic character of the event; the dramatic quality is equally the consequence of the method of description, which, in narrating an episode that is happening in the here and now, advances a tacit claim to realism. Fabre offers this description as of something real, in the way that images on film are of something real. Its jolting effect—as the reader sees the events "not without emotion"—derives from this cinematographic quality, a textual invitation to the reader to co-witness the episode. The reader's witnessing is perceptual on a double level, in that the encounter between the wasp and the cricket is both seen and enlarged in the mind's eye. Fabre's powerful representation of insect life invites the merging of reading and seeing; his words may be likened to an acorn from which an oak tree grows.[10]

In Fabre's description of the wasp and the cricket, as with the Peckhams' portrayals, there is a brazen immersion of the naturalist into the animal's world. In the naturalist's genre there is little room for so-called disinterestedness. The knowledge of naturalists is thus at odds with the idea that objective knowledge ought to display a veneer of emotional and intellectual disengagement. Fabre's and the Peckhams' ardor is reminiscent of the idea of a "feeling for the organism" expressed by the biologist Barbara McClintock (see Keller 1983). Evelyn Fox Keller cites how McClintock conceptualized her "participant observation" of the chromosomes of a cell:

> I found that the more I worked with them the bigger and bigger [they] got, and when I was really working with them I wasn't outside, I was down there. I was part of the system. I was right down there with them, and every-

thing got big. I even was able to see the internal parts of the chromosomes—actually everything was there. It surprised me because I actually felt as if I were right down there and these were my friends. (Keller 1983: 117)

There are two ways to understand the notion of the "feeling for the organism." One sense implies the cultivation of an empathic connection between organism and observer. If considered to be the sole sense, however, this denotation of empathy can be misleading, diverting attention from the more central meaning of the "feeling for the organism," which is McClintock's: of intimate and, at the same time, rational knowledge of an organism acquired after years of close association and study (Keller 1983: 198). Like McClintock becoming "part of the system," the Peckhams relate how they throw themselves on the ground to observe the wasps, and Fabre, with his inimitable style, is even able to bring the reader "down there" with him. Naturalists' understanding celebrates participation in the nature that is studied and, especially at its best, exemplifies the notion that in the pursuit of knowledge the virtues of passion and rationality are not mutually exclusive.

THE EFFECTS OF FABRE'S DESCRIPTIVE STYLE: A GRUB AS SUBJECT

Jean Henri Fabre is undoubtedly among the most brilliant of naturalists, a keen observer, experimenter, and writer whose oeuvre on insect life is an extraordinary legacy of a passionate and rational intellect. One commentator appositely refers to Fabre's work as "epic." [11] In the passages cited below, I illustrate his exceptional power to bring the reader within the presence of the scenes he describes. I provide a lengthy example of his portrayal of the life of the grub to elucidate further the ramifications of two aspects of Fabre's language: his use of active verbs in the description of animal action and the imagistic intimacy of his depictions, which bring the reader perceptually into the presence of the animal's life. The grub described is the larva of (what becomes) the great Capricorn beetle—"the chief author of the oak's undoing":

> Strange creatures, of a verity, are these grubs, for an insect of superior organization: bits of intestines *crawling about!* At this time of year, the middle of autumn, I meet them of two different ages. The older are almost as thick as one's finger; the others hardly attain the diameter of a pencil. I find, in addition, pupae more or less fully colored, perfect insects, with a distended

abdomen ready to leave the trunk when the hot weather comes again. Life inside the wood, therefore, lasts three years. How is this long period of solitude and captivity spent? In *wandering* lazily *through* the thickness of the oak, in *making roads* whose rubbish serves as food. The horse in Job swallows the ground in a figure of speech; the Capricorn's grub literally *eats its way*. With its carpenter's gouge, a strong black mandible, short, devoid of notches, scooped into a sharp-edged spoon, it *digs* the opening of its tunnel. The piece cut out is a mouthful which, as it enters the stomach, yields its scanty juices and accumulates behind the worker in heaps of wormed wood. The refuse leaves room in front by passing through the worker. A labour at once of nutrition and of road-making, the path is devoured while constructed; it is blocked behind as it makes way ahead. (1918: 44–45, emphasis added)

Fabre then proceeds to describe the grub's physique and sensory capacities in detail. Concluding that the grub's senses are "limited to taste and touch," he continues:

What can be the psychology of a creature *possessing* such a powerful digestive organism combined with such a feeble set of senses? . . . What have the lessons of touch and taste contributed to that rudimentary receptacle of impressions? Very little; almost nothing. The animal *knows* that the best bits possess an astringent flavor; that the sides of a passage not carefully planed are painful to the skin. This is the utmost limit of its acquired wisdom. . . . Does the drowsily digesting paunch remember? Does it compare? Does it reason? I defined the Capricorn-grub as a bit of intestine that crawls about. The undeniable accuracy of this definition provides me with my answer: the grub has the aggregate of sense-impressions that a bit of intestine may hope to have. (1918: 50–51, emphasis added)

For Fabre, even while the grub has practically no psychology, it is not an "organism," but a "creature possessing an organism"; despite its lack of sensory impressions, the grub is still portrayed as a subject. At this point in the story, the grub has been demoted to a creature that knows "almost nothing" and has been likened to a "bit of intestine." This temporary disparagement of the grub's life prepares for a dramatic reversal in the final denouement.

And this nothing-at-all is capable of marvelous acts of foresight; this belly, which knows hardly aught of the present, sees very clearly into the future. Let us take an illustration on this curious subject. For three years on end the larva *wanders about* in the thick of the trunk; it *goes* up, goes down, *turns* to this side and that; it *leaves* one vein for another of better flavor, but *without moving too far* from the inner depths, where the temperature is milder and greater safety reigns. A day is at hand, a dangerous day for the recluse *obliged to quit* its excellent retreat and *face* the perils of the surface. Eating is not everything: we have to get out of this. The larva, so well-equipped with tools and muscular strength, finds no difficulty in *going where it pleases,* by boring through the wood; but does the coming Capricorn, whose short spell of life must be spent in the open air, possess the same advantages? Hatched inside the trunk, will the long-horned insect be able to clear itself a way of escape? . . .

Despite his stalwart appearance, the Capricorn is powerless to leave the tree-trunk by his unaided efforts. It therefore falls to the worm, to the wisdom of that bit of intestine, *to prepare* the way for him. . . . Urged by a presentiment that to us remains an unfathomable mystery, the Cerambyx-grub *leaves* the inside of the oak, its peaceful retreat, its unassailable stronghold, *to wriggle toward* the outside, where lives the foe, the Woodpecker. . . . At the risk of its life, it stubbornly *digs* and *gnaws* to the bark, of which it leaves no more intact than the thinnest film, a slender screen. Sometimes, even, the rash one *opens* the window wide.

This is the Capricorn's exit-hole. The insect will have but *to file* the screen a little with its mandibles, *to bump against* it with its forehead, in order *to bring it down;* it will even have nothing to do when the window is free, as often happens. The unskilled carpenter, burdened with his extravagant head-dress, will emerge from the darkness through this opening when the summer heats arrive.

After the cares of the future come the cares of the present. The larva, which *has just opened* the aperture of escape, *retreats* some distance down its gallery and, in the side of the exit-way, *digs* itself a transformation-chamber more sumptuously furnished and barricaded than any I have ever seen. It is a roomy niche, shaped like a flattened ellipsoid, the length of which reaches eighty to a hundred millimeters. . . . The two axes of the cross-section vary: the horizontal measures twenty-five to thirty millimeters . . . ; the vertical measures only fifteen. . . . This greater dimension of the cell, where the thickness of the perfect insect is concerned, leaves a certain scope for the action of its legs when the time comes for forcing the barricade, which is more than a close-fitting mummy-case would do.

The barricade in question, a door which the larva *builds to exclude* the dangers from without, is two- and even three-fold. Outside, it is a stack of woody refuse, of particles of chopped timber; inside, a mineral hatch, a concave cover, all in one piece, of a chalky white. Pretty often, but not always, there is added to these two layers an inner casing of shavings. Behind this compound door, the larva *makes its arrangements* for the metamorphosis. The sides of the chamber are rasped, thus providing a sort of down formed of raveled woody fibers, broken into minute shreds. The velvety matter, as and when obtained, is applied to the wall in a continuous felt at least a millimeter thick. . . . The chamber is thus padded throughout with a fine swan's-down, a delicate precaution taken by the rough worm on behalf of the tender pupa. . . .

When the exit-way is prepared and the cell upholstered in velvet and closed with a three-fold barricade, the industrious worm *has concluded its task.* It *lays aside* its tools, *sheds* its skin and becomes a nymph, a pupa, weakness personified, in swaddling clothes, on a soft couch. The head is always turned toward the door. This is a trifling detail in appearance; but it is everything in reality. *To lie* this way or that in the long cell is a matter of great indifference to the grub, which is very supple, *turning easily* in its narrow lodging and *adopting whatever posture it pleases.* The coming Capricorn will not enjoy the same privileges. Stiffly girt in his horn cuirass, he will not be able to turn from end to end; he will not even be capable of bending, if some sudden wind should make the passage difficult. He *must* absolutely *find* the door in front of him, lest he perish in the casket. Should the grub *forget* this little formality, should it *lie down* to its nymphal sleep with its head at the back of the cell, the Capricorn is infallibly lost: his cradle becomes a hopeless dungeon. (1918: 51–57, emphasis added)

Fabre begins with the grub's movements inside the wood. The grub "wanders lazily through the thickness of the oak," "eats its way"; "the path is devoured while constructed," "blocked behind as it makes its way ahead." Even though these activities are not observable, Fabre brings his readers to the grub's roadways inside the oak, into the presence of its slow work of "scooping the wood," "digging the tunnel," and leaving "wormed wood" behind. Every sentence consolidates the bridge between grub and human observer. A shared language of action and living, coupled with descriptions that are richly detailed, transforms reading into a kinesthetic experience whereby the reader-observer enters an alien lifeworld. The distance between human and grub is even explicitly renounced when, referring to the grub, Fabre writes: "Eating is not everything: *we* have to get out of this."

Having penetrated the grub's world, Fabre next considers its psychological experience. Assessing its sensory limitations, he concludes that the animal knows "very little—almost nothing." While he sustains the grub's difference in this anti-anthropomorphic assessment of its mental limitations, in Fabre's account it ceases to be a mere grub—a "nothing-at-all." Rather, the grub becomes an active subject through two interconnected features of the writing. The first is the imagistic intimacy of its lifeworld effected in the merging of reading and seeing. Fabre opens a visual field onto the landscape, such that the grub's activities and way of life are magnified in the reader's eyes. In this magnification, the grub commands attention, and the existential distance between it and the reader is abated. The grub is witnessed as owning a world and authoring the work of its world. It thus becomes a subject.

The second facet of the grub as subject is the portrayal of its movements as actions through the use of a diversity of action verbs. The cumulative effect of the sustained usage of verbs to which the grub is subject—"crawling about," "wandering through," "making roads," "eating the way," "digging," "leaving," "gnawing," "filing," "bumping against," "concluding a task," "retreating," and so forth—is to position the grub at the center of action. Despite the insignificance of its being, the grub is the sentient force from which action radiates. Its actions embody intentionality, in the sense of being directed distinctively and meaningfully, in a timely manner, to objects in its environment.

This intentionality is manifested particularly in the grub's activities surrounding its upcoming metamorphosis. These activities are work in virtue of altering the world in skillful and useful ways. Indeed, they are presented as carpentry, as Fabre suggests from the outset: "with its carpenter's gouge, a strong black mandible, short, devoid of notches, scooped into a sharp-edged spoon, it *digs.*" The grub fashions useful objects, such as a "slender screen," a "window," and an "exit-way"; a "transformation-chamber" is "upholstered in velvet," with a "wall" that is "rasped" and "padded" with "continuous felt" or "fine swan's-down"; and a "barricade" or "compound door" is made of "woody refuse," a "mineral hatch," and "shavings." While the vernacular of objects and actions of carpentry erases the boundaries between the worlds of humans and grubs, the two are never confounded. It is the anonymity and universality of courses of action and work that allow admission of the grub's activities into the fold of carpentry. At the same time, the grub never appears humanlike, nor is new light shed on human carpentry after the description of the grub's work.

The nonconflation of the human and insect realms is due partly to the fact that not all significations of work map onto the grub's activities. Although the notion of work is conceptually connected with purposefulness in human affairs (Schutz 1962: 212), this signification is not altogether passed on to the grub, since the objective of its work—that of altering space in preparation for its transformation into pupa and then beetle—is not conceivable as its deliberate premeditation. It does not appear tenable, from a human vantage, that a grub can anticipate and thus make preparations for its metamorphoses; hence Fabre's assessment of the grub as "urged by a presentiment that to us remains an unfathomable mystery." This exclusion of foresight in the grub's preparations—a consequence of the limits of our imagination, knowledge, generosity, or whatever—prepares the conceptual ground that will allow technical-causal accounts to flourish in animal behavioral science. So the perplexity about *why* the grub does what it does is relieved by the explanatory appearance of technical notions, such as the classical ethological "fixed action pattern" or the sociobiological "genetic program." Under the auspices of such bodily mechanisms, apparently rational behavior for which no "reasons" or "plans" are forthcoming can be enacted by ostensibly nonrational organisms.

Implications Regarding Anthropomorphism

Anthropomorphism is taken to be the unwarranted or erroneous attribution of human mental experiences to animals. This understanding is dubious, however, for the notion of "attribution" suggests deliberate intention on the author's part, while the blanket term "human mental experiences" begs the issue by positing, a priori, the existence of mental experiences that are ostensibly exclusive to human beings. In contrast to this definition, I suggest that the anthropomorphism of naturalists is the effect of representing animal life in the language of the lifeworld. In rendering action meaningful and authored, animals emerge as subjects. In turn, the portrayal of animals as subjects allows the existence of mental life to supervene with forcefulness and credibility. Mental life may either emerge specifically in the ascription of particular mental predicates or shine through in the more diffuse sense of mindfulness in the animal world.

The *Verstehen* perspective on animal life as "meaningful from the outset" and its subsequent description in the language of the lifeworld often do draw the charge of "anthropomorphism" (see, for instance, Kennedy 1992). Anthropomorphism is viewed pejoratively as an erroneous likening of animals and humans or, more specifically, as an uncalled-for imputation of mental states or capacities to animals. The objection to anthropomorphism is commonly cast as a heightened expression of skeptical misgivings about *Verstehen* more generally. The accessibility of a subjective orientation is declared troublesome in connection to *both* human and animal action; subjectivity is then pictured as especially intractable in the latter case. Skeptical misgivings about animals as subjects are aired vociferously, since the relative privacy of the meaning of human action ostensibly becomes absolute inscrutability in the case of animal action.

The analysis of naturalist writing allows for a detailed appreciation of the meaning of anthropomorphism and of how it is constituted in writing. What immediately becomes clear with naturalists such as the Peckhams and Fabre—as well as in the previously examined case of Darwin—is that anthropomorphism is more complex than simply imputing mental experiences or, as Barnett puts it, "attributing our own awareness, feelings and thoughts" to animals (1963: 9). While naturalists are unabashedly "anthropomorphic" in the sense that their portrayals create a strong alignment between human and animal worlds, such attributions of human awareness are not prominent in the writings. And yet awareness, feelings, and thoughts are far from irrelevant to the naturalist genre. The important qualification (alluded to earlier) is that such notions do not appear as attributions *in* the writing as much as they emerge as effects *of* the writing.

Awareness surfaces in virtue of the way an action, or a sequence of actions, is perceived and depicted. To illustrate with an example, Fabre describes a wasp that, upon returning to her burrow with captured prey, finds a praying mantis on a blade of grass near the burrow's entrance. The wasp takes notice of the mantis—"she lets go of her game and pluckily rushes upon the Mantis." The mantis, however, stays where it is, and Fabre observes:

> The Sphex goes back to her capture, harnesses herself to the antennae and boldly passes under the blade of grass whereupon the other sits perched. By the direction of her head *we can see* that she is on her guard and that she holds the enemy rooted, motionless, under the menace of her eyes. (1915: 189–90, emphasis added)

Here Fabre does not directly attribute the mental state of awareness to the wasp. Nevertheless, to say that "the direction of the Sphex's head" shows that she "holds the Mantis rooted with her eyes" delivers the wasp's awareness as a viewable facet of the tension of the animals' engagement. Awareness emanates from the totality of prior conditions, unfolding events, and future possibilities: the setting of the mantis near the burrow and the wasp returning with her prey, the subsequent actions of the wasp with respect to the mantis, and the tension of an uncertain future, closely monitored and negotiated with the eyes' focused gaze. In short, without any mention of the concept, Fabre's description aligns the reader's attention to the wasp's demeanor such that its awareness is integral to the life of the scene perceived. The main vehicle of this alignment is the *Verstehen* reasoning that sustains the subjective cohesiveness of the successive actions of "rushing upon," "passing boldly," being "on guard," and holding "the enemy" under the "menace of eyes."

The indirect yet vivid presence of mind here may be further underscored with the observation that Fabre's description could not be used to support the view of insect behavior as instantiating, in the words of J. L. Gould and C. G. Gould, "mindless programming" (1982: 271). This view of insects as automatonlike has been quite widespread in contemporary biological science (Griffin 1992). The Goulds' overall conclusion is that "insects stand . . . as testaments to the power of blind behavioral programming, and as such remind us to be wary of attributing to vertebrates anything more than larger, more interesting on-board computers" (1982: 269). If this view of insects as executing "blind behavioral programming" is taken to stand as a serious ontological claim, then the wording of Fabre's account of the wasp-mantis interaction collapses into a mere literary, even fanciful, description.

Gould and Gould's standpoint not only provides an illustrative contrast to Fabre's "anthropomorphism" but is also useful in bringing into relief the idea of "mechanomorphism," which I develop in the next chapter. Gould and Gould endorse a *mechanistic* viewpoint of insect behavior. Yet mechanomorphic presentations need not involve a committed affiliation to a mechanistic philosophy, nor do they entail an explicit rejection of animal mentality. Instead, I argue that mechanomorphic portrayals—or rendering behavior in a language that likens animals to machines—are effected by the application of a technical language in combination with an interest in causal explanation. The logical corollary of a technical-causal language is the presentation of animals as puppetlike, guided by theoretically explained forces that are beyond their control and understanding. The consequence of technical-causal idioms of representation is that animals appear mindless; otherwise put, the conceptual space that might admit a vision of inner life drastically shrinks.

Returning to the naturalist genre, the *direct* attribution of ostensibly human mental experiences is not a defining or even necessary feature of anthropomorphism. In the writings of naturalists, anthropomorphism is an effect of the consistent reliance on the language of the lifeworld—of a meaningful world-in-common replete with action—in the representation of animals. The significant consequence of portraying a lifeworld where animals exist and act is the creation of a conceptual environment within which modalities of mind are natural, scenic, and commanding constituents. It is therefore far from coincidental that active critics of anthropomorphism do not simply warn against, and attempt to purge, the use of mental vocabulary, but offer as a remedy the construction, or importation, of a technical language of behavior to replace, insofar as it is possible, ordinary action concepts (see Kennedy 1992: 160ff.). The marshaling of technical idioms as a way to ward off or at least contain anthropomorphism is a central theme in the chapters on classical ethology and sociobiology that follow.

CONCLUSION

The investigation of naturalists' portrayal of animals reveals that they understand animal life as subjectively meaningful. Their task is to grasp and communicate that meaning, which can range from being directly and confidently detected, to being interpreted on the basis of scenic evidence in combination with other sources of knowledge, to being tenuously inferred and thus contestable and uncertain.

The writings of the Peckhams and Fabre reveal seminal features of the understanding of animal action as meaningful: a focus on the fullness of life in the depiction of action as a perennial dimension of sentient existence; the portraiture of the animal's world as a lifeworld populated by singular actors with an everyday life that is (often) shared and (always) replete with action; the play of the Here and There between the human and animal perspectives, accomplished especially via the shared vocabulary of objects, actions, and events. Central methods of the *Verstehen* approach to animal life are episodic description, that is, the narration of concrete here-and-now events, revealing that action is always an achievement; imagistic intimacy in virtue of a thickness of description that virtually transports the reader into the scenery; and the plethoric use of action verbs, in the active voice, which presents animals as authors of their actions.

Animal action is portrayed as subjectively meaningful with the use of the rich ordinary language of action. The logic of its concepts has the property of being internal to action, thereby suggesting that the perspectives of the observer and the actor are linked—so that what "I" see from *here* as an observer is what "you" experience over *there* as an actor. In the genre of ordinary-language accounts, exemplified by naturalist depictions of the animal world, action is depicted as originating in an irreducible form from animals as actors. It is both *initiated* and *directed* by the actor, and in that sense it is authored: the initiation of action and the direction of action toward some aspect of the environment by the actor are understood and represented as sufficient to account for the occurrence of action.

Language is the reader's medium of navigating in the animal world, and the naturalists' language of the lifeworld is galvanizing in its color, movement, composition, ambiance, and texture. The language of peerless observers and scientists such as Charles Darwin, Jean Henri Fabre, and George and Elizabeth Peckham creates a vision of a coherent and beautiful world. The reality of the vision of that world is not guaranteed simply by its intrinsic cohesion, but is equally a matter of the reader's willingness to persist in holding on to that vision long enough to consolidate it. What I will argue in the next chapters is that when behavioral investigators displace the language of the lifeworld with a technical idiom, all the elements of the animal world change, and readers find themselves hovering over a very different landscape.

3   The Ethological Constitution of Animals as Natural Objects

I NOW turn to the writings of the chief founders of classical ethology, Konrad Lorenz and Nikolaas Tinbergen. In contrast to their naturalist predecessors' representation of animal life as immanently meaningful, ethological accounts are external to any possible vantage point of animals, deriving their meanings from models that are theoretical and technical. From naturalist studies to classical ethology, the form of knowledge of animal behavior shifts radically, from an interest in understanding animals' experience within their world to the task of arriving at a theoretical comprehension of their behaviors. With ethology, then, the depiction of animal behavior becomes epistemologically equivalent to that of the behavior of inanimate phenomena. Just as there is no intrinsic meaning to a falling object or a swinging pendulum, so an internal point of view is eradicated from animal life with the use of technical language. I argue that the elimination of an internal, experiential perspective and the constitution of animals as "natural objects" are the effects of the application of a technical idiom to animal life.

Lorenz and Tinbergen began their behavioral research in the 1930s. Their work gave rise to the school of classical ethology, which formally established the study of naturally occurring animal behavior as a subfield of biology, with university teaching positions and courses, professional societies, and journals. Prior to its establishment as a scientific discipline within the academy, the study of naturally occurring animal behavior was largely the domain of naturalists such as Fabre and the Peckhams, discussed in the previous chapter. Naturalist studies remained outside, or marginal to, the world of academic science. Yet naturalists were engaged in making realistic inventories of animals' behaviors and providing explanations of what they observed. Their work was scientific in the sense of aspiring to deliver true representations of animals through the natural-historical method of long-term observation and, to a certain degree, field experimentation. Naturalists were thus protoethologists. Their intimate affiliation with the tradition of classical ethology can also be seen in Tinbergen's and Lorenz's knowledge and recognition of their pioneer studies.[1]

There was intellectual continuity between the naturalists and the classical ethologists in their focus on naturally occurring animal behavior, and particularly in their common interest in the nature of innate (or "instinctual") behavior, in contrast to comparative psychology's interest in learning. These two historical moments of ethology also shared a common methodology of long-term, careful observation and recording of behaviors occurring in a normal environment, as unaffected as possible by human intervention. Both traditions employed experimentation for the purpose of shedding light on the nature of innate behavior, rather than with the comparative psychologist's interest in the scope of behavior modification. The shared interests and methods of naturalists and ethologists, and the ethologists' acknowledgment of naturalists as their source of inspiration, place them within a common scientific-intellectual tradition.

Despite their intellectual continuity, there is great disparity between ethologists and naturalists with respect to their uses of language. In contrast to the naturalists' language of the lifeworld, ethologists use a technical vocabulary, in part constructed by themselves and in part appropriated from behaviorist psychology. The linguistic and argumentative edifice created by the pioneer ethologists led to the representation of animals as natural objects. Yet it is quite certain that neither Tinbergen nor Lorenz wanted to "desubjectify" animals. In using a technical, highly theoretical language, they aimed to establish the study of animal behavior as a rigorous science; they presupposed a specific idea of "science," on the model of natural science as well as of comparative psychology, which was already a successful discipline at the time (see Boakes 1984; Dewsbury 1984). The inexorable if unwitting consequence of applying a technical language was the epistemological objectification of animals and ultimately their mechanomorphic portrayal. Mechanomorphism was the price of the idiom that ethologists opted for; it did not involve the ethologists' deliberate endorsement of a mechanistic view of animals, but was an effect of the representational medium that they elaborated.

The aim of this chapter is to show how animals become portrayed through a technical language. When these analyses are considered in conjunction with naturalists' portrayals, it becomes evident that in the representation of animal life language use is neither a neutral tool nor simply ancillary to the worldly phenomena depicted. Divergent vocabularies and forms of reasoning actively configure different ways to witness animal being: animals as authors of their actions, with a unified view and experience of their world, or animals as vessels upon or through which forces act to determine the emission of behaviors. This is the heart of the antithesis between subject and object, and my aim is to show how images of subjectivity and objectification emerge through the details of different ways of wording.

At the heart of the conflict between these two pictures of animal being lies the theme of animal mind. This tension has been expressed by Griffin as the difference between viewing animals as "thinking and feeling" and regarding them as "limited to existing and reacting" (1992: 234). Wittgenstein has drawn a similar distinction, although with the different aim of illustrating a connection between language and perception. He writes: "We say: 'The cock calls the hens by crowing.' . . . Isn't the aspect quite altered if we imagine the crowing to set the hens in motion by some kind of physical causation?" (1953: para. 493). The comparative analysis of representations that I undertake in this work reveals how the distinction between "thinking and feeling," on one hand, and "existing and reacting," on the other, is linked to language use. Different linguistic mediums can transmit the nonequivalent images of a hen coming to a calling rooster as a result of answering a summons versus being set in motion by a stimulus. The first portrayal is anthropomorphic in displaying an understanding comparable to that of human episodes. The second view is mechanomorphic in representing the hen as lacking a purview on her world and actions, as a quasi automaton that is passively steered by an external force, which is designated by the technical term *stimulus*. In comparing different writings, therefore, the task is to explore the detailed aspects of style and reasoning whose compounded effects lead to such disparate images of animals. In what follows, I focus on the representations and forms of argument of ethological reports.

GENERIC DESCRIPTION AND THEORY-LADENNESS IN ETHOLOGICAL ACCOUNTS

In ethological writings descriptions of animal behaviors are largely generic, representing behavioral patterns in terms of how they *generally* appear in *any* member of a species in *similar* circumstances. In contrast to the attention to some actual here and now of episodic description, generic description factors together many different heres and nows to yield a report that describes none in particular. In ethological writing, generic description is often theory-laden as well, as descriptions of animal behavior are interlaced with technical concepts. As the compounded effect of describing the typical case and applying technical concepts, particular behaviors can become presented as instantiations of theoretical constructs. The behavior is described for the purposes of illustrating a technical concept, or for clarifying the theory that explains the behavior.

A passage from Lorenz illustrates the generic, theory-laden presentation of animal behavior. This example demonstrates how animals' behavioral responses can be framed so as to illustrate theoretical terms. (The meaning of Lorenz's technical terms are clarified in the course of discussion.)

> The innate [releasing mechanisms] are, from the very first, built into an overall system of instincts; this system is specific to the species, and its essential characteristics are determined in advance. Therefore, it is only consistent with the principle of economy if as few cues as possible are included in the releasing mechanism. The sea urchin *Sphaerenchinus* has a very highly specialized escape-and-defense reaction to his chief enemy, the starfish, *Asterias*. A single, specific chemical stimulus emitted by the starfish suffices to set off this reaction. This type of release of a highly complicated motor pattern, adapted to a specific biological process, by one single stimulus, or at any rate by a relatively simple set of stimuli, is typical for the majority of innate reactions. (1957a: 86)

What is striking here is the theory-laden character of the discussion of the sea urchin and the starfish. The sea urchin's response is presented as a "specialized escape-and-defense reaction." This quasi-technical, packaged phrasing transmutes the ordinary connotations of the words *escape* and *defense*, which in the vernacular strongly implicate intention and feeling. While the sea urchin's reaction must perforce be described in these or comparable terms—so that the antagonistic character of its relation with the starfish is conveyed—not all connotations of the terms are retained. Ordinarily, the terms *escape* and *defense* are intentional, indicating a particular orientation to some object or circumstance (namely, escape *from* and defense *against* something). These terms also suggest that the situation encountered is meaningful, in that it is dangerous, and arouses feelings such as fear or terror. In the case of the sea urchin and the starfish, however, Lorenz hyphenates the terms *escape* and *defense* into a single unit and places them between *specialized* and *reaction*. With the technical ring of the phrase "specialized escape-and-defense reaction," the connotations of intention and feeling are lost. Their ellipsis is further underscored by treating the phrase "specialized escape-and-defense reaction" as interchangeable with "highly complicated motor pattern."

The behavioral phenomenon under consideration, which Lorenz uses to illustrate his theoretical view, is the sea urchin's response to the starfish. Yet the reader comes away with no concrete picture of precisely what the sea urchin *does* when a starfish is in the vicinity. There is no interest in a photographic realism of the encounter, but rather a paramount concern with specifying the behavior in theoretical terms. The sea urchin's reaction is positioned within a theoretical matrix, where technical notions play the leading part. The behaviors are of relevance only insofar as they illustrate the theory, exemplifying technical terms such as "innate releasing mechanism," "highly complicated motor pattern," "stimulus," and "innate reaction." Part of these terms' association in theory derives from the use of what may be referred to as an "idiomatic vocabulary," in particular verbs such as *release, set off,* and *emit*. The linguistic status of an idiomatic vocabulary—as ordinary-language terms that present the appearance of being technical—is discussed below.

The pervasive deployment of such mechanism-related verbs in ethological writing displaces the use of action verbs that have animals as grammatical subjects. This is one way that technical accounts defuse authorship. Another, clearly evident in Lorenz's example, is that the encounter does not take place between the sea urchin and the starfish, but seems to transpire between the referents of the technical terms—that is, between chemical stimuli, releasing mechanisms, and the emission of innate reactions. For the sea urchin, the stimulus is not the starfish as such, nor the starfish as "chief enemy," but a "single specific chemical stimulus" that works as the "releasing mechanism" of a "complicated motor pattern." The agents in this text are not the animals but highly technical constructs.

The technical language of description dominates the account, while the animals and their interactions recede from visibility. A noteworthy feature, then, of technical descriptions is that they restrict the visual participation of the reader. There are two steps in this process. First, generic description relays the behavior of any member of a species under similar circumstances. By extracting only the general, common elements from many different observations, generic description is inevitably much thinner than episodic description. This, by itself, discourages visual contact. If, second, the description is theory-laden—like Lorenz's—then visualization is obliterated, for the reader's cognitive efforts become fully engaged in the demanding task of comprehending complicated and abstract accounts.

The episodic description of naturalists, which tends to be more thickly textured and nuanced for the purposes of accommodating specific episodes observed in all their local modulations of expression and circumstance, affects the imagination of the reader very differently. Episodic description opens a visual scene on the behaviors described, for it is about concrete episodes involving actual animals. The greater the detail given, the more intense and alive is the imaged picture. This visual quality of episodic description, encountered in naturalist writing, tends to appresent animals as agents, for their vivid presence commands the reader's full attention. Describing actual episodes of animal interaction highlights the individuality, idiosyncrasies, and atmosphere of embodied activity, which in turn support a picture of mindfulness in animal life. On the other hand, an inadvertent effect of discussing examples of animal behavior generically is to exaggerate the invariance of behavioral patterns. What is lost is that every particular instantiation of a behavioral pattern is different. And of course the overemphasis on invariance and fixedness can bolster a mechanomorphic image of animals.

In comparison to the early naturalists, it is also evident that there is a marked shift in what motivates the study of animal behavior for ethologists. With naturalists, or "protoethologists," there is a desire to understand animal life directly, to grasp the meaning and feeling of action from an experiential perspective. With Lorenz and Tinbergen, preoccupations become far more intensely theoretical, overshadowing a concern with an immanent perspective and eliding to a large extent the visual, phenomenological icon of behavioral events. A passage from Nikolaas Tinbergen exemplifies certain ramifications of theory-ladenness and generic description in ethological writing.

> An animal in which an instinctive urge or drive is activated, starts "random," "exploratory" or "seeking" behavior. . . . It is continued until the animal comes into a situation that provides the sign stimuli necessary to release the motor response of one of the [nervous] centers of the lowest level. To mention an instance: a peregrine falcon in which the hunting drive be-

comes active, searches for prey until it is found. The sight of prey releases the motor response of catching, killing and eating, which is a chain of simple, relatively rigid, responses. Or, a female rat runs through a maze, keeps searching, until it finds its young, which releases the maternal motor responses. (Tinbergen 1950: 307)

The examples of the falcon and the rat are provided as illustrations of the theoretical idea that innate behaviors, conceptualized as somehow present in centers of the nervous system, are released by stimuli. The generic description of behaviors resonates with Tinbergen's substantive claim that "catching, killing and eating is a *chain of simple, relatively rigid, responses.*" In other words, the generic depiction of typical behavior patterns, occurring under abstractly conceived circumstances, is well suited to the theoretical claim of behavioral rigidity and invariance; such a method of depiction provides an icon that tacitly bolsters that claim.[2] The effects of two grammatical features in this passage are noteworthy. First, the use of quotation marks around the words *exploratory, seeking,* and even *random* signifies the active evasion or qualification of mental vocabulary. Second, the avoidance of the active voice of verbs is affiliated with the elision of authorship. Thus, for instance, the animal does not *feel* an instinctive urge, but the urge *is activated* within it, and the falcon does not *catch, kill,* and *eat* its prey, but rather the sight of prey *releases* these "motor responses." These grammatical forms of scare-quoting and the use of the passive voice work in different but mutually reinforcing ways toward effacing subjectivity.

All facets of Tinbergen's passage, then, reinforce and resonate with one another, conjuring a picture of animals as natural objects, guided by forces they can neither know (physiological factors) nor control (environmental stimuli). The view advanced is that appropriate environmental stimuli inhibit or release specific mechanisms in the neurophysiological makeup of the animal. This theoretical perspective, garnered and constituted through a set of technical terms, functions as an adequate, if not complete, explanation of the emission of behavior patterns. In virtue of the work of a technical language, meaning is thus transferred from the purview of the actor to the theoretical categories that are designed to explain its behaviors.

In both Lorenz's and Tinbergen's examples, discussions of behavior are structured on the matrix of impinging stimuli, intermediate mechanisms, and elicited responses. The assimilation of the "stimulus-response" connection from behaviorism, and its consequences on the portrayal of animals, deserve closer inspection.

THE STIMULUS-RESPONSE CONNECTION AND THE IDIOMATIC LANGUAGE IT SUPPORTS

Ethological methods and concerns were forged partially in opposition to the behaviorist school of comparative psychology of the early twentieth century (see Burkhardt 1981; Lorenz 1950). While behaviorists focused on the malleability of behavior and studied animals in laboratory settings under controlled and largely artificial conditions, ethologists turned their attention especially to innate behaviors, observing animal life in its natural environment. Despite these important differences, the formative influence of behaviorism is discernible in the language of ethologists. Perhaps in their endeavor to legitimate and institutionalize the scientific study of natural behavior, it was expedient for ethologists to assimilate aspects of terminology and thinking from the closely affiliated discipline of comparative psychology, which was already well established in the scientific community of the time. The work of classical ethologists shows the influence of the behaviorist school in two important respects: the adoption of the language of stimulus-response and the concurrence that skepticism is a legitimate stance toward animal mind. The stimulus-response connection is the abstract vector used pervasively by ethologists to articulate the relationship between internal and/or external environment and the production of behavior. Intimately connected with the adoption of stimulus-response as the central matrix is the avoidance of allusions to mentality, for both on the plane of language use and in its conceptual ramifications beyond direct textual experience, stimulus-response does yeoman's work in supplanting mental predication.

Under the influence of behaviorism, the idea that mental phenomena are unobservable and hence their existence is unverifiable acquired axiomatic status. A central injunction regarding the study of animal behavior dictated the scrupulous avoidance of any reference to mental phenomena. To this end, adopting the stimulus-response connection was extremely effective in displacing an understanding of a mindful relation of animals to their surroundings—in terms, for example, of knowledge, understanding, purpose, emotion, belief, and so forth. A "stimulus" is conceptually constructed to signify the touching off of a "reaction," and thus tropes of awareness, consciousness, or attention are not required in the contact be-tween animal and world. Moreover, in addition to mobilizing the men-tality-effacing effects of stimulus-response, ethologists explicitly validated the skeptical stance in their careful avoidance or qualification of mental language.[3]

The technical concept of "stimulus" has two central logical features. First, it is conceived as a unit that impinges on the sensory apparatus of an organism and lacks intrinsic meaning. Thus Lorenz maintains that "what we ordinarily call an object is created in our environment in some-what the following way: we gather the stimuli that come to us from some one thing, and refer them collectively to that thing as a common source of stimulation" (1957a: 83). Here Lorenz underscores the atomistic quality of "stimulus" by decomposing the object encountered in human and ani-mal environments into basic units, conceived as purely physical and in-trinsically meaningless. The second feature of the notion of stimulus is that it is general and indefinite, referring to *any* element that arouses a "re-sponse" from the organism. This broad quality of the concept allowed ethologists to extend the behaviorist conception of an external, envi-ronmental stimulus to include internal, physiological states as stimuli.[4] Through its tight affiliation with the technical notion of stimulus, the con-cept of response becomes altered vis-à-vis its vernacular meaning. As a complement to the notion of stimulus, "response" becomes technical as well, remaining largely only a homonym to the ordinary concept of re-sponse. As a component of the stimulus-response connection, the response no longer corresponds to a performative action but is more akin to an involuntary reaction. Indeed, in his work *The Study of Instinct,* Nikolaas Tinbergen uses *response* interchangeably with *reaction* (1989: 54–55 and passim).

Because the connection between stimulus and response is so broadly applicable, it is readily available for pervasive use. It permeates ethological thought and may be characterized as the backbone of its technical lan-guage. The stimulus-response connection forms a conceptual home where more explicitly mechanical notions can reside. Although the language of stimulus-response is nested in at least partially vernacular descriptions, it comprises a fundamental step away from the ordinary language of lived action. It is important to note the deterministic quality of the connection between stimulus and response (see Watson 1970: 183), stemming from the kinship of the idea of "response" to the notion of "reflex." As the historian Roger Smith points out, "Behaviorist explanation is deterministic, linking one set of physical changes ('the stimulus') with a second set ('the response'). The possibility of describing organisms in these terms developed historically with the concept of the reflex, already associated after Descartes with the elimination of mind from animals. The reflex described how mechanism produced an appearance of purposiveness and hence of mind" (1990: 420).

Indeed, by envisioning the direct impact of stimuli upon the body, René Descartes did more than simply deny the existence of animal mind: he created a story for the production of behavior that effectively nullified the need for mentality. What he succeeded in doing was to give a novel picture of how animal existence could be essentially different from human existence:

> My view is that animals do not see as we do when we are aware that we see, but only as we do when our mind is elsewhere. In such a case the images of external objects are depicted on our retinas, and perhaps the impressions they leave in the optic nerves cause our limbs to make various movements, although we are quite unaware of this. In such a case we too move just like automata. (Descartes 1970: 36)

The birth of the conceptual transfiguration of "action performed" into "movement caused" is fully visible here. In ethological (and of course behaviorist) writing the concept of response, through its affiliation with stimulus, permits the bypass, if not the elimination, of the presence of mind. By contrast, reliance on ordinary vocabulary and reasoning of action authorizes the potential or actual inclusion of mental phenomena by representing the link between animals and worldly affairs as meaningful rather than deterministic (cf. White 1968).

Another point of contrast between the stimulus-response framework and the ordinary language of action involves indefiniteness and specificity of sense, respectively. The stimulus-response framework can be deployed as a general descriptor, with "stimulus" as the placeholder for any object or event in the (internal or external) environment and "response" as the placeholder for any (re)action of the animal with respect to the stimulus. In other words, the language of stimulus-response has no indexical limits. The stimulus-response framework articulates a ubiquitous and abstract link between any state of affairs and the behavior it triggers. Because the language of stimulus and response does not speak to the specifics of behavioral events but rather structures those specifics, it cannot be apprehended as *constitutive* of particular behavioral scenes. The indefinite and abstract quality of stimulus-response thus has the effect of rendering animals "meaning-blind" with respect to the particular conduct and circumstances so described; as physiological or surrounding stimuli impinge upon, and guide, animals to behave in certain ways, they do not have to apprehend the meaning of objects, actions, or events.[5] While ethologists rejected the behaviorist view that external environmental stimuli alone could evoke responses, they did not question the logic of the behaviorist conception; instead, they altered and broadened its domain, making stimuli inclusive of internal (physiological) events. In this way, classical ethology accounted for "spontaneous" behaviors—behaviors appearing without any obvious external stimulation. However, in keeping the causal origins of spontaneous acts within the conceptual confines of the stimulus-response matrix, they remained stripped of any implications of authorship. It is worth underscoring that these effects of effacing authorship and meaning from the animal's world derive from conceptual features of the stimulus-response connection.

The stimulus-response connection is the linguistic backbone of ethological reports about animal behavior. It forms the central axis around which an entire linguistic style and an armory of technical concepts are spun. The deterministic quality of the concept of stimulus affords the complementary usage of the affiliated verbs *release, activate,* and *trigger,* which have strong mechanistic overtones. In ethological writing, these words are employed ubiquitously as verbs with behavioral patterns as their objects. Just as the notion of "stimulus" works as the intermittent, yet pervasively used, placeholder for anything to which an animal reacts, so *release, trigger,* and *activate* are placeholders for specific action verbs, and they are used consistently in presenting behavioral patterns. The employment of vernacular action verbs with animals as grammatical subjects is massively curtailed, and thus their effect of authorship in animal action is preempted.[6] The recurrent verb-concepts of *release, trigger,* and *activate* may be characterized as idiomatic to ethological writing, which is to say that their use is neither ordinary nor technical, but straddles these two domains. While they are metaphorically imported from the context of operating machinery and thus are not technical per se, their ubiquitous usage, as well as their resonance with the technical notion of "stimulus," gives them the appearance, and hence the authoritative force, of being scientific-technical concepts. Thus the tacit transformation from metaphoric to technical status not only contributes decisively to the mechanomorphic portrayal of animals but also contributes to presenting such a portrayal as scientific—with concomitant truth effects—by internally marking itself as a technical linguistic usage.

The Technical-Explanatory Concept of the IRM and the Elimination of an Epistemic Relationship Between Animal and World

Central to the study of behavior is the concern with the connection between the actor and the (animate or inanimate) surrounding objects and events. In the case of the naturalist genre discussed in the previous chapters, this connection is understood, on a par with human action, under the auspices of a meaningful orientation of animals to their surroundings. For classical ethologists, the connection between actor and world is centrally mediated through what they term "innate releasing mechanisms" (IRMs). IRMs are conceived as built-in, species-specific neurophysiological mechanisms, which correspond to different behavioral patterns possessed by the organism (see Tinbergen 1989: 41–42).

The IRM is the interface between stimulus and response. It is pictured as a kind of inner switch that, when activated by a particular stimulus, releases the appropriate corresponding behavioral response. According to Lorenz, "several stimuli are usually merged in a very simple stimulus combination, to which an 'innate releasing mechanism' (IRM) responds" (1957a: 85). The relationship, then, between a stimulus and its corresponding IRM is like that of a key and its lock: as the key fits the lock and opens the door, so the stimulus triggers the specific IRM and releases the behavior that is the appropriate response to that stimulus. For Lorenz, the metaphor of the key and lock is apposite, because "the form of such a releasing mechanism must have a certain minimum of general improbability, for the same reasons that a bit of key is given a generally unusual form" (ibid.). The value of improbability is that of "preventing 'mistaken' responses to other, accidentally similar stimuli" (1957a: 88), just as the unique form of each key prohibits illegitimate access to its lock.

The behavioral response of the animal occurs when stimuli act upon the IRM ostensibly corresponding to that behavior. To clarify with an example from Lorenz, the throat markings of a nestling grosbeak are strangely colorful because they are "the key to the parents' innate feeding reaction" (1957a: 88). In ethological language, the throat markings of the nestling bird gaping for food constitute the stimulus that releases the parental innate reaction of feeding. The action of the parent bird does not reflect, nor even obliquely evidence, knowledge of the state of affairs toward which the action is directed. The grosbeaks' feeding of their nestlings is conceived as a behavioral pattern released by the sensory configuration of the throat markings. The act of feeding does not indicate that the birds have any understanding of the situation within which they behave in specific ways. Lorenz acknowledges that the exclusion of understanding from the animal's world is entailed by his theoretical viewpoint. Thus he writes:

> Man endeavors to master his world and its phenomena through insight into their causal relationships. For him, it is essential to unite the single stimuli into objects of his world. In fact it constitutes the basis of all his knowledge.
>
> The animal on the other hand, and the lower animal in particular, is essentially fitted into his world by innate behavior. . . . A material or objective comprehension of his world is not a biological necessity. (1957a: 85)

The ethological "innate releasing mechanism" fulfills the task that in the human case is accomplished through knowledge. While human action in and upon the world is mediated by knowledge, animal action is mediated largely through the IRMs. Along with the elimination of a knowing connection between actor and world effected by the IRM, there appears simultaneously a linguistic displacement of agency to the postulated mechanism. Lorenz, for example, writes that "out of all the stimuli which the object emits, the IRM of an instinctive act *chooses* a small number . . . and *reacts* to them selectively, thus *initiating the action*" (1957a: 86, emphasis added). This phenomenon of the dislocation of agency from actors to technical concepts is recurrent. Behavioral phenomena thus call forth the relevance of agency so powerfully that if it is denied to the animals themselves, then it must surface elsewhere—be it in their innate mechanisms or, in more recent conceptions, in their genes.

"THE BABY CRIED. THE MOMMY PICKED IT UP."

According to Lorenz, a single object that emits two different stimuli is not the same object from the animal's perspective. One of the consequences, therefore, of the IRM as mediator between action and environment is that the external world of objects and events does not possess experiential unity and continuity for animals. An example from Lorenz demonstrates the logic by which the construct of the IRM undercuts the understanding of animals as subjects with an outlook upon the world and a continuity of experience. Close analysis of this example shows that the consequence of the loss of animals' unified perspective fosters a mechanomorphic icon of animal being.

Lorenz gives an example of a female mallard duck that "comes to the rescue" upon hearing a musk duckling's "cry for help" (1957a: 87). The mallard duck's response to the musk duckling is explained in terms of her "defense reaction . . . [being] elicited by the alarm call of young birds of different species" (ibid.). On Lorenz's explanatory model, the duckling's call releases the IRM of the maternal defense reaction of the female duck. Additional "fostering reactions," such as protecting the duckling or attacking whatever might be threatening it, "are highly specific to the species" and are determined, for Lorenz, by "definite colors and markings on the head and back" (ibid.). Thus the female mallard duck "comes valiantly to the rescue," but upon *seeing* the calling *musk* duckling she treats it indifferently, attacks it, or may even kill it, "solely because it does not have the mallard head and back markings which elicit further care" (ibid.). On the ethological view, the specific head and back markings form the combination of stimuli corresponding to the IRM's release of "fostering reactions." Hence the innate behavior patterns—first, coming to the rescue of the duckling, and next, indifferent or hostile treatment of the duckling—are released by two different sets of stimuli coming from the same object (the musk duckling). Therefore, ethological reasoning continues, the musk duckling is *not* a unified object of experience from the point of view of the female mallard duck, since her two reactions are directed to different objects.

According to the model advanced by Lorenz, the mallard female duck encounters *two* objects in this episode. Two distinct sets of stimuli elicit two distinct behaviors that correspond to different objects—to offspring, on the one hand, and an alien animal, on the other. The *calling* musk duckling, therefore, is a different object from the *sighted* one. On this view, the meaning of the object is not assembled, from a subject's perspective, as the selfsame, unitary object. Rather, a single object, at different moments, projects distinct combinations of stimuli (in this case, auditory and visual, respectively) that, like keys unlocking different doors, release different behaviors. If the same object projects two sets of stimuli that release behaviors corresponding to two different objects, then the object, while the same from a human standpoint, is not the same from the animal's standpoint. The calling musk duckling and the sighted one are not the same for the mallard duck, since "one object may release two antagonistic reactions, each of which should, biologically, have a separate object" (ibid.). On Lorenz's construction, then, the female mallard's actions, while unfolding *in tandem,* are semantically disconnected. They do not constitute a *sequence,* in the sociologist Harvey Sacks' sense of having some organization between them (1987: 54). The action of coming to the rescue of the calling duckling and the indifference toward, or attack of, the duckling upon seeing it are entirely disconnected events. The animal's adjacent actions are not tied to each other, but occur as separate behaviors released by separate, specific stimuli combinations (the releasing stimuli, or "releasers," are the duckling's call, on one hand, and its markings, on the other). This conception of behavior is given explicit theoretical articulation by Tinbergen when he writes that "consistent study of the dependence of behaviour on sensory stimuli has . . . revealed the fact that many reactions, even relatively short and simple ones, are in reality a chain of separate reactions each of which is dependent on a special set of sign stimuli" (1989: 47).

The alternative view of the female duck's responses as sequentially continuous would yield a very different understanding of her actions. She responds to the alarm call of a duckling only to find upon arrival that the calling duckling is not one of her own; at this point her response changes from a protective one to an indifferent or hostile one. This manner of tying together her two contradictory actions—of coming to the rescue of a duckling and then mistreating it—implicates the idea that the female duck misrecognized the duckling caller for one of her chicks. The notion of "misrecognition" conveys the sense of an achievement, "recognition," which turned out to have been incorrect. This alternative view embeds not only knowledge of the object (mis)recognized, but also a temporal extendedness of the knowledge of the object that is recognized.

For Lorenz, the possibility of misrecognition on the female duck's part cannot even arise, because her two actions are construed as disconnected from the outset. At each separate moment the animal is guided by the stimuli at hand. Because those moments are discontinuous, the resulting picture is that of an animal that does not coherently assemble the objects present and the events unfolding around it. When the sequential logic of linked actions is repudiated, a picture of subjective coherence becomes unsustainable—as though it were logically blocked. On Lorenz's model—and without any explicit endorsement of a mechanistic thesis—the duck is almost puppetlike, with the stimuli acting upon it like steering strings.

In his investigations of the ties between language and social relations, Sacks used an example similar to Lorenz's duck and duckling example. In a lecture on how people accomplish and recognize descriptions, he investigates two simple sentences from a children's storybook: "The baby cried. The mommy picked it up." Sacks begins by noting that, on the surface, these are separate sentences describing two entirely different events. Yet they are immediately heard in conjunction and understood as forming a unit: the "mommy" is the mother of *this* baby (it is not that she just happens to be a mother); the *it* of the second sentence refers to the baby in the first; and the mother of this baby picks it up *because* it is crying (and not for some other reason). The knowledge that makes this shared, immediate hearing possible includes what is known about mothers and babies; what is known about how categories co-occur in descriptions, namely, consistently with respect to each other and bound relevantly to activities they predicate; and what is known of how sequences of adjacent actions are tied together observably and reportably (see Sacks 1972). This simple datum from a child's story illustrates what Sacks calls "the fine power of culture," for, in his words, "you all just heard what I said you heard, and I don't even know you" (1992: 237).

Indeed, this "fine power" is all the more evident in the witnessing of a "mallard duck *leading her young . . . com[ing] valiantly to the rescue* of a musk duckling crying for help" (Lorenz 1957a: 87, emphasis added). The immediate apprehension of the interconnection of the actions described is equivalent to the direct way the propositions "The baby cried. The mommy picked it up" are heard as connected. The perception of "the duck coming to the duckling's rescue" is a first-level description in the ordinary language of living, and it resonates with what is known about "mommies" and "babies." This phrasing expresses the immediate and pretheoretical availability of the sense of the specific scene. Such a description, then, works as the scaffolding for a theoretical overlay; further analysis of behavior requires, and is generally built upon, some first-order intelligibility. Here, the first-order intelligibility of the scene depends upon the availability of the reported actions—"A mallard duck leading her young hears a duckling cry. She comes to the rescue of the duckling crying for help"—as sequenced. Lorenz's subsequent theoretical construct, while built upon this first-order view, removes any sequential logic from the duck's actions; rather, there are different sets of stimuli impinging upon the duck at discrete moments.

The break of temporal cohesiveness, effected largely through the stimulus-response-cum-IRM framework, is consequential for how animals are pictured. It denies that knowledge is embodied in the mallard duck's actions—knowledge initially implicated in a description employing the terms *defense, alarm, cry for help,* and *rescue.* In the place of familiar experiential fields of action, populated by objects and (possible) events about which the animal has knowledge, there is the work of the machinery of "ready-made IRMs" (1957a: 88) activated by stimuli, thereby releasing appropriate reactions. Awareness is effaced in this model of behavior, for it is no longer required for the contact between subject and object. The object gathers all the necessary and sufficient features for the elicitation of the proper behaviors; it need not be known, assessed, understood, recognized, misrecognized, or witnessed by the subject of action. Moreover, the subject does not *perform* actions, since the object's features, the stimuli, work upon the inner machinery, releasing the behavior. Authorship is thus expunged, for the animal does not cause events in the world, but rather is at the mercy of a causal constellation of stimuli, IRMs, and innate reactions.

A picture of animals as unaware and passive is created through the fragmentation of temporal continuity. On the other hand, when the unfolding unity of temporally contiguous actions is preserved, the resulting sequential coherence of actions reflects back on the actor. Animals are then understood as assembling and experiencing objects and events in the world in their temporal and spatial continuities. Thus, on the alternative interpretation of Lorenz's example, the applicability of the mental notion of (mis)recognition hinges more on the acknowledgment of the coherence of actions across the temporal spectrum than on the postulation of some inner representation or other cognitive process. There is, therefore, a profound difference between viewing actions *sequentially* versus *serially.* The first pictures the duck as knowing that the duckling she hears calling is the same one that she encounters, though misrecognized as one of her own, while the second (Lorenz's) pictures that for the duck the two objects—of her concern and of her indifference—are distinct and disconnected.

With this example of the mallard duck and the musk duckling, Lorenz is not simply explaining an extraordinary or uncommon episode of two serially placed, inconsistent behaviors. The account is advanced as having far-reaching implications. For Lorenz this unusual case, where it happens that the calling duckling turns out to be a different species from the female duck that responds to its calls, exposes the behavioral mechanisms that are always at work. He mobilizes the example to propose the following general thesis:

> Consistent treatment of another member of the species, therefore, as it occurs in natural conditions where instinctive activities function normally, is not necessarily the result of an inherent connection of reactions in the acting subject. Rather, it is often achieved by the purely extraneous circumstance that the releaser, the fellow member of the species, emits all the stimuli correlated to the various releasing mechanisms collectively. The functional design of innate behavior patterns localizes the biologically necessary element of unity in the stimulus-emitting object, rather than in the acting subject. (1957a: 87)

There is no unity and consistency of objects from the animal's experiential perspective. So in the normal, routine case where the female duck "comes to the rescue" of her own ducklings "crying for help," it only *appears* that her actions manifest an understanding of objects, events, and their connections: that a given call from her offspring duckling is summoning her and indicating alarm or need of protection. What the unusual case reveals for Lorenz is that the duck's reactions are generally elicited by distinct sets of stimuli, occurring in discontinuous—even if contiguous—pockets of time. The stimuli release the responses by triggering IRMs. The calling mallard duckling triggers the female mallard's IRM for coming to the rescue and, in the next moment, the female's visual encounter of the duckling's markings triggers her IRM for caring reactions.

The unusual case is taken to unveil the world of temporally fragmented sets of stimuli that animals perennially inhabit. The fragmented character of the animal's world is portrayed as cloaked by the usual, overall consistency of objects in that world. Thus Lorenz writes that "in the natural life of a species, releasers and innate responses together secure consistent treatment of its members, even though the latter are not conceived as entities" (1957a: 89). The consistency of an animal's behavior around its fellows is a consequence of all the appropriate releasers being (more or less) functional at all times, activating the IRMs and thereby releasing the corresponding behaviors. With this picture, there is neither necessity nor conceptual space for animals as witnesses of their surroundings or authors of their actions. Inquiry into animal behavior becomes epistemologically equivalent with inquiry into the behaviors of objects. Mentality falls out of the interpretive picture, for within the ethological view it has no function that is not already fulfilled by the interface of responses and stimuli through the IRMs.

The Invocation of Experimental Support in the Depiction of Animals as Natural Objects

The construct of the innate releasing mechanism and the example of the female mallard duck and the musk duckling illustrate how the temporal fragmentation of actions severs the epistemic connection between animals and their world. The resulting mechanomorphic effect is strengthened by the overall linguistic environment, especially of stimulus-response and its accompanying mechanical concepts of releasing, activating, and triggering. The retraction of an epistemic connection (of knowledge, understanding, belief, recognition, and related notions), the replacement of specific objects and events with the category "stimulus," and the displacement of action verbs by mechanical verbs render animals meaning-blind. The idea that the meaning of objects, actions, or events is beyond animals' purview, in turn, invites a mechanical icon of their behaviors.

Tinbergen's description of a herring gull sitting on her eggs may clarify how animals become meaning-blind and how mechanomorphism is thereby entailed: "The *reaction* of sitting down on the nest to incubate *is released* by *sign stimuli* from the eggs" (1989: 50, emphasis added). Rather than an action performed, brooding is conveyed as a "reaction released"; the eggs are not whole, meaningful objects for the gull, but emit "sign stimuli." While Tinbergen's account is not motivated by the desire to eliminate meaning from the animal's perceptions and actions, the supervenient effect of a deterministic explanation couched in technical terminology is the elimination of subjective meaning. A number of questions arise: What warrants Tinbergen's description of the brooding gull? Why is sitting on the eggs a reaction rather than an action? Why is it released and not simply done? Why are there sign stimuli coming from the eggs, rather than simply the eggs being there? The general impression conveyed is a deterministic portrayal of brooding. But how is this portrayal justified? If ethological language suggests that inquiry into animal behavior is epistemologically equivalent to inquiry into the behavior of natural objects, what supporting grounds are invoked? In this section, I discuss the role of the results and interpretation of ethological experiments in corroborating the presentation of animals as natural objects.

The design and interpretation of experiments is tightly knit up with the theoretical framework of ethology. The idea that animals "react to stimuli" leads to the design of experiments in which the objects of an animal's environment are transformed in order to isolate and expose the specific aspects that function as effective stimuli. Ethological experiments are ingenious in targeting a circumstance or object of the natural environment and altering it, so that the animal's responses may be observed. The fact that animals often do respond to these altered objects then works to legitimate the descriptive and explanatory force of technical terms such as *stimulus* or *innate releasing mechanism*. In this sense, experimental results and theory mutually generate and support each other. The discussion of certain experiments should make this point clearer.

Ethological experiments begin with the object to which an animal is known to respond, artificially modeling and then modifying that object. The aim of the experimental design is to isolate the "releaser," the feature of the object that is critical in evoking the behavior under consideration. How closely this experimental aim is entangled with theoretical concerns can be seen in Tinbergen's own words. He writes that "releasers . . . are properties—either such of shape or colour, or special movements, or sounds, or scents, &c.—serving to elicit a response in another individual" (1989: 56). Experimental results are thus interpreted as showing that the animal responds not to the whole object, but rather to a certain property of the object. That the behavioral response is provoked by a property of the object, in turn, reinforces the credibility of the ethological lexicon— *stimulus, releaser, fixed action pattern,* and the like.

In ethological experiments the model objects are representational variations of certain aspects of the entity to which an animal normally responds. The object may be copied, decomposed, simplified, or exaggerated in artificial substitutes or object dummies; or the action of the object—tactile or chemical, for example—may be simulated by an artificial replacement. The male stickleback, for example, is known to respond aggressively to other males who display "nuptial markings" (1989: 27). In one experiment, a series of increasingly abstract and dissimilar replicas of the original was presented to a male stickleback in order to isolate the feature that elicits the aggressive behavior:

> Some of the models were very crude imitations of sticklebacks, lacking many characteristics of the species or even of fish in general, but possessing

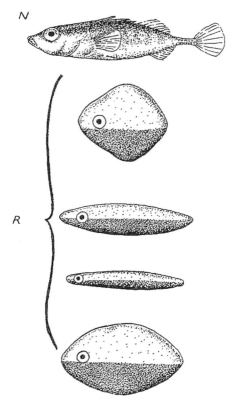

Figure 7 Stickleback model dummies

a red belly (Series R). Others were accurate imitations of sticklebacks, but lacked the red (Series N). The males attacked the first group of models much more rigorously than they did the others. In this experiment the red colour was put into competition against all other morphological characters to-gether. The results prove that the fish reacted essentially to the red and ne-glected the other characteristics. Yet its eyes are perfectly able to "see" these other details. (Tinbergen 1989: 28)

The model presented to the animal is a minimal and abstract representa-tion of the original object. The whole, meaningful entity—a live male stickleback with its red nuptial markings—is replaced by a look-alike dummy. The dummy is next refashioned into an abstract object, bearing little resemblance to the original—an oval shape with a red underside (corresponding to the red belly and throat of the male stickleback). This minimal object, with the intrinsically meaningless feature "red," draws the fighting response of a male stickleback to a greater extent than the look-alike imitation of a stickleback lacking "red."

The results of this kind of experiment are deciphered as isolating what Lorenz calls the "key stimulus," and Tinbergen the "sign stimulus," releasing the particular behavior; in the stickleback case, the stimulus "red" releases aggression. This decomposition and reduction of the object into its atomized component(s) is then conceptually translocated onto the animal: rather than responding to the whole meaningful object (a competing male), the stickleback is conceived as reacting to a key meaningless component of it (red). According to ethological reasoning, moreover, it is not even that animals react to stimuli, but rather that key stimuli release their reactions.

> The carnivorous water beetle *Dytiscus marginalis,* which has perfectly developed compound eyes . . . , *does not react* at all to visual stimuli when capturing prey, e.g. a tadpole. A moving prey in a glass tube never *releases* nor *guides* any reaction. The beetle's feeding response *is released* by chemical and tactile stimuli exclusively; for instance, a watery meat extract promptly *forces it* to hunt and to capture every solid object it touches. (Tinbergen 1989: 25–27, emphasis added; see Figure 8)

Experimental designs confront animals with largely unprecedented and unnatural situations. These retain selected elements from the natural life of the animals with the aim of seeing whether and how they respond. At first the beetle is exposed to a tadpole in a tube. The beetle thus encounters an object that is prey in its normal environment, but from which scent has been experimentally subtracted; the beetle shows no response to the tadpole. Next the beetle is exposed to the scent of meat extract, but an object that would normally carry such a scent has been subtracted; the beetle now shows a "feeding response," despite the absence of prey. The experiment indicates that scent, not sight, triggers the behavioral response. The idea of a "physiological trap" appearing in the legend of Figure 8, and the textual reference to the meat extract "forcing" the beetle to hunt, underscore the ethological view that the stimuli work as *causes* of animals' responses.

The experiments are taken to reveal the stimuli that are causally effective in triggering behavioral patterns. As the key stimuli appear to be unveiled through the isolation of different component elements, the experimental design corroborates the adequacy of the technical term *stimulus* in

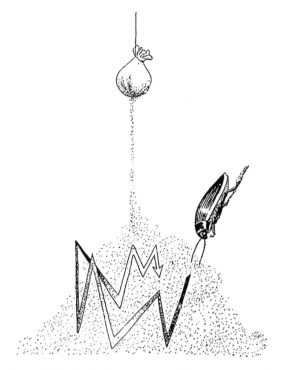

Figure 8 Beetle feeding response: "physiological trap"

describing the impact of a property of some object on the animal. The design and results of the experiment suggest that animals react not to whole objects, but only to certain features or parts. This allows for the corollary implication that animals do not experience objects in a meaningful way, but instead components of the objects—meaningless in themselves—set off their reactions. This picture is conveyed also in the description of the dragonfly's hunting of mosquitoes:

> In the visual domain, motion may often be a powerful stimulus. One of the earliest studies of this type concerned the "recognition" of prey by dragonflies. . . . Mosquito-hunting species do not react to properties of shape, although their highly developed compound eyes certainly enable them to see even minor differences in shape. They react specially to the type of motion of flying mosquitoes. Mosquitoes are not hunted when walking on solid ground. Small scraps of paper of varying shape but of approximately the right size promptly release the hunting responses when they are thrown in the air. (1989: 31–32)

The dragonfly is represented as responding to the *motion* of the mosquito, rather than to the mosquito itself as a meaningful entity. The treatment of motion as a stimulus and the placement of quotation marks around the word *recognition* are tacitly portrayed as warranted by the dragonfly's response only to mosquitoes in motion; indeed, that motion alone "promptly releases" a response is experimentally confirmed by throwing pieces of paper in the air. The theoretical features of the stimulus as both abstract and determining appear borne out by the dragonfly's response being directed to "motion" rather than to "mosquito," as well as by the dragonfly's pursuit of moving pieces of paper—interpreted in terms of the part (i.e., the stimulus of motion) "promptly releasing" the insect's "hunting response."

What appears as animals' inability to notice that the experimental object is not an entity actually deserving of the intense behavior directed to it—that a tuft of red feathers, to mention another experimental instance, is not a male robin, and thus does not merit territorial display or attack—becomes a tacit warrant for abrogating the epistemic connection of animals to the world, or at least affirms skeptical misgivings with respect to such a connection. If the male robin does not see through the lack of realism of a tuft of red feathers (positioned conspicuously in its territory by the ethologist), then doubt may be cast on whether his relation with *actual* male robins is mediated by knowledge and understanding. Therefore the fact that in experimental setups animals respond to crude or partial models in the same way they do to real and whole objects of their world has two significant consequences: (1) it can be used to legitimate conceptualizing the animal-environment relationship on the stimulus-response matrix, and (2) it works to reinforce a skeptical stance regarding the epistemic connection of animals to their world.

The experiments that aim to expose what ethologists interchangeably have called the releaser, the effective stimulus, the sign stimulus, or the key stimulus reinforce a mechanomorphic portrayal of animals. Mechanomorphism is affiliated with several features of these experiments. A response from an animal is provoked with the presentation of a model of an original entity. The reduction of the original is first from the whole, real entity to an artificial imitation; then the reduction is taken a step further, from an artificial imitation to a partial model, having a single component or property of the original. It turns out that animals not only react to the artificial copy, but allegedly sometimes react even more vigorously to the crude model with the "releasing" component. The reductions from the real whole to an artificial whole, and then to an artificial part, imply that animals do not apprehend the meaning of the real entity they encounter and interact with in natural circumstances.

"Fooling" animals into responding to inauthentic replicas suggests that animals lack understanding. This insinuation of ignorance supports, but is also forcefully underlined by, the linguistic constitution of the key feature as a "stimulus" that "releases a reaction." The deterministic implications of the stimulus-response connection are reinforced by a language of causation that pervades ethological writing. For example, Tinbergen writes of the "prompt release of the dragonfly's hunting response" and of the "prompt forcing of the beetle to hunt," suggesting that the stimuli are forces beyond animals' comprehension and control and inexorably guide animals' reactions.

The causal efficacy of the stimulus is also propped with grammatical constructions that circumvent having animals as subjects of sentences.[7] One such construction involves using the passive voice in behavioral descriptions. To reiterate a couple of examples, Tinbergen maintains that "the beetle's feeding response is released by chemical and tactile stimuli," and he writes of "the 'recognition' of prey by dragonflies." A cognate grammatical device involves positioning the stimulus as the subject of the sentence with quasi-mechanical verbs such as *release, trigger,* or *elicit* predicating the behavioral response; for example, "the scraps of paper promptly release the hunting response." These grammatical forms would perhaps not be noteworthy if they occurred only sporadically. However, this is not the case. Ethological writing systematically uses grammatical constructions that build in the elision of animals as subjects of the sentence. This style of writing is consistent with the skeptical stance toward animal mind that classical ethologists embraced. Whether deliberate or unintentional, it comprises a collection of grammatical forms that avoid or prescind intimations of experience and authorship in the animal world.

The argument that classical ethologists' portrayals implicate a mechanomorphic picture of animal being involves two aspects. First, mechanical behavior connects with the notion of a behavioral response being provoked by an intrinsically meaningless component rather than the whole object. This suggests that animals have a sort of knee-jerk reaction to one key feature—for example, to "red" rather than to the living, trespassing male competitor—and in turn, this may be taken to entail that animals are blind to the entire complex of meanings and implications of the situation they encounter. Second, the image of cajoling an animal within an experimental situation to respond to some crude model of the real invokes the sense of mechanical behavior that, in D. W. Hamlyn's words, "is applicable to behavior . . . equivalent to 'stupid' or 'unthinking'" (1981: 69). Thus certain experiments inevitably (and, of course, irrespective of the ethologists' intentions) make the animal appear stupid or foolish. This is sometimes reflected in the language of the description of the experiment:

> The courting behavior of a male stickleback before a pregnant female is . . . dependent on at least two sign stimuli: the swollen abdomen and the special posturing movement of the female. When a crude fish-like model with a swollen abdomen is presented to the male, it will vigorously court this *ridiculous* dummy, whereas its response to a complete stickleback which has a normal belly is much less intense. (Tinbergen 1989: 38, emphasis added)

This picture of "foolishness" is also pronounced in the experimental set-ups that led to the ethological idea of "supernormal releasers." In certain cases, when some feature of the original object is exaggerated, animals show a preference for the exaggerated ("supernormal") "stimulus situation" over the "natural situation" (Tinbergen 1989: 44). The classic example in this regard is the oystercatcher's preference for incubating a gigantic decoy egg over her own normal-sized clutch of eggs.

While it appears that such misdirected actions demonstrate that animals lack comprehension of the meaning of the objects they encounter, the background theoretical interpretation and the language of descriptions powerfully support such a picture. In other words, misdirected behaviors do not by themselves dictate how such behaviors are to be interpreted. A passage from Darwin illustrates that there are alternative ways of seeing and describing infelicitous actions:

> Ornaments of all kinds . . . are sedulously displayed by the males, and apparently serve to excite, or attract, or charm the females. But the males will sometimes display their ornaments, when not in the presence of the females, as occasionally occurs with grouse at their balz-places, and as may be noticed with the peacock; the latter bird, however, evidently wishes for a spectator of some kind, and will shew off his finery, as I have often seen, before poultry or even pigs. All naturalists who have closely attended to the habits of birds . . . are unanimously of opinion that the males delight to display their beauty. (Darwin 1981, 2: 86)

Darwin understands the male peacock's misdirected displays as expressing his zealousness to show his beauty. He does not interpret the bizarre behavior of displaying to poultry and pigs as revealing that the peacock is oblivious to the meaning of his courtship presentations. Quite to the contrary, Darwin sees the behavior as indicating that the peacock is so vividly present to the fact that the display is for showing his beauty that he himself decontextualizes the action from its proper occasion, for the sake of "shewing off his finery." On Darwin's portrayal, the male peacock, an inhabitant of an aesthetic and exhibitionist world, is the author of his ("ridiculous") action. As a consequence of being performed, his action comes through as a *gesture*. In virtue of being initiated and directed by the peacock himself, the gesture emerges as immanently meaningful, despite the fact that it is out of proper context. The splendor of the display is within the purview of its author. An image of mindfulness comes through Darwin's description: not as an inference about events "in" the animal's mind, but as corollary to the icon of a male peacock who fully extends a gesture.

When the same behavior of the peacock is considered from a classical ethological standpoint, its import changes radically. The ethologists conceptualized displays as "fixed action patterns," that is, innately given behavioral patterns with certain "inner specific energies" associated with them (see Lorenz 1950; Tinbergen 1989). The behavioral pattern (the male's display) is released by the appropriate stimulus (the presence of the female peacock). Ethologists then reasoned that if the appropriate stimulus is absent for a long enough period, the inner specific energies accumulate and can finally trigger—by themselves, or in the face of a minimal, inappropriate stimulus, like a chicken or a pig—the expression of the behavioral pattern. As discussed in Chapter 1, this is the stipulated mechanism of what ethologists have called a "vacuum behavior," or a response appearing in an irrelevant or inappropriate context. The peacock's behavior of displaying to animals other than female peacocks is exemplary of what counts as a vacuum behavior for ethologists.

The identical behavioral expression of the peacock from an ethological perspective is quite different from Darwin's portrayal. The technical terms and their logical interconnections fully account for the *eruption* of this odd behavior. The male peacock is oblivious to the meaning of his actions and the unsuitability of the context: displaying to a pig is something that might happen to a male peacock quite unwittingly. He is compelled to execute a fixed action pattern by inner physiological forces that are beyond his control and, of course, outside the pale of his understanding. Once the peacock's behavior becomes theoretically accounted for in this manner, configured as a blindly executed vacuum behavior, the perceptibility of the display as an immanently meaningful gesture is extinguished. The peacock's odd display is no longer a misfired performance, but something he cannot help doing. The behavior looks empty, meaningless, and mechanomorphic—in a word, *mindless.*

In the mechanomorphic portrayal of animals, all elements—experimental facts and interpretations, technical and idiomatic terms, and grammatical forms—work together in a mutually sustaining and elaborating fashion to build the image of animals as natural objects. It should be noted that while an experimental design that provokes an animal to respond in what looks like a meaningless or foolish manner props such a mechanomorphic picture of behavior, it cannot establish the validity of such a picture, for a number of reasons: on account of the nature of the data of ethological experiments, which always represent the typical case, thereby masking individual variations of response; on account of the irremediably "metaphysical" quality of the replicated and reduced objects from the animal's perspective; because a mechanomorphic picture is a totalizing picture, subsuming the understanding of animal being, and is thus not at the level of a fact that can be proven or disproven; and finally, as the example from Darwin indicates, because infelicitous actions can be alternatively interpreted. Yet while inducing a response to inauthentic objects cannot stand as proof that behavior is mechanical, it can persist as powerfully suggestive of a lack of vision on the animal's part. The unforgettable images of ethological experiments—such as the oystercatcher trying, in vain, to sit on a gigantic decoy egg—tacitly work to place animals on the other

Figure 9 Oystercatcher with supernormal releaser

side of a border, with this side of the border standing for the human tropes of intelligence or rationality.

THE INTRANSIGENCE OF THE VERNACULAR: TENSIONS BETWEEN TECHNICAL AND ORDINARY LANGUAGE IN ETHOLOGICAL WRITING

Since a meaningful link between the actor and some state of affairs is often captured with mental language—the language of knowledge, understanding, thinking, intention, purpose, memory, or emotion—the displacement of the vernacular by the stimulus-response connection functions as a device to deflect mental vocabulary and to suspend the commitments it entails. This relates to the classical ethologists' concurrence with a skeptical attitude about animal mind. Skepticism is premised on a metaphysics of mind that holds mental states to be interior and unobservable phenomena. Tinbergen puts forth this premise right at the beginning of his work *The Nature of Instinct*:

> Subjective phenomena cannot be observed objectively in animals, [so] it is idle either to claim or to deny their existence. . . . Hunger, like anger, fear, and so forth, is a phenomenon that can be known only by introspection. When applied to another subject, especially one belonging to another species, it is merely a guess about the possible nature of the animal's subjective state. By presenting such a guess as a causal explanation, the psychologist trespasses on the domain of the physiologist. (1989: 4, 5)

Alongside the idea that mind cannot be objectively observed comes the mandate to be on guard against mental terms such as *hunger, anger, fear,* and so on, infiltrating accounts of animal behavior.

It is not surprising, then, that ethologists use various means to monitor carefully the (hardly avoidable) appearance of mental notions. Constant vigilance is required, for the eradication of mentality from the language of behavior is an endless task. To give an example of the deliberate supervision of language, Tinbergen writes that "the peculiar behaviour of the stickleback results in frightening other males away . . . Or, *to put it more objectively,* the biological significance of its behavior is that it drives off other males" (1989: 2, emphasis added). The stickleback's behavior is first conveyed with the word *frightening;* immediately this wording is revoked as nonobjective, and the statement is recast. This is one of the monitoring devices used by ethologists—a kind of on-the-spot translation of "subjective" language into "objective" language. It exemplifies the tension in ethological writing between "language speaking," on one hand, and the attempt to guard against the ostensibly unverifiable or unwarranted denotations of "mental language speaking," on the other.[8]

The tension is between the autonomy of language and the struggle to contain its errant wanderings into the territory of the mental. The spontaneous allusion to mental phenomena arises on account of the coherence of the link between behavioral and contextual evidence and the perception and ascription of mental modalities. This link is an evidential resource relied upon and cultivated in the writings of Darwin and the naturalists previously discussed. The skeptical move, however, is precisely to sever the connection between behavioral evidence and mental life. Returning to Tinbergen's example, the link between certain territorial-type behaviors and associated events—such as fighting, posturing, attacking, retreating, or swimming away—can be worded as "frightening other males away." "Language speaks" in the intelligibility and force of this expression to convey not only what happened, but the atmosphere and the image of what happened as well. But because Tinbergen accedes to the skeptical premise that mind is accessible only to introspection, the term *frightening* becomes problematic—an unwarranted slip of language that needs to be set right.

Tinbergen's next move, therefore, is an attempt to regain control over an unruly language that speaks as though of its own accord. Purging the language of the obstinate mental expression ("frightening away") involves three aspects of its translation into "objective" language ("to put it more objectively, the biological significance of its behavior is that it drives off other males"). First, the problematic subjective description is recast into a more physical description, with the notion of "driving off" replacing "frightening away." But the idea of "driving off"—even though apparently more neutral than that of "frightening away," which also delivers an emotional constituent of the action—continues to express an intentional action. The second move, then, is to attenuate the potential reading of "driving off" as an intentional action by having the stickleback's behavior, rather than the stickleback itself, as the subject of the action. The final aspect of Tinbergen's translation of the male stickleback's action into "objective" language is to invoke the biological significance of the behavior, relaying that the function of the behavior is captured from a theoretical perspective, as opposed to its function being identified with the purpose it expresses from the animal's point of view.

Hence one way of regulating mental language is to use its vocabulary and then immediately revoke, translate, or problematize it in some way. The following examples from Lorenz illustrate this point:

> Young birds of most species, if reared in isolation, *do not recognize* other birds of their species when brought together. *In other words*, another individual of the same species *does not release* the behavior that normally responds to it. (Lorenz 1957a: 102, emphasis added)

> If I am walking along with a tame greylag goose which suddenly stretches, extends its neck and softly utters a harsh warning-call, I may say "now it is *alarmed*." However, this subjective abbreviation *only means* that the goose has perceived a *flight-eliciting stimulus*. (Lorenz 1971: 323, emphasis added)

This writing exemplifies both the artifice of immediately translating recalcitrant mental terms into "objective language" and the way a technical language can facilitate such a translation by directly substituting for— and so averring to do the conceptual work of—a mental vocabulary. The same type of device, namely, use-cum-negation, is also seen in the ubiquitous application of scare-quotes as a technique for problematizing certain connotations of a term, for expressing skepticism, and, in general, for withdrawing ontological conviction from the mental vocabulary used. In short, mental language is simultaneously used and discarded, needed and denied.

A nondeliberate opportunism is involved in these moves, since the ideas and imagery of mental words—which are, when apposite, among the most powerful of words—inform the reader's understanding of the behavioral scenery, regardless of whether these are qualified with on-the-spot translations or enveloped in quotation marks. Once stated, mental concepts have a perceptual and interpretive effect that can never be completely undone by accompanying caveats.

Yet the ambivalence of letting language speak and then negating what it expresses signifies something deeper than mere unwitting opportunism. The tension between a technical idiom and the language of action it displaces relates to the view of science that ethologists embraced. On this view there is, and even ought to be, a disjunction between the practical theorist of everyday actions and the scientific theorist. The former "seeks an interpretation of . . . [daily] affairs while holding a line of 'official neutrality' toward the interpretive rule that one may doubt that the objects of the world are as they appear. . . . By contrast, the activities of scientific theorizing are governed by the strange ideal of doubt toward the belief that the objects are as they appear" (Garfinkel 1967: 272–73). The "strange ideal of doubt" is a pervasive element of ethological behavioral science. So, for example, while Tinbergen writes of pursuing "the investigation of the external stimuli releasing the pecking response of a herring gull chick," the figure referred to in this connection has the legend "herring gull chick begging for food" (1989: 5). The expression "begging for food" presents the chick's behavior in a very different light from the "release of its pecking response." While the first formulation expresses a performative action, embedding the desire for food and the intention of getting it, the latter formulation is clearly removed from any possible perspective of experience, and thus tacitly expresses doubt about whether such an experience exists at all.

In Garfinkel's terms, the statement "herring gull chick begging for food" can be seen to stand for the object-of-the-world-as-it-appears, while the statement "the external stimuli releasing the pecking response"— which nonequivalently references the same behavior—is launched on the basis of a suspension of the belief that objects actually are as they appear. By representing "how things appear in the world," the legend "herring gull chick begging for food" has a paradoxical status: on one hand, it conveys the first-level intelligibility of what can be seen in the picture, while on the other hand, it stands as a reminder of precisely the kind of expression whose adequacy or veridicality in representing "things as they really are" is brought into doubt. "Herring gull chick begging for food," then, has a double rhetorical role. It conveys what is the case at a glance by calling upon the reliable forces of practical reasoning and practical seeing to grasp the meaning of the action. Simultaneously, the expression brings into contrasting relief the technical account of "the external stimuli releasing the pecking response," implying that this latter conception is scientific—expressing what really is the case, in contrast to how things merely appear. Thus one aspect of the tension between a technical idiom and the ordinary language of action is corollary to a particular conception of science; the creation of this tension is actively pursued, for it serves to strengthen the claim that technical depictions reveal how things really are as opposed to how they only appear to be.

Another expression of the tension between the two representational mediums seems less deliberate. It relates to the appearance of certain depictions that are not encompassed by the ethological technical-theoretical framework; they appear residual, either not translated or not translatable into that framework. An example of this can be seen in Lorenz's narration of the story of two storks, of different species, who were a couple in the Vienna Zoo. The two species of stork, Lorenz explains, have slightly different greeting ceremonies when entering the nest, as white storks clapper while black storks hiss; according to Lorenz, these greeting displays are innate and fixed patterns that function as "social releasers." Despite their possession of distinct fixed action patterns, the storks remained paired over the years. Their greeting ceremonies were nevertheless always misfitted. "As a result," notes Lorenz, "the two storks, who had been married for years, always *eyed each other suspiciously and anxiously* throughout the greeting ceremony. The white female in particular often seemed about to attack her mate when he absolutely refused to clapper" (1957a: 112, emphasis added). The storks' "eyeing each other suspiciously and anxiously" exemplifies the sort of observation that is adventitious with respect to ethological concepts and theoretical explanations. It suggests that the greeting interaction is experienced as a strained exchange, but that it is somehow negotiated and muddled through by the two birds. These ideas are not easily made consonant with the model of display exchange in terms of the matrix of social releaser–IRM–subsequent response.

The storks' "eyeing each other suspiciously and anxiously" is reminiscent of what in the previous chapter was described as the *Verstehen* approach of naturalists. It pinpoints and brings into view a moment of experience in the life of the birds. Even as it is incommensurate with ethological theory, the beauty of Lorenz's description is that it bundles the feeling of the storks' vexed communion within a single image. This example, like similar ones strewn amid technical depictions of animals, shows one important way in which the division between description in a technical idiom and description in ordinary language is not absolute.

CONCLUSION

For a subject, the typological range of action, exemplified by the human case, runs from avowedly voluntary (chosen and pursued after deliberation) to starkly involuntary (in the sense of either obliged or coerced by the force of circumstance). At the same time, actual instances of conduct fall overwhelmingly between these antithetical types. The categories of "voluntary" and "involuntary" are much more like poles on a continuum than like mutually exclusive and exhaustive types. Thus most courses of action do not require a prelude of careful assessment or scrutiny; at the same time, not even the most familiar, routine, or habitual actions preclude elements of reflective deliberation. By contrast, the effect of technical-causal representations of animals may be characterized as the constitution of animal behavior as "involuntary" in a profoundly different sense from the involuntary behavior of a subject, for animals are not represented as either obliged or coerced. Instead, a technical language of behavior leads to the presentation of animals as natural objects, driven by forces outside the ken of their experiential and authorial possibilities, steered and propelled by interior states and exterior stimuli beyond their control and comprehension. A technical idiom, in combination with a proclivity to provide a causal explanation of behavior (especially in terms of proximate physiological mechanisms), leads to a mechanomorphic view of animals. Through technical-causal accounts, animal behavioral patterns lose the typological breadth and qualitative admixture of elements of subjects' actions, emerging far more monolithically and akin to impersonal events.

The mechanomorphic imagery of classical ethological depictions does not derive from a commitment to a mechanistic view of animal behavior, nor does it entail the explicit denial of animal mind. Rather, mechanomorphism may be understood as a particular conception of involuntary action. "Voluntary action," according to White, "is to do x with the awareness that one has an alternative course open to one" (1968: 6). "Involuntary action" is to be made to do something by either force or obligation. This antithesis, of course, does not exhaust the gamut of action. As White states, "If what I do is unintentional, unknowing, or in certain ways nonattentive, then, though it is still an act of mine, it is neither voluntary nor obliged, since it is not done in the knowledge either that there is or that there is not a choice" (ibid.). Hence the language of (human) action allows three possibilities—voluntary, obliged, or neither; regardless of which alternative is operative, the human actor is always the author of action, in the sense of being the cause of what is brought about through his or her action. The mechanomorphic conception of animal behavior, on the other hand, corresponds to none of these options; even preceding the positing of these alternatives, it annihilates the view of the animal as actor. Thus it is not that animals' activities are involuntary in the sense that the animal is obliged to do what it does, but rather that they are non-voluntary, as causes act on or through the animal, bringing about what the animal does as something that happens to it. This is what it means to be portrayed as a quasi automaton.

Despite the discrepant effects of the two mediums on the portraiture of animals, the distinction between a technical idiom and the ordinary language of action and life does not describe insular domains. A technical description must be built upon the scaffold of the first-order intelligibility of ordinary natural language, for the purposes of securing and maintaining a fundamental level of understanding. A technical idiom is created through operations upon ordinary terms (for example, "highly specialized escape-and-defense reaction"); or it respecifies an ordinary description (for example, the explanatory matrix of releasers–fostering reactions transfigures the initial observation that "the mallard duck comes to the rescue of the musk duckling crying for help"); or it translates problematic, subjective terminology (for example, to say a goose is "alarmed only means that it has perceived a flight-eliciting stimulus"). In the next chapter, I argue that sociobiology capitalizes upon the permeability between technical and ordinary languages by applying an idiom that extends simultaneously into both domains.

4   Genes and Their Animals
The Language of Sociobiology

IN THE analysis of the behavioral writings of Darwin, Fabre, and the Peckhams, I argued that the affirmation of a subjective perspective in the animal world precedes the possibility of a compelling acknowledgment of mental phenomena, namely, phenomena of intention, memory, understanding, thinking, and emotion. Knowing animals as subjects, that is, with an experiential perspective and with authoring force, assembles a world within which inner life has a part to play and is scenically present. A subjective viewpoint becomes accessible in the presentation of observations in the language of the lifeworld—the shared language of objects and events, actions and relations, community and individuality. In turn, the understanding that animals experience events and actively perform their actions allows mentality to surface as what Schutz calls "wide-awakeness" and Griffin "conscious awareness." Once this sense of mindfulness is diffusely present in the portrayal of behaviors and events, specific mental predicates can subsequently be cogently ascribed or insinuated. It goes without saying that the relevance and authenticity of recounted observations must be beyond reproach for the language of the lifeworld to unveil the landscape of animal life as the naturalist has witnessed it.

In the investigation of classical ethological writings, I examined the ramifications of a technical idiom in the portrayal of animals. Technical languages are historically subject to change, and they vary with disciplinary commitments. They are characterized by a vocabulary of specially defined terms (for example, *stimulus-response* or *innate releasing mechanism*); an idiomatic vocabulary of concepts taken from ordinary language and implicitly advanced as technical via semantic affinity with formally technical terms (for example, verbs such as *trigger, activate,* and *release*); and finally, a theory, or set of theories, explaining the production of behavioral patterns and providing a broad context of meaning for technical terms. Classical ethology represents animals on the model of natural objects of the physical sciences by describing their behaviors in technical terms that are extrinsic to fields of action—that is, it is not conceivable that the meaning of the terms could be within the province of animals' experiential world. Indeed, only the specialist is privy to their sense, after being initiated into and mastering the specific theoretical frameworks that give technical terms their sense.

The implicit message of ethological depictions, and perhaps of technical renditions of animal life in general, is that the generation and meaning of behaviors is fully accounted for by the proposed theories; the proponents of such theories do not aspire to leave residual or unexplained areas. An immanent, subjective view is thus suspended, for it has no part to play in the production of animal behavior. The consequence of an interpretive framework that is extrinsic to their phenomenal world is that animals appear oblivious to the actual meaning of what they do, and the authorship of their actions is translocated to the referents of technical constructs. The supervenient effect of a language that constitutes animals as natural objects is a picture of mindlessness, a landscape where agency and experience are banished by the all-consuming logic of a technical idiom. Animals are inevitably disempowered, for technical idioms make them out to be "epistemic dopes"—that is, without knowledge, awareness, or control of the contexts or relevancies of their behaviors.[1] In short, the conceptual ecologies created through technical idioms are hostile to inner life, for such idioms tend to banish mentality either by force or by obviation. Inner life is banished by force when the logic of the technical idiom is incompatible with the language of subjectivity, and it is banished by obviation when the technical idiom renders subjective experience redundant, that is, without a significant part in the production or character of action.

In the same spirit as the previous three chapters, I turn to examine the sociobiological view of animal life via the linguistic and argumentative means that underlie the sociobiological portraiture of animals, with special attention to the understanding of animal experience and mind that sociobiology advances. In sociobiology two representational mediums figure centrally: the use of an economic idiom and the deployment of social-category concepts. Sociobiology diverges from its twentieth-century behavioral-science predecessors in that it does not construct a technical language, but instead appropriates, and respecifies on a genetic level, the already extant and connotatively potent economic and social-category idioms. Much of the analysis focuses on what I regard as the unique peculiarity of the language use of sociobiology, namely, its mobility across domains of meaning. In the case of economic language, while a clear boundary between technical definitions of terms and their ordinary meanings is enunciated, that boundary is at the same time constantly trespassed. In the case of social-category terms, sociobiology builds a bridge between evolutionary and commonsense reasoning, both utilizing and explaining commonsense knowledge. In this chapter, I argue that sociobiology creates a total picture of animal life: a worldview erected on the cornerstone ideas of success, competition, and selfishness. My aim is not to submit a direct evaluation as to whether, or to what extent, this worldview is a faithful representation of animal existence. Rather, I am more interested in showing how the sociobiological vision is created and given internal coherence, and what its ramifications are in the portrayal of animals.

The effect of implementing idioms that are already in use and extremely familiar to the reader is that sociobiological reasoning embeds multiple layers of meanings. This multiplicity of meaning has been a major source of trouble for sociobiology, for it is readily interpreted as a form of "rhetoric," in the underhanded sense of the term. The approach taken here, however, is not critical, for I do not regard sociobiology as violating proper language use. Quite to the contrary, the extension of concepts across semantic boundaries, the ability to operate within different meaning domains, is sociobiology's characteristic form of language craft, the mark of its analytical ingenuity, and the shifting but far from unstable foundation of its argumentative force. My interest is to elucidate the conceptual structures of sociobiology in order to understand what is distinctive and powerful about its reasoning, and how that reasoning maps the landscape of animal life. Before turning to a close linguistic analysis of economic and social-category language use, in what follows I provide a brief introductory discussion of certain central themes in sociobiology.

In his landmark work *Sociobiology: The New Synthesis,* E. O. Wilson defines sociobiology as "the systematic study of the biological basis of all social behavior" (1975: 4). He declared sociobiology a new disciplinary formation, synthesizing ethological, ecological, and population-genetics approaches in a systematic study of social behavior and structure in the animal world.[2] An intellectual descendant of ethology, sociobiology has retained the conception of behavior as biological trait. As E. O. Wilson puts it, "Konrad Lorenz and his fellow ethologists . . . convinced us that behavior and social structure, like all other biological phenomena, can be studied as 'organs,' extensions of the genes that exist because of their superior adaptive value" (1975: 22). The interest of both classical ethology and sociobiology is to arrive at a theoretical comprehension of the causation of behavior. However, the classical ethological postulation of physiological mechanisms—of innate releasing mechanisms, fixed action patterns, and inner specific energies—has given way in contemporary behavioral science to a preoccupation with the genetic stratum of behaviors. Whereas ethological terminology was more focused on what biologists refer to as "proximate causation," stipulating underlying physiological mechanisms of behaviors, sociobiological accounts are concerned with "ultimate causation," conceptualized in terms of the inheritance of a genetic makeup that reflects advantages accrued in the past by certain behavioral patterns. In the words of sociobiologist David Barash, "sociobiology is typically concerned with the adaptive significance of the genetically-influenced behavior (the *why*) rather than the proximal question of *how* that behavior is produced" (1979: 33; see also Barlow 1989; Gould 1982).

While both ethology and sociobiology treat behavioral patterns as indices of antecedent conditions, there is a shift from the former's language of mechanisms to the latter's calculus of genes. Yet an intimate relation between the two fields persists, particularly as ethology's focus on innate behavior provided a pathway for the respecification of "innate" as "genetic" in contemporary behavioral science. In this way behavioral science has aligned itself with the prominent position given, in general, to the gene in contemporary biology.[3] Like anatomy or physiology, behavior and social structure are conceptualized in terms of their contribution to fitness. Through the manifest forms of behavioral expression and social configuration, natural selection is understood to operate, and have operated, on an underlying genetic base.

For sociobiologists, regularly occurring and especially clearly advantageous behavioral patterns are indicative of genetic action; hence their paramount preoccupation with the adaptive function of behaviors and inferred genetic basis. Sociobiology enthusiastically embraces the neo-Darwinian view of evolution, according to which the chief mechanism of evolutionary change is that of natural selection acting on the genetic basis of an organism's phenotype—the phenotype consisting of the set of traits that are manifest. Behaviors are considered phenotypes, which, insofar as they vary and have a genetic component, are subject to natural selection.

Genes underlying behaviors contributing to survival, and especially to reproduction, proliferate, while genes underpinning maladaptive behaviors tend to be selected against, thereby disappearing from the gene pool. Behavioral patterns that give animals an advantage in reproduction and survival are more likely to be preserved, and eventually diffused throughout the population, as a consequence of the selection and subsequent spreading of their heritable base. In accordance with neo-Darwinian reasoning, sociobiology sees natural selection as inevitably favoring individuals adapted to maximize the spread of their genes. This genetic calculus makes selfishness the ground rule, for individuals who put their own survival and reproductive interests *first* tend to leave their genes behind. Conversely, sociobiologists argue, genes of altruistic individuals, individuals who would be inclined to sacrifice their lives or reproductive interests for the benefit of others, will be extinguished from the gene pool.

Sociobiologists reason that extant, widely shared behaviors must have been advantageous to animals in the past. "The central principle of sociobiology," therefore, is that "insofar as a behavior reflects at least some component of gene action, individuals will tend to behave as to maximize their fitness" (Barash 1979: 29). In examining adaptive behaviors of a species, the operative assumption of sociobiologists is that these proliferated on account of having been selected for in the course of evolution. The genetic emphasis of this assumption is reflected in the maxim that animals are expected to behave in ways that maximize their "inclusive fitness"— an evolutionary concept that was pivotal for the emergence of sociobiology (Hamilton 1964; Wilson 1975: 415). Inclusive fitness signifies that what is considered crucial is not simply the fitness of the individual organism, but rather that of its genes, which are largely shared among relatives.

With the idea of inclusive fitness sociobiology has expanded the conceptual territory of the idea of selfishness. Selfishness is manifest not only in putting the reproductive and survival interests of the individual before those of others, but also in behaviors that promote the interests of the individual and/or the individual's relatives before all others. For sociobiology, a quintessential expression of this axiom—the logic of the "selfish gene"—is patterns and strategies of parental care. In the words of sociobiologists T. H. Clutton-Brock and Paul Harvey, "Natural selection produces individuals which are adapted to maximize the spread of their own genes—sometimes through relatives but more commonly through their own offspring" (1978: 37). So, for example, in species where parents provide nutrition, protection, and care for their offspring, they maximize their own fitness, for the offspring are carriers of their parents' genes, including the genes for successful behavioral patterns of parental care.

Behaviors are consequently scrutinized for the advantages they provide animals and their kin. It is generally assumed that dispositions to act, aggregate, and compete in certain ways have been selected for and refined in the course of evolution, such that chances of survival and opportunities for successful reproduction have increased. The game of maximizing inclusive fitness runs itself, for its logic is inexorable: the genes that maximize reproduction proliferate and take over because they get reproduced. This state of affairs is portrayed as unconditionally competitive, impersonal, and amoral. Barash, for example, writes that "even reproducing is merely a special case of the more general evolutionary requirement of selfishness. Parental love itself is actually but an evolutionary strategy whereby genes replicate themselves" (1979: 25). And the primatologist and sociobiologist Sarah Blaffer Hrdy offers the following etiological account of the occurrence of infanticide among certain primates:

> By eliminating a baby unlikely to be his own, the male reduces the number of offspring sired by his competitor; by inseminating the mother himself, he increases the rank of his own progeny. But the male, seemingly in control, is in fact no less a prisoner in this system than females are. A male born or immigrating into an infanticidal population who failed to eliminate the offspring of his competitors would be at a reproductive disadvantage. Both sexes, then, are trapped by the exigencies of natural selection, and have been since their origin. (1981: 82)

As these passages so starkly illustrate, in the animal world of sociobiology the main players are the genes and the form of life is selfishness. Natural selection favors the genes that operate to increase their own numbers—whether it takes parental love or infanticide to do so.

THE ECONOMIC IDIOM: SUCCESS AND COMPETITION OF MALE AND FEMALE RED DEER

In this section I focus on T. H. Clutton-Brock, F. E. Guinness, and S. D. Albon's *Red Deer: Behavior and Ecology of Two Sexes* (1982). The analysis of this particular work allows the elucidation of the sociobiological use of economic language. The sociobiological concern with adaptation— that is, the fit between animals and the environmental forces they encounter—is the starting point of Clutton-Brock and colleagues' study of the behavior and ecology of male and female red deer. What are the animals adapted to do? ask the authors. "The short answer is to reproduce" (1982: 2). Reproductive success is the key to the exquisite adaptation of animals to their surroundings, and it is thereby made the unifying theme of all analyses, including the measure according to which the differences between the sexes are assessed: physical differences of size and body structure, as well as behavioral differences in patterns of feeding, mating strategies, relating to offspring, affiliating within and across the sexes, and the like. According to the authors, the origins of most anatomical, physiological, behavioral, and ecological differences between hinds and stags are to be found in the divergent factors affecting their reproductive success (1982: 287). In the background of reproduction, both driving force and consequence, are the genes. "The genetic material of an individual that fails to reproduce is lost . . . [while] genes that increase the reproductive success of their carriers will spread through successive generations until they occur in all members of the species" (1982: 2). Widespread behavioral strategies of female and male deer, and the differences between these strategies, are taken to reflect this inexorable process of the spreading of genes that have contributed to reproductive success. "Ultimately," they write, "it is the genes that endure, that spread or become extinct" (1982: 3).

Various factors influence the reproductive success of stags and hinds, but all are mediated by one constant parameter—competition. Competition is considered the all-important factor in the success of male and female deer. However, the types of competition that they engage in differ, because their reproductive success is limited by different factors. The limiting factor for males is access to females, while the limiting factor for females is access to nutritional resources. I briefly sketch the reasoning behind this difference between males and females, for it is central both to the particular study of red deer and to sociobiological thought in general.

Male deer can potentially father a great number of offspring at virtually no cost. For stags (and male mammals in general) the energetic cost of fertilization is minimal, involving only the expenditure of sperm. The fact that the cost of the reproductive act is low and that males are able to father many offspring means that stag reproductive success correlates with maximizing the number of offspring, rather than with investing in the care and successful upbringing of each. Stag reproductive success, then, entails

Figure 10 Male and female red deer

maximizing access to hinds, which in turn accounts for the evolution of
the deer social structure of the "harem." During the rut, the harem provides the male with access to a number of females. According to Clutton-
Brock and colleagues, acquiring and safeguarding a harem involve stags
in direct, intense competition. Selective pressure for males to win access
to females—given the practically win-all or lose-all social structure of the
harem—accounts for a variety of characteristics such as the evolution of
antlers, the greater body size of males, the speedier growth of male calves,

and the nature of male fighting contests. What ties these physiological and behavioral aspects together is the unmitigated requirement of successful reproduction, which, given resource limitations, always involves competition. On this logic, natural selection will, and has, favored the genes of the winners of direct competitive contests for access to females; the bottom line for the reproductive success of male deer is *efficiency in fighting*.

Factors influencing the reproductive success of females differ, for female deer (and female mammals more generally) have vastly more stringent physiological limits in the number of offspring they can produce in a lifetime. In contrast to the male case, the cost of the reproductive act for the female is maximal, for she becomes pregnant, carries the offspring in her body, and cares for it after it is born; the energetic output involved in gestation, birthing, and lactation is extremely high. The fact that the cost of the reproductive act is high and that females are limited in the number of offspring they can bear in a lifetime means that hinds should invest heavily in each of their offspring. Selective pressures, then, favor the increase of female fecundity and the decrease of calf mortality, both of which depend on the body weight and condition of the hind, which in turn depend on quantitative and qualitative access to nutritional resources. Female reproductive success, therefore, hinges on procuring the nourishment that will allow her to best provision and guard her offspring both in utero and after birth. According to the authors, the requirement of access to resources puts females in competition with one another. The competition between hinds, however, is "indirect" or "scramble" competition for the resources that give them the physical stamina to raise their young successfully. Natural selection will, and has, favored hinds that compete successfully in securing or monopolizing nutritional resources; the bottom line for the reproductive success of female deer is *efficiency in feeding*.

This sociobiological overview of the different reproductive strategies of males and females is at the heart of the analyses of deer behaviors, interaction, ecology, and physiology. Its significance for sociobiology is that it describes a pattern that is common in vertebrates and widespread in mammals. Two points about it may be highlighted. First, what is of utmost importance in animal life is reproduction and the competitive endeavors that it involves. Reproductive success, which involves winning in the struggle of survival and proliferation, is the core theme that structures the understanding of most, if not all, of the factors in the lives of animals. For sociobiology, the game of winners and losers is played against the impersonal and amoral backdrop of a genetic infrastructure having survived and proliferated or, conversely, stagnated and disappeared. To win is to parent offspring successfully. Winners are immortalized in projecting the blueprint of their makeup into the future. To lose is to fail to reproduce (adequately). Losers have a mortal configuration of genes—it dies with them. The animals that win in direct or indirect competition succeed in leaving behind (more) copies of their genes. These genes perpetuate not only the physical constitution of the winners, but the very behaviors and strategies of competition insofar as these have a genetic basis; and sociobiologists tend to assume they do have a genetic basis, especially when such behaviors and strategies are widespread and obviously adaptive. According to sociobiological reasoning, this is what counts in the behavioral repertoires of stags and hinds—and not without reason: without a relentless, competitive drive to reproduce at the heart of their existence, there would exist no deer to observe. For sociobiology, this view is more than truth; it captures necessity. Sociobiology conjures a hard image of animal life—the nonnegotiable requirement to compete well so as to survive and above all to reproduce—as the rock-bottom fact upon which to erect its total vision of animal life.

The second point of interest regarding the sociobiological analysis of stag and hind behavioral strategies is that the theme of reproductive success mediated by competition allows the elaboration of a nexus of interconnected economic terms. The twin ideas of success and competition create a conceptual environment wherein economic terminology can flourish. Terms such as *monopoly, advertising, budgets, efficiency, investment, value, costs, benefits, maximizing, minimizing, winning, losing,* and the like are pervasive. The justification of an economic language of costs, benefits, and investment is rooted in the evolutionary exigency to reproduce in a competitive environment of limited resources—resources being females for stags and food for hinds. The core theme of the proliferation of genetic material, requiring success in competitive endeavors, thus allows for the natural elaboration of an economic idiom that simultaneously becomes the dominant representational means of animal action and life and develops into a conceptual medium that strengthens a success-oriented, competitive neo-Darwinian vision of evolution. In examining the effects of an economic language in greater detail, I address two questions. With what intent is it used by sociobiologists, and what consequences does it have on the portrayal of animals?

Sociobiologists do not use economic language figuratively, but for realist representation, that is, as a literal, impartial, and objective medium. The realist import of economic terminology is secured via its immanent transformation into a technical idiom. Sociobiological economic terms are accorded technical status (1) by consistently underscoring that the meaning of economic terms is not applicable at the level of animal experience or awareness and (2) by explicitly providing specialized and/or operational definitions, which guarantee that the economic terms have stable meanings and can be assigned numerical values replicable by any trained observer. These features confer technical status and thereby scientific authority on economic terms. Once such a status is bestowed on the economic idiom, it can then be accredited as a medium of realist description and explanation of the facts of animal life.

Sociobiologists frequently caution that ideas such as "success" and "failure," "benefits" and "costs," or "investment" and "value" are inoperative at the level of deliberate animal orientation. To give an example of this type of caveat, David Barash writes that "although a clear-cut goal is achieved—maximum fitness—neither the genes nor their carriers need have any picture of what they are doing or why" (1979: 22). At the same time, since economic terms semantically include a calculating attitude, they can be used in lieu of a language of intentionality. The implementation of an economic language is thus consilient with the twentieth-century behavioral science injunction to refrain from reference to mentality in the depiction of what animals do. The following passage, which sketches the idea that females expend more energy per individual offspring than males, illustrates how an economic term that refers to a genetic calculus can displace an intentional concept:

> The general principle is . . . stated by saying that a female allocates a greater proportion of her total reproductive effort to each offspring than does the male. . . . However, since *"effort"* is a word that sits uneasily on the tongues of biologists, it has been replaced by the term *"parental investment,"* defined as a process or action by a parent that increases the reproductive value of its offspring but reduces its own ability to invest further in the future. (1982: 4, emphasis added)

The objectivity of the term *parental investment* is certified by its ability to replace the objectionable term *effort*. The authors imply that *effort,* which "sits uneasily on the tongues of biologists," has anthropomorphic connotations, presumably as it may be taken to suggest intentional exertion. The notion of parental investment is counterproposed as the valued, scientific alternative. Its technical status is exhibited by both its contrast to the ordinary concept of effort and its prompt assignment of a special definition.

Bestowing technical status on *parental investment* and cognate terms implies that the discourse is elevated to an overall greater level of accuracy and clarity. The authors are thus effectively claiming that, in contrast to *effort*, the term *investment* has been purged of connotative effects when applied to parental behaviors. This promotional introduction of *investment*, in opposition to the word *effort*, facilitates the elision of the effects that economic terms themselves have on the portrayal of animal life. The evaluative asymmetry of the concepts "effort" and "investment" insinuates, authoritatively and almost in passing, that while the former is suspiciously connotative, the latter is straightforwardly neutral. In short, one way the validity claim of the impartiality and objectivity of economic terms is advanced is by replacing, or rendering pleonastic, descriptions in terms of animals' intentions. With an economic idiom as its chief representational means, sociobiology can abide by the institutionalized injunction against anthropomorphism—in the sense of avoiding the ascription of mental concepts to animals.[4]

The presentation of the economic idiom as impartial and objective could be assessed as a sociobiological argumentative strategy. However, sociobiologists do not cloak figurative language as realist representation, but rather transform the economic idiom of success and failure, investment, cost-benefit trade-offs, and the like into a nexus of technical terms that are firmly connected to the neo-Darwinian evolutionary perspective, on one hand, and can be given endogenous definitions, on the other. The realist import of economic language is thus achieved immanently, by giving that language strong roots in the theory and statistical methods of contemporary behavioral science. To clarify with an example from the study of red deer, the central idea of "lifetime reproductive success" is operationalized through a straightforward measure: it is the total number of calves surviving to the age of one year produced by an individual in its lifetime (Clutton-Brock, Guinness, and Albon 1982: 46–47). This number is unproblematically ascertainable for the offspring of hinds, and can be reasonably estimated for those of stags, in the kind of long-term study carried out by Clutton-Brock and colleagues, where, ideally from birth to death, the reproductive activities of individual animals (tagged for recognition purposes) are monitored and surveyed via a systematic methodology. Once the "lifetime reproductive success" of specific animals in a given population is measured, then the variables accounting for differences between them can be determined. In the case of hinds, for example, differences in reproductive success correlate with differential fecundity and with calf birthdate and birth weight; these factors are connected to maternal body weight and condition, which, in turn, are affected by her home range or the quality of available resources (1982: 98–99). In the case of stags, a major contributing factor is harem size, with lifetime reproductive success shown to be "closely related to the number of hinds he was able to collect and defend during his peak years of breeding activity" (1982: 149). Reproductive success, then, has to do with the perpetuation of genetic material, and it is calibrated via operational definition and standardized methods of measurement; it is a measure that enables the articulation of comprehensive claims. "Reproductive success" is not intended to express animals' experiential viewpoint. At the same time, the character and intensity of the animals' lived actions, especially during the rut, are conveyed as reflecting high evolutionary stakes.

In short, the literal, impartial, and objective import of economic terms is secured by their transformation into a technical language. The economic idiom as a whole resonates with a vision of evolution in which reproductive success, with competition inescapably at its core, are practically all that matter. Moreover, ideas such as reproductive success, parental investment, and energetic costs are declared irrelevant vis-à-vis the perspective of animals. And finally, the meaning of specific economic terms is provided explicitly through specialized definitions that allow the application of statistical operations, and subsequently the formulation of general statements and predictions.

The bona fide avowal, however, that economic language references what transpires on the evolutionary level of the selection and operation of genes cannot entirely offset the effects of its concepts on the portraiture of animal life. Language use can be qualified, and qualifications do make a difference, but the autonomous and diffuse effects of language are not entirely contained through addended caveats. Securing technical definitions for economic terms such as *parental investment* and *reproductive success* and imbuing them with meaning immanent to the content and methods of contemporary behavioral knowledge cannot arrest the expansion of this terminology into semantic areas outside their official demarcations. Official definitions are genuine attempts at delimiting open-ended concepts, but success can be only partial: since economic language is already opera- tive in the vernacular, sociobiology cannot deploy that language without partaking of the extant knowledge of its meanings. As a consequence, once implemented, economic terminology operates as a mixed idiom that is mobile across the semantic domains of technical definition, on one hand, and the ordinary language of action, on the other. The use of eco- nomic terminology thus intertwines different layers of meaning. This se- mantic mobility confers on sociobiology a great deal of argumentative force, for the simultaneous engagement of technical and ordinary senses of economic terms makes its reasoning both authoritative and evocative. While this effect is rhetorically achieved—in the sense that it involves marshaling compelling dimensions of language use—it certainly does not implicate sociobiological deviousness.[5] Language use itself permits the multilayered constitution of meaning; the argumentative artfulness of so- ciobiology is simply to avail itself of the open-endedness of language, so as to create an arresting view of animals. Indeed, the application of an economic language that engages both technical and ordinary dimensions of meaning contributes significantly to the nondeliberate elaboration of a sociobiological worldview. The intrinsic expansiveness of this language, coupled with its peculiar connotative effects, makes it an idiom that im- parts an engulfing picture of animal existence.

The consequence of the semantic mobility between technical and ordi- nary dimensions is that sociobiological accounts are redolent with mean- ing. Economic language has a secure technical status backed by the authoritative weight of science, for through the provision of technical definitions terms have consistent and delimited meaning and/or replicable numerical values. At the same time, through excursions into the ordinary- language counterparts of economic terms, and by the perennial invocation of their diffuse connotations, an imagery and atmosphere that envelops animal life is created. The structuring of the domain of animal experience and lived action via economic ideas has two recurring manifestations, which I consider in turn, illustrating them with specific examples.

The first manifestation of how technically defined economic terms sur- face in the phenomenal world of animals may be exemplified by a passage discussing the fighting of stags during the rut. The idea of a calculus of compromise between the energetic costs and reproductive benefits of fighting—a trade-off tuned by natural selection over evolutionary time—

becomes the medium that guides the observer's (and reader's) *perception* of the bodily comportment of the stags.

> On account of the *costs* of fighting, there were likely to be strong selection pressures favoring individuals that *minimized* the frequency with which they were involved in fights, so far as this was compatible with *maximizing* their *reproductive success*. [//] As would be expected, stags generally appeared *reluctant* to fight, especially when they were unlikely to *gain* by doing so. (Clutton-Brock, Guinness, and Albon 1982: 135, emphasis added)

I have inserted the marker [//] to indicate a shift of levels occurring in the transition from the first sentence to the second. First, frequency of fighting is roughly calibrated as a trade-off between selection pressures to minimize the costs of fighting (loss of harem, injury, or, very rarely, death) and to maximize reproductive success (defending one's harem, or, infrequently, appropriating another's). Next, this evolutionary conception, which is applicable at a genetic level, barely noticeably turns into a lens for seeing the comportment of stags: the economic ideas of "costs" and "benefits" become embodied in an image of reluctance and of reckoning gain. The first manifestation, then, of the mobility across technical and ordinary semantic domains involves a subtle or obvious slippage from technical conception into phenomenal embodiment: the evolutionary pressure to minimize costs is crystallized perceptually as "reluctance," while the evolutionary pressure to maximize success opens a pathway toward viewing the orientation of action along the vector of "gain." The passage that follows is another illustration of how economic language can surface into the landscape of animal experience through the embodiment of economic ideas.

> Nearest-neighbor distances were consistently less between hinds than between stags, and hinds often *tolerated* other individuals feeding within a few centimeters of their heads. (1982: 214, emphasis added)

This is a vivid example of the transmutation of an interpretive register into a mode of perceiving the behavioral scenery. Given the authors' analysis of "indirect" or "scramble" competition between female deer, which I summarized above, the observation of two hinds feeding with their heads close together, far from being seen as a sign of possible affiliation, is witnessed as their *tolerating* one another. The apparent suspension of competition is visualized as "tolerance." These examples of reluctant stags and tolerant hinds illustrate how economic terms become manifest within animal experience by *seeing* animal activities in ways that are cognate with economic ideas. These kinds of shifts into the level of embodiment are unavoidable, because there is no watershed between theorizing animal life and the way the (observer's and reader's) gaze assembles animal action.

What also happens in sociobiological texts is that a calculating attitude —affiliated with economic action—is sometimes passed on to the animals. This is the second manifestation of how the economic idiom moves from the domain of technical definition into the lived world of animals. Sociobiological depictions slide from the level of genes to that of inner life in the occasional direct imputation of a competitive and selfish ethos to the animals themselves. This introjective move is connected to the theme of animal mind. Sociobiologists largely avoid mental language, endeavoring to remain faithful to the behavioral science mandate against implicating mentality in animals and especially against giving an intentional orientation a causal role in the production of action. An intermittent yet recurrent exception to this rule, however, is a degree of willingness to attribute to animals either the intention to deceive and manipulate, or the shrewd ability to weigh advantages and disadvantages. This tendency is so visible in contemporary behavioral science more generally that a theoretical term has been coined for such a mental orientation, namely, "Machiavellian intelligence" (Byrne and Whiten 1988). The imputation of a Machiavellian mind-set is exemplified in the passages below, where a calculating shrewdness is conveyed in the forms of implication, prediction, and conjecture, respectively.

> Though the rut gave the impression of frantic activity, it was less disorganized than it appeared, and the frequency of most *displays* and *interactions* was closely related to variation in the *benefits* of performing them. (Clutton-Brock, Guinness, and Albon 1982: 123, emphasis added)

> Stags would be expected to *assess* their opponents carefully, fighting only in the cases where they were likely *to win*. (1982: 105, emphasis added)

> Stags roared infrequently when they were distant from their harems, perhaps *avoiding advertising* that their harems were unprotected. (1982: 126, emphasis added)

These passages illustrate the movement of language from the competitive field of genes to the cunning of animals in virtue of direct or insinuated ascriptions to the animals themselves. The invocation of a Machiavellian ethos can hardly be deterred, for it stems from the resonance between economic concepts and the calculating, gainful orientation of an investing or merchant mentality. The second manifestation, then, of crossing the boundary between technical usage and ordinary connotation involves this transposition of an ethos of cunning and selfishness into animal life (see Krebs and Dawkins 1984).

The sociobiological representation of animals oscillates between locating the authorship of action within the matrix of a cost-benefit calculus of genes and allowing that calculus to surface as embodied or even as a facet of animal awareness. In sociobiological thought animals become what, in reference to human beings, social theorists call "purposive-rational actors."[6] The sociobiological counterpart might be referred to as "behavioral purposive-rationality," with animals emerging as units that variously execute, embody, and/or connive the efficient calculation and pursuit of self-interest. While these shifts between execution, embodiment, and conniving sound sizable, their occurrence is often barely noticeable, for there is conceptual fluidity in the textual transmutations between genetic calculus, bodily comportment, and mental stance.

The official sociobiological level of behavioral purposive-rationality is neo-Darwinian: the genetic makeup of animals, their inheritance from reproductively successful ancestors, compels them to execute behavioral patterns that maximize fitness. The rationality of genes is pictured as the invisible hand that—via the programming of neurophysiological machinery—guides behaviors so as to optimize the chances of survival and maximize the reproductive output of their carriers. In this picture, nothing about an experiential or inner perspective need be implied, and sociobiologists can thereby stand by the claim of agnosticism with respect to the question of animal mind. However, the second level of behavioral purposive-rationality is manifest with the transposition of the genetic level into an embodied form that is visually available. For example, the technical term "minimizing costs" becomes apperceived in the ordinary idiom of the stags' "reluctance to fight," while the interpretive framework of "indirect competition" designs an image of hind "tolerance." The final level of behavioral purposive-rationality brings the pursuit of self-interest into animal life itself via the introjection of a Machiavellian mentality, as in the example of the wiliness implied in the assessment that stags are silent so as to "avoid advertising" that they are not close to their harems. With the transposition of economic language from genetic calculus into incarnate image or mental stance, behavioral purposive-rationality moves into the phenomenology of the animal's world. This move is hardly avoidable, for economic ideas cue the eyes to see how incarnate actions reflect their truth.

The economic idiom of sociobiology, and of neo-Darwinism more broadly, has been compelling, for it succeeds in combining the strengths of two domains of meaning in language. On an explicit level, sociobiology claims scientific authority in accrediting technical status to economic terms, while tacitly it rallies the connotational force of economic concepts that are familiar to the modern reader. In Clutton-Brock and colleagues' study of the red deer there is a deluge of expressions representative of sociobiological writing—*successful males, monopoly of females, costs of lactation, benefits of fighting, parental investment, intense competition, time budgets,* and the like. Even as such terms are assigned special sociobiological meaning, their significations unavoidably flow into their ordinary-language cognates and extensions. For the reader, then, understanding is the outcome of a process that involves the figurative parataxis of technical specification and the ordinary meaning of these economic concepts. This relation is found both intraconceptually and interconceptually: thus the term *investment,* as such, is simultaneously a technically defined concept and an ordinary-language one. In addition, *investment,* qua technical term, allows a cognate ordinary term such as *gain* to slip into the writing with impunity.

In short, economic terms are operative both on technical and ordinary levels of meaning. This is seen in how technical economic language expands into the phenomenology of animal life, surfacing in the bodies and attitudes of animals. Far from rendering meaning duplicitous, equivocal, or indeterminate, the sociobiological facility to operate with two dimensions of language use is a seminal source of its argumentative power. On the one hand, technical definitions, along with frequent reminders that the calculating intent of economic terms references only the genetic level, confer on economic language its authoritative weight. On the other hand, ordinary-language extensions and connotations of economic terms create an arresting picture of behavioral purposive-rationality in the animal world. Being an alloy of the technical and ordinary, the economic language of sociobiology simultaneously captures the intellect and hooks the imagination. It lays a grip on the reader's mind that is iron strong.

Indeed, not only is economic language semantically expansive, from technical definition to ordinary meaning, it is also syntactically expansive. I quote the passage below to illustrate the density of economic terms sometimes encountered in sociobiological writing. The ubiquity of the economic idiom is discernible in its virtual takeover of the syntax: it is a grammatical avalanche of active verbs, infinitives, and adverbs, as well as subjects and objects of sentences.

> Several evolutionary theories have predicted that parents should *invest* more in their offspring as their own potential for future reproduction *fails*. In its crudest form, the idea (which we refer to as the theory of *terminal investment*) suggests that a female that has reached the stage in her life where she is unlikely to raise further offspring *successfully* should *invest* her remaining *resources* in her existing progeny. In practice, the proportion of her *resources* a mother should transfer to her offspring in order to *maximize* her *lifetime reproductive success* will be affected by age changes in the *costs* and *benefits* of *energy investment,* and no precise prediction concerning the relationship between maternal age and parental *investment* is yet possible. However, under most conditions, the proportion of the *resources* a mother should *invest* is likely to increase toward the end of her life span, when the number of offspring she can expect to rear in the future is low, and some evidence from vertebrate studies supports the existence of a trend of this kind. (Clutton-Brock, Guinness, and Albon 1982: 93–94, emphasis added)

The authors are proposing the hypothesis that the relation between the hind and her calves should change in the course of her lifetime; she is expected to increase investment in her existing progeny as her reproductive potential becomes smaller. This prediction is based on a sociobiological model of a behavioral-reproductive strategy that would maximize her investment returns. While this calculus of maximizing fitness is technically operative at a genetic level, which is outside the phenomenal world of experience or awareness, what it references is the character of animal relations. This economic structuring of animal interaction has a profound impact on the reader's understanding of animal life. In the above passage, it conveys that what is most important about the connection between the hind and her offspring is deliverable in a language of investment. This message is then intensified via the syntactic expansion of economic language into virtually every grammatical niche. In short, economic terminology is so pervasively deployed that it simply takes over animal life. The open-endedness of economic language, its ability to expand both semantically and syntactically beyond the core of specially defined terms, is precisely what makes it an *idiom*.[7]

The semantic and grammatical ubiquity of the economic idiom entirely consumes the explanatory, interpretive, descriptive, and perceptual space in which animal life is grasped. Not only do the economic ideas become embodied in the actions of animals or surface in their inner lives, their ubiquitous presence also contributes to the exclusion of other modalities of depicting animal life. Since the conceptual space of grasping animal relations is expended, an alternative understanding of the social life of animals, especially through tropes of the lifeworld, is preempted. The impact of the economic idiom on the domain of experience and lived action involves the erasure of an animal lifeworld—an everyday world of experience of activity and leisure, pleasure and pain, abundance and hardship, exhilaration and fear, rivalry and affection. Tropes of the lifeworld are not denied in any direct sense, but simply swept aside, preempted by the absolute priority of reproductive success, its corollary of competition, and the economic idiom that delivers them.[8] States of being of the individual within the lifeworld, such as happiness, misery, joy, wonder, dignity, triumph, grief, or defiance, evidenced in the countenance and conduct of animals by Charles Darwin, are effaced in the neo-Darwinian sociobiological view of animal life. For sociobiology, the kinds of affect and attitudes referenced by state-of-being concepts are simply not relevant to the big picture. As discussed in the analysis of Darwin's language, the effect of acknowledging states of being in animal life is to convey a fullness and breadth of living, a temporal extendedness of experience in the present. Obversely, the extinction of the landscape of the lifeworld is manifest in the trivialization of quotidian experience.

The view of animals as inhabitants of a lifeworld is precluded by the saturation of sociobiological writing with economic concepts. This effect of extinguishing the lifeworld is intuited by the reader in a pronounced characteristic of sociobiological imagery, namely, the vivid absence of *feeling*. A chill permeates the sociobiological representation of animal life. Whether run by selfish genes, wary bodies, or crafty minds, animal life exudes an atmosphere of unrelenting coldness. Even as animals aggregate in permanent or seasonal social formations, the exigencies that an economic language expresses—of success, competition, investment, and cost-benefit trade-offs—create a picture of essential isolation. The form of life conjured by sociobiology is incompatible with a lifeworld in which meaning is shared and action is concerted. The message of sociobiology—or perhaps more accurately, its worldview—is that to be an animal is essentially to live alone, to fight hard, and to die, often prematurely. It is a grand-scale and austere picture, which sociobiologists often recognize as cynical, but which, by the same token, could also be characterized as romantic. Thus on one level, sociobiological discourse is about formulating hypotheses and correlating variables to arrive at general statements about animal life. The "ultimate goal" of sociobiology, Wilson writes, is a "stoichiometry of social evolution" that "when perfected . . . will consist in an interlocking set of models that permit the quantitative prediction of the qualities of social organization—group size, age composition, and mode of organization, including communication, division of labor, and time budgets—from a knowledge of the prime movers of social evolution" (1975: 63). Yet beyond pedantic proclamations of intent and the production of straightforward, often dry, and heavily statistical scientific reports about different species, sociobiology creates a worldview that engages both imagination and affect. It is a vision of animal life that is epical— hard, heroic, and lonely.

PERSONAL KNOWLEDGE, SOCIOBIOLOGICAL OBJECTIVITY, AND FREQUENCY-LADEN DESCRIPTION

In the study of natural behavior, that is, of the behavior of animals as it occurs in their normal and undisturbed environments, the methodology of natural history is prolonged, close, and patient observation. Indeed, the naturalist Jean Henri Fabre, discussed in Chapter 2, frequently interjects commentaries about the perseverance and long hours of work that the observation of animal life entails. This personal commitment to protracted observation, through the hours of day and night, over the months and years, is integral to the form and endurance of the naturalist's knowledge. It creates a bond between the naturalist and the animal world that is reflected both in the diligence of description and in the delicate affection that suffuses the writing. The naturalist's predilection for representing animal subjectivity with bold and often penetrating assessments is neither conceited nor reckless: rather, this predilection flows precisely from the naturalist's merging into the animal's world, from the heightening of awareness and receptivity that stems from intimate knowledge. Michael Polanyi's conception of "personal knowledge" is an apposite description of the form of knowing that the work of a naturalist such as Fabre embodies. Polanyi writes:

> We may distinguish between the personal in us, which actively enters into our commitments, and our subjective states, in which we merely endure our feelings. This distinction establishes the conception of the *personal,* which is neither subjective nor objective. In so far as the personal submits to requirements acknowledged by itself as independent of itself, it is not subjective; but in so far as it is an action guided by individual passions, it is not objective either. It transcends the disjunction between subjective and objective. (1962: 300)

For Jean Henri Fabre nothing is more real than the world of insects that he observed and nothing more urgent than recording that world with fidelity. His portraiture of animal life is not a projection of his feelings and beliefs; on the contrary, it reflects a deference and a dedication to conveying with exactitude the way things are. At the same time, his writings comprise a unique knowledge, a personal testimony of what he witnessed, that is unrepeatable. Guided by individual passion, as Polanyi puts it, Fabre delivers tropes of the beautiful, the grotesque, the bizarre, the ludicrous, the marvelous, the cunning; watching insects, he entered their world completely and brought it back as poetry.

In continuity with the tradition of natural history, the methodology of contemporary behavioral science retains the requirement of protracted observation over an extended period. This endeavor, however, is no longer *defined* in terms of personal commitment, as an act of solitude and a labor of love, but rather is institutionally and organizationally regimented. Observation is systematized, in accordance with disciplinary prescriptions, so as to compile data replicable by any trained observer or team of observers. In Clutton-Brock and colleagues' sociobiological study of the red deer, hypotheses to be tested are formulated prior to going into the field; day and night are broken down into observation periods; activity patterns are inventoried; and specific individuals or types of individuals are identified for observation. Methodological tools include charts where variables of interest—as, for example, activity type, age group, or sex— are already inscribed. Gathering data, to a large extent, is a matter of recording frequencies of events or behaviors. In the chapter titled "Methods, Samples, and Definitions," the authors summarize methods of data collection that are the standard fare of sociobiologists, and of contemporary behavioral scientists more generally. The following passages reflect certain salient characteristics of their methodology:

> To measure activity patterns, we watched particular individuals continuously for a day at a time. When an animal was selected for observation, its activity was recorded at the end of every minute during the daytime or at the end of every five minutes at night (using infrared viewing equipment) by teams of two to four observers taking four-hour shifts. Day watches began at dawn or soon afterward . . . and lasted till dusk . . . , and night watches began at dusk and lasted till dawn. . . .
>
> During the day watches, the frequency of social interactions involving the target animal was recorded, as well as the animal's distance from its two nearest neighbors and their identity. In addition, we collected data on the activity and composition of the group they were in. At 15-min intervals we recorded the identity of all animals in the group, their activities, and (in some watches) their positions relative to each other, using a check sheet with a series of concentric rings on which the position of all animals was recorded. . . .
>
> During the rut, we also carried out a number of full day watches of stags and hinds. Samples included seven day-watches and five night-watches of mature stags (six years and older) when they were holding harems, seven day-watches of five- and six-year-old stags not holding harems, ten day-watches of anestrous hinds, and four day-watches of hinds in estrus. In addition, the activity of all hinds belonging to the harems of the stags that were watched at night were recorded at 15-min intervals, giving a measure of nighttime activity among hinds. (1982: 42–44)

The central aim of the methods outlined is the collection of data amenable to quantitative treatment. The information collected on charts, concerning predetermined questions and variables, is designed to streamline into statistical operations that will then translate into propositions about general trends. Procedures, tools, and categories of recording are standardized, so that a near-identical study could be carried out by any observer trained in behavioral science. This requirement of the replicability of obtained results is reflected in the alternation, and hence interchangeability, of different observers assigned to the four-hour shifts.

The methods of sociobiology are clearly not designed to create "personal knowledge," in the sense Polanyi has identified. Quite to the contrary, "objective knowledge" here signifies results that are intersubjective and impersonal, namely, gathered simultaneously by at least two observers and gatherable by any trained observer. The methods of studying the deer are disciplined for the pragmatic purposes of both interobservational consistency and acquiring the targeted data. If the agreed timetable of recording the activity of a specific animal is, for example, at the end of fifteen-minute intervals, then this regime is strictly followed. The observer will not be sidetracked into recording events that occur at a time other than the one set.

I contrast this methodological regime to the naturalist's enterprise, for it is interesting to see how strikingly divergent are the forms of knowledge that these approaches foster. The naturalist goes into the field to record the stream of life as it occurs. The sociobiologist goes to the field to collect the data that are required by the hypothesis formulated and the experimental design. The naturalist seeks to record singular events witnessed in great detail. The sociobiologist will deliberately refrain from collecting information that is outside the purview of the specific task and timetable, so that if a specific animal has been targeted for observation, the sociobiologist will not be beguiled into attending to another animal, even if what it is doing is of interest. For a naturalist like Fabre, "objective knowledge" is a personal achievement, stemming from an intensity of immersion that grounds his authority to speak for the insect world with which he has become intimately acquainted. For sociobiologists such as Clutton-Brock and colleagues, "objective knowledge" is accredited by interobservational agreement, involving emphasis on quantitative information, procuring observational data, and producing general claims that are founded in impersonal measurement. The naturalist wants to glimpse inside the animal's experiential world. The sociobiologist wants to submit claims that any behavioral scientist can verify.

The purpose of the red deer study is the collection of data that can be statistically analyzed so as to lead to the establishment of comprehensive claims about deer life, and/or mammal life, and/or harem social structure, and/or hormonal correlates of behaviors, and the like. General statements and predictions about social behavior—often referred to as "theorems" or "models" in sociobiology—are the main goal of such field studies. For example, the "reproductive success" of an animal is operationalized as the number of its offspring. In the words of the authors, "it is reasonable to assume that the number of surviving offspring an individual produces in its lifetime provides a measure of its success in passing on its genetic material to the next generation" (1982: 3). The numbers of offspring of dif-

ferent individuals, which vary considerably, are then collated against a
variety of factors that have contributed to their determination, in order to
arrive at propositions regarding the determinants of reproductive success
that are general, testable, and potentially extendable to other species. For
example, do birthdate and weight of calves correlate with female reproductive success? Does male body size or antler size correlate with reproductive success? Does the average size of the harem held by a stag correlate
with the number of offspring he sires? These and similar questions can be
posed and given at least provisional, if not highly certain, answers by
means of quantitative analyses. The resulting claims can then inspire and
guide the study of their applicability to other species.

Given the generality and abstract nature of the knowledge pursued, the
individual animal as a realistic entity is almost completely absent in sociobiological accounts. The individual disappears, while the type it represents
takes its place. Thus, a deer is "male" or "female"; if female, she can be a
"milk-hind," "anestrous," or "estrous"; if male, he can be a "harem-
holder" or "non-harem-holder." Both sexes can also be broken down into
different "age groups" corresponding to different life stages. Such categories subsume and articulate everything that needs to be known about the
individual; in other words, individuals become absolute incumbents of
categories. Behavioral repertoires, especially those pertaining to reproduction, are then streamlined along the axes of these category types to discern
correlations with reproductive success and failure. Descriptions of animals'
activities are always generalized, delivered through quantification markers
such as *often, frequently, regularly, rarely,* and the like. Thus the idiosyncrasies and peculiarities of individuals, the ways in which their uniqueness
is expressed, are factored into the analyses only indirectly to the extent that
they are pooled into quantitative operations. In a discourse that is fundamentally statistical in character, individual variability, as such, is minimally
significant; it does not appear within the descriptive apparatus. In sociobiology, variability is important only as it factors into the mathematical
computations, not as itself a central message extracted from the data.

Indeed, statistical operations precisely sink individual variation and
cancel out idiosyncratic expressions, for the purposes of discerning and
mapping out general patterns and trends. This interest and form of knowledge is reflected in the sociobiological inscription of behavioral events and
activities:

From the first week of October onward, harem-holding stags interacted *regularly* with the hinds—sniffing, licking, chivvying, and herding them. . . . On the whole, stags distributed their attentions evenly among the mature members of their harem, though they interacted with calves, yearlings, and two-year-olds *less frequently* than with adult hinds. Stags also paid particular attention to hinds that had recently joined their harems, and the *frequency* with which they licked and chivvied them was *higher than average*. Stags holding larger harems did not compensate by chivvying hinds more *often,* and the *frequency* with which individual hinds were chivvied or licked was *negatively related* to harem size. However, on days when particular stags held large harems, they *tended* to stay closer to them and spent *less* time feeding. (1982: 126–27, emphasis added)

Emphasis on the statistical processing of data generates a descriptive style that may be characterized as "frequency-laden." This passage is replete with quantitative markers that deliver the average circumstance or overall trends. Identifying behavioral trends of both males and females, at different life-cycle stages and seasons, is a central descriptive motif. In the chapter "The Rutting Behavior of the Stags," the displays and interactive behaviors of the stags are named, inventoried, and then explicitly typified by definition. "Chivvying" identifies the stag's chasing hinds over short distances, with his neck outstretched and sometimes extending his tongue (1982: 112). Description subsequently focuses on how often chivvying occurs and toward which types of hinds. What is of interest is the extent to which a behavioral pattern occurs in correlation with particular categories: how much chivvying is directed toward "estrous" vis-à-vis "non-estrous" females, or toward "newly arrived" vis-à-vis "already present" hinds. The specific form of the behavior, the feeling of its expression, and the interactional atmosphere it projects are themes that are not addressed. There exists no representational machinery to deliver them. In contrast to naturalist descriptions, displays are not illustrated episodically through a specific context of their occurrence or as part of a stream of events. The descriptions of displays are typified, and information about behavioral patterns is quantitatively collated to general variables.

    The focus on category types of animals and typified behavioral patterns yields abstract descriptions, while the emphasis on quantitative correlations between variables and category types yields statistically mediated or frequency-laden descriptions. The individual animal as a concrete medium of description—exemplified in the naturalist's episodic description, discussed in Chapter 2—disappears, and statements about general trends, expressed via quantitative markers, emerge as primary. The consequence of this mode of description is an intensification of the erasure of the life-world. It is important to note that states of being can be witnessed and attributed only through a focus on the individual; such states are certainly not "measurable" in any sense whatsoever, nor deliverable through quantitative markers. Thus the economic idiom, statistical methodology, and frequency-laden descriptions of sociobiology are mutually reinforcing in the effect of the erasure of the lifeworld.

A New Anthropomorphism?

Much of the language of twentieth-century behavioral science has been forged in deliberate avoidance of the anthropomorphism of early naturalists, including that of the founder of modern biology, Charles Darwin. As discussed in the previous chapter, ethologists acquiesced to the stance of skepticism regarding animal mind, carefully shielding their writing from mental language. In doubting or denying animal mind, skepticism expresses a deep distrust of, and prohibition against, a reflection between human and animal realms. The use of discrepant representational mediums precisely serves to keep these realms largely insulated. The construction of a technical language of behavior is the most effective insulating device, for it both directly displaces mental terminology and indirectly suggests that animal life can be fully comprehended through an interpretive framework divergent from that ordinarily used for human action. Obversely, a language commonly applicable to the two domains operates like a mirror between them.

As seen in the overall avoidance of mental language, sociobiology inherited the skeptical stance. Sociobiologists continue to honor the mandate to eschew anthropomorphism: the focus on reproductive success and competition, and the economic idiom it sustains, displace a language of intentionality and translocate agency to the level of the genes. Moreover, frequency-laden description constitutes behavioral phenomena as data to generate general claims or theorems, rather than as iconic descriptions to guide the reader's imagination onto a landscape of actions and events. And yet, at the same time, a stringently prohibitive attitude toward the idea of animal mind is presently giving way to a greater open-mindedness within behavioral science. This is due to various overlapping and interconnecting factors, partially independent of sociobiology: the decline of behaviorism, the influence of primate studies, the emergence of cognitive ethology, and changes of thinking and attitudes in the broader culture. Sociobiology reflects this shift in the academic and broader culture, and has also contributed to its advancement with its ambition to encompass human and animal social behavior in a single biological-evolutionary framework. With its application of a common theoretical and conceptual framework—and especially the use of social-category concepts that I discuss in this section—an alliance between human and animal worlds is created. A common language of society allows echoes and reflections to crisscross the two worlds, thereby tying them together in various ways. This facet of sociobiology, by itself and however indirectly, has promoted the corrosion of skepticism regarding animal mind.

In other words, while there is a language and descriptive style in place to eschew anthropomorphism, there is also a tendency within sociobiology to deviate from the strict commitment against it. As discussed, economic ideas occasionally surface in the guise of Machiavellian cunning. John S. Kennedy, a neobehaviorist committed to opposing animal mind, obliquely criticizes what he sees as an anachronistic and antiscientific trend in contemporary sociobiology toward a "new anthropomorphism."[9] He notes that certain sociobiologists interpret terms such as "decision-making" and "strategizing" as proximate, mental causes (1992: 57). Kennedy maintains that he would not object to the use of concepts such as "decision-making" and "strategizing" in connection to animal behavior as long as these were used as a shorthand to describe the genetic steering of behavior in the direction of maximizing fitness. He calls shorthand use of anthropomorphic language in contemporary behavioral writing "mock anthropomorphism"; he finds this sort of use acceptable, for on his view "natural selection has produced animals that act *as if* they had minds like us" (1992: 94).[10] What Kennedy fails to recognize, however, is that a mental dimension is already part and parcel of the concept of "decision-making," and the invocation of this dimension is neither a matter of sloppy reception on the reader's part nor one of careless use on the part of certain sociobiologists. The most extraordinary conceptual precautions could not undo the implications of mentality in the concept of "decision-making," and contemporary behavioral scientists are no longer so hardened against the idea of animal mind to engage in endless self-censoring vigilance. Indeed, they tend to prevaricate when it comes to mental capacities or predilections that resonate with the themes of success, competition, and selfishness. It is not surprising, therefore, that a major topic in the study of animal communication in contemporary behavioral studies is the extent to which it is characterized by deception and manipulation (for example, Dawkins and Krebs 1978).

Apart from the resonance between economic ideas and the introjection of a Machiavellian orientation, an even more pervasive dimension of the "new anthropomorphism"—to borrow Kennedy's expression—is the application of concepts of social action, structure, relations, or attitudes to animals. I have been referring to this nexus of terms as social-category concepts. Examples of social-category terms are *adultery, altruism, caste, cheating, class, contest, cooperation, cuckoldry, desertion, division of labor, dominance, exploitation, harem, infanticide, infidelity, kinship, nepotism, promiscuity, rape, sacrifice, selfishness, weaning,* and so on. The conceptual constitution of the social life of animals through this terminology has provoked the criticism that such language use is anthropomorphic. The use of social-category terminology has been one of the most controversial aspects of sociobiology—second only, though intimately related, to the direct application of sociobiological reasoning to human life. So, for example, the well-known anthropological critic of sociobiology, Marshall Sahlins, avers that

> the anthropomorphic inclination is not confined to the vulgar sociobiology. To take a random and limited sample from Wilson's *Sociobiology: The New Synthesis,* we read of animal societies that have "polygyny," "castes," "slaves," "despots," "matrilineal social organization," "aunts," "queens," "family chauvinism," "culture," "cultural innovation," "agriculture," "taxes," and "investments," as well as "costs" and "benefits." (1976: 6–7)

Ruth Bleier, a feminist critic of sociobiology, also provides a (somewhat less random) list of such ostensibly objectionable terms. "A central problem of sociobiology," she maintains, "is the anthropomorphism of its concepts and language—rape in plants, machismo in insects, prostitution in apes and birds, homosexuality in worms" (1985: 29). Social-category terms are a shorthand for describing social relations; they tend to summarize complex interactions or attitudes; they may describe constellations of relationships sustained through the exercise of force; and they are often concepts that have pronounced moral connotations, invoking sensibilities or strong beliefs and responses about the "is" and the "ought" of human social arrangements. The kinds of concepts that Sahlins and Bleier object to as anthropomorphic are not mental concepts, and anthropomorphism is most commonly associated with the ascription of mental terms to animals. If anthropomorphism is restricted to the idea of ascribing mental experiences to animals, then it is unclear why the application of social-category concepts should be off-limits to animals, for these concepts do not directly or necessarily implicate mental qualities. This may in part explain why sociobiologists—who are heir to the twentieth-century apprehension against anthropomorphism—have no qualms employing social-category terms, for the most part, without cautionary qualifiers.

The criticism of the sociobiological application of such concepts to animals provides an opportunity to revisit the idea of anthropomorphism from a new angle. I regard the critique of sociobiological language use as anthropomorphic to be unconvincing, for it reveals more about the beliefs and assumptions of the critics than about why we ought to feel epistemically or morally affronted by the sociobiological application of social-category terms to animals. In what follows, I discuss the use of social-category terms in sociobiology, first by evaluating its denunciation as anthropomorphic and next by offering an analysis of its effects on the representation of animals and humans.

The fall into anthropomorphism is often depicted as a kind of conceptual seduction. Marshall Sahlins condemns sociobiology for giving into the "temptations of anthropomorphism." Philip Kitcher, as well, even though he is far friendlier toward the sociobiological enterprise than Sahlins, maintains that "because we have so rich a vocabulary for describing the activity of fellow human beings, it is tempting to use similar expressions to discuss animal behavior that seems very like pieces of human behavior" (1987: 184). Anthropomorphism is presumed to be a naive view, an illusion generated through superficial analogies between human and animal behavior, a deluded projection of the wealth of human experience onto a world that is putatively less rich. The charge of anthropomorphism, then, signifies that—from either nescience or naïveté—the complexity and subtlety of human reality are erroneously projected onto animal life. As though it were too obvious a point to defend deliberately, critiques such as those of Sahlins and Bleier merely affirm the tacit conviction that animal life is simple, if not indigent, in comparison to the world that humans create and inhabit. The suggestion is that authors who "commit" anthropomorphism see the mirage of a sumptuous abode where, in reality, stands a minimally outfitted shack. It is not possible to experience the force of the charge of anthropomorphism without partaking of these assumptions, which lie at its very foundations.

Beyond its discrediting connotations, however, the concept of anthropomorphism actually has no *substantive* content. In labeling sociobiological language as anthropomorphic, critics are simply stating their objection to the use of a language that violates the border between human and animal worlds. As a way of driving the point home that the charge of anthropomorphism lacks content, I compare two passages, one by Charles Darwin, the other by E. O. Wilson. Both thinkers have been accused of anthropomorphizing animals, and the point of reading them side by side is to note how markedly their portrayals diverge. I begin with Darwin's wonderful portrayal of ants:

> To describe the habits and powers of a female ant, would require, as Pierre Huber has shewn, a large volume; I may, however, briefly specify a few points. Ants communicate information to each other, and several unite for the same work, or games of play. They recognize their fellow ants after months of absence. They build great edifices, keep them clean, close the doors in the evening, and post sentries. They make roads, and even tunnels under rivers. They collect food for the community, and when an object, too large for entrance is brought to the nest, they enlarge the door, and afterwards build it up again. They go out to battle in regular bands, and freely sacrifice their lives for the common weal. They emigrate in accordance with a preconcerted plan. They capture slaves. They keep Aphides as milch-cows. They move the eggs of their aphides, as well as their own eggs and cocoons, into warm parts of the nest, in order that they may be quickly hatched; and endless similar facts could be given. (Darwin 1981, 1: 186–87)

E. O. Wilson offers the following general description of ant life:

> The higher social insects, comprised of the ants, termites, and certain wasps and bees, form societies that are much less than perfect. To be sure, they are characterized by sterile castes that are self-sacrificing in the service of the mother queen. Also the altruistic behavior is prominent and varied. It includes the regurgitation of stomach contents to hungry nestmates, suicidal weapons such as detachable stings and exploding abdomens used in defense of the colony, and other specialized responses. The castes are physically modified to perform particular functions and are bound to one another by tight, intricate forms of communication. Furthermore, individuals cannot live apart from the colony for more than short periods. They can recognize castes but not individual nestmates. In a word, the insect society is based upon impersonal intimacy. (Wilson 1975: 379)

While there are points of similarity between the passages, their alternative semantics deliver a fundamentally different tenor. Darwin depicts ants in the language of the lifeworld, an everyday world in which actions, communal life, objects, and events are meaningful for its inhabitants, and the meanings are shared. Darwin's description delivers an intersubjective life-world, for his language of communal activities embeds what Schutz calls the "reciprocity of perspectives," the fundamental assumption that what I see from over Here is essentially the same as what you experience over There. Transferring this language to animals carries with it the feature of shared meaning. Building great edifices, keeping them clean, making roads and tunnels, enlarging the doors, collecting food—all these descriptive tropes suggest that activities are not only achieved together by the ants, but also shared in signification.

The tempo of Darwin's account is set by a series of action verbs, with the ants as grammatical subjects: the ants build, keep clean, close, make, collect, enlarge, emigrate, battle, capture, and move. The reiteration of this pattern creates an image of ceaseless and concerted action. In Wilson's description this grammatical construction is absent. His account is guided by structural-functionalist concerns, conveyed through social-category terminology. Social structure is delivered with the idea of a colony, ruled by the queen, and kept running by castes. Function comes through with the social-relational terms *altruistic behavior, service, defense, self-sacrifice*, and *suicidal*. The social life of the ants is presented in terms of a stratified society, composed not of a collective of individuals but of types enacting a physically based division of labor. The finesse of Wilson's description is that it is wonderfully tailored to lead up to his synopsis of ant life as one of "impersonal intimacy."

The impetus to compare these passages arises from the consideration that both Darwin and Wilson have been accused of anthropomorphism. The stylistic and conceptual divergence between Darwin's and Wilson's passages demonstrates that "anthropomorphism" has no specific substantive content. Indeed, there exists no inventory of concepts, or classes of concepts, for which the categorical case could be made that they should *never* be applied to animals. The only feature of its application that is constant and consistent is the disparaging function of the word *anthropomorphism*. Its meaning, therefore, is strictly its performative function, which is to cast aspersion, in an ad hominem fashion, upon any linguistic usage that lifts a mirror between animals and humans. The criticism that sociobiologists use ostensibly anthropomorphic language thus says nothing specifically informative about sociobiology. Rather, it lays bare the ingrained presupposition of the critics that any discourse permitting a reflection between the human and animal worlds should be dishonored—tagged as erroneous, dangerous, or superficial—because human and animal life are so far removed as to prohibit the application of a shared language of representation. A second problem with the charge of anthropomorphism is that it embeds two problematic assumptions about the nature of language. The first is that speakers of language are sovereign over its use and therefore can self-consciously refrain from using purportedly anthropomorphic terms. The autonomy of language, however, is revealed in the spontaneous and apposite applicability of concepts to circumstances or conditions witnessed by the observer. Speakers of a language do not *decide* what words to use, but apply those that language suggests. The second presupposition of the critique of sociobiological language as anthropomorphic is that concepts are bounded, whole packages of meanings, so that when they are transferred across different contexts of use they retain identical meanings. Yet the application of the same concepts in different domains involves not only transference but also shifts of meaning: the meaning of concepts is not rigidly stable but, rather, largely context-dependent. Placed in new posts, the same words signify somewhat differently; thus across different domains of applicability, they may, for instance, lose or gain denotational extensions. Extended into a novel domain, the field of meaning of a word shifts to resonate with what the particular domain affords; certain dimensions of its meaning may become highlighted, while others fall away as irrelevant or not applicable. Clutton-Brock and his colleagues' lack of anthropomorphic worry in using the term *harem* in relation to deer life is corollary to both these aspects of language. They define it as "the group of hinds defended by a stag at a particular time on a given day during the rut" (Clutton-Brock, Guinness, and Albon 1982: 44). The stag defends his reproductive priority over the group of hinds against other males, with frequent displays and occasional fighting, and he herds females attempting to run away. The authors do not choose to employ the term *harem* from a range of alternatives. It is not only that the use of the term is established in the literature; there simply is no other single word to convey how the particular social constellation is witnessed. Moreover, not all dimensions of the meaning of the harem in connection to human affairs are transferred to animal life in the application of the concept. The morally aversive implications of *harem*, at least for modern Western readers, do not carry into its extension to deer. To censor the extension of social-category terms to animals, as certain critics of sociobiology seem to enjoin, can never suppress the knowledge that their applicability is intelligible and arises naturally for speakers of the language.

Yet a third problem with the notion of anthropomorphism as a discrediting label is that it implicitly assumes that a neutral language exists, or can be created, and that this can be applied unproblematically as a realist representational means in writings on animal behavior. However, as I have endeavored to show through the examination of different uses of language, from Darwin and early naturalists to classical ethologists and contemporary sociobiologists, language is never a neutral medium in the portrayal of animals. It may be possible to avoid anthropomorphic language by devising a technical idiom for the description and explanation of animal behavior. Technical languages, however, impart their own connotative and imagistic effects on the portrayal of animals. Certain technical idioms, such as that of classical ethology, are able to avoid anthropomorphism by deploying a technical and causal vocabulary, but the effect of this language is a mechanomorphic view of animals. The economic language of sociobiology also has its own peculiar impact, consuming the entirety of animal life and annihilating the possibility of a lifeworld—an everyday world replete with activities, objects, and events whose meanings are shared by its inhabitants. In short, whatever language is employed entails consequences in terms of how animal life is understood and how it is pictured in the reader's imagination. Language choice comes with certain commitments, not only because each language use has its own specific effects, but also because it invariably excludes the imagery, atmosphere, and message of other sorts of accounts.

Finally, the charge of anthropomorphism fails to be compelling for one additional reason. Even in the case of constructing and deploying a technical language of behavior, the ordinary language of action can never be entirely erased from behavioral texts. And this language, being the everyday language of human affairs, carries with it potentially anthropomorphic connotations. A *purely* technical language is just as unrealizable in the description of animal behavior as it would be in that of human behavior. As the ethnomethodologist Roy Turner aptly puts it in connection to the depiction of human action, the intelligibility of " 'reports' or 'descriptions' are so constrained . . . that . . . technical descriptions of events would . . . be treated as bizarre, humorous, in bad taste, or in some way incompetent" (1975: 200). In the analysis of classical ethology, I showed that a first-order description of animal behavior in the ordinary language of action is required in order to convey the fundamental intelligibility of a behavioral event. Technical languages cannot sidestep the ordinary language of action; they perforce either use it with accompanying transformations or move into its domain in virtue of connotational and semantic extensions of technical terms. The use of scare-quotes is also a common device in behavioral literature, a way of simultaneously using a concept and attempting to cancel its application. This device, however, does not so much screen out semantic features of the word as it expresses the author's lack of conviction in using it. The ultimate indispensability of the ordinary language of action, and even of mental concepts, is the reason that "anthropomorphism" is increasingly recognized as ineradicable in the description of animal behavior (see, for example, Asquith 1984; Fisher 1990, 1991).

In short, the critique of the sociobiological application of social-category terms to animals as anthropomorphism is not compelling. It does not articulate a coherent argument against the application of such terms, but instead reveals the presuppositions of the critics of sociobiology: the highly suspect a priori conviction that the difference between animals and humans is so fundamental as to prohibit a shared language of representation in the depiction of action; the erroneous belief that words transfer as whole units of meaning across different contexts; the equally erroneous assumption that authors are sovereign over their conceptual choices; the untenable idea that a neutral language offering, in Thomas Nagel's words, a view from nowhere (1986), exists or might be fashioned; and finally the unrealizable hope that anthropomorphic concepts can be completely eradicated from behavioral accounts.

I turn now to an analysis of how sociobiologists use social-category concepts and what their peculiar effects are on the portrayal of animals *and* human beings. Critics of sociobiology claim that social-category terms refer to culturally acquired, linguistically bound, or institutionally mediated social relations that are socially and ideationally constructed rather than naturally given. In other words, they deem the application of social categories to animal relations and interactions to be a category mistake: the mapping of contingent culture onto universal nature. This critique, however, misses the analytic point that sociobiological thinking naturalizes these concepts—that the application of the language of human society to animals precisely intends to undermine the demarcation between "culture" and "nature."

Just like economic terms, social-category concepts are used with realist intent. They are not, however, transformed into technical concepts, but rather respecified as "natural-kind" terms, which refer to phenomena that exist independently of human agency or will (Hacking 1991). The naturalization of social concepts is achieved in sociobiology, not by deliberate argumentation, but through the implicit demonstration that these concepts have literal and credible applicability in the context of animal life. Their applicability to animals, in turn, has a powerful upshot for human affairs: it reflects back on human society, indirectly exposing the animal dimension of human relations, practices, and attitudes. The sociobiological use of social-category terms for animals thus entangles a number of tasks and consequences. It is a representational medium, with robust capacities for generalizing about social structures and relations across many different species; it presents those concepts as referents of phenomena that have a substantive existence independent of human will or agency, thereby transfiguring the concepts into natural kinds; and finally it transforms the status of social-category terms as they apply to human beings themselves, revealing such terms to refer to phenomena whose manifestations in human cultures are refractions of evolutionary history. In sociobiological reasoning, words such as *selfishness, nepotism, harem,* or *polygyny* represent phenomena far older than the emergence of human language that has crystallized those phenomena in symbolic articulation.

I focus on two argumentative techniques in sociobiology that achieve the respecification of social categories as natural kinds. Both make use of commonsense knowledge, one doing so tacitly, the other deliberately.[11] The first might be called the "double-entendre" technique. It consists of describing behavioral strategies found in the animal world, while implicitly relying on the readers' recall of the same sorts of behaviors encountered in human society. An example from Clutton-Brock and Harvey may be useful in explicating this technique. In this particular passage, the authors are introducing certain of the ideas of biologist Robert Trivers.

> To provide a functional explanation of variation in parental care, it is necessary to understand the costs and benefits to each sex of *deserting* its mate after egg laying or parturition. Trivers (1978b) argues that, at any point during rearing, the sex which has invested less may be *tempted to desert,* thus forcing the partner to complete the rearing alone while it mates again. He goes on to suggest . . . that it may be adaptive for males to *desert* females since the female's initially heavy investment is likely to commit her to further

investment. One possible strategy that a female can adopt is to require heavy male investment prior to mating (e.g. by *playing "coy"* and extending the process of courtship), thus increasing the risks of subsequent *desertion* to the male. (1978: 42, emphasis added)

This passage exemplifies a number of characteristics of sociobiological thought. I want to look specifically at the use of the social-category terms *desertion* and *coyness,* but it is worth noting briefly certain general striking features. The relations between mates is mediated by an economic arrangement of costs, benefits, and investment. This matrix displaces any other conceptualization of the bond between them. The idea of "the sex which has invested less," usually the male, being "tempted to desert" once again echoes a Machiavellian stance of self-interested action. Genetic selfishness and its calculus of an inverse relation between degree of investment and desertion leave no room for the possibility or relevance of other ways of relating. So while the idea of "desertion" can be applied unproblematically as a natural cognate of the economic idiom, its isomorphic antonym of "loyalty" could find no suitable conceptual space in sociobiological discourse. The nonoccurrence of desertion, prompted by heavy investment, is simply "nondesertion" and cannot signify an attitude or feeling of "loyalty."

The passage cited is advancing a general proposition—applicable to certain birds or mammals—about behavioral strategies of an individual with respect to their mate that maximize the individual's reproductive success. Finding "desertion" and "coyness" in the context of bird and mammal life transforms them from morally loaded concepts into referents of widespread, evolutionarily based phenomena. The invocation of common-sense knowledge, or of the stock of widely shared knowledge, involves an indirect but unmistakable allusion to human affairs—namely, to men "who leave" and women "who play hard to get." Hence it is nearly impossible to read this and similar passages in sociobiology without reflecting upon human affairs—in this case, relations between women and men. This exemplifies the effect of "hearing double," for while animals are being discussed, human life is obliquely brought into the general picture that is created. The transformation of the social-category concepts "desertion" and "coyness" into natural-kind terms thereby boomerangs into the world of human affairs, where male desertion after mating, and female coyness before, become another instantiation of a general behavioral-biological phenomenon.

In the above example from Clutton-Brock and Harvey, commonsense knowledge is implicitly invoked. However, sociobiologists also call upon commonsense knowledge quite deliberately to strengthen their conceptual edifice. A passage from Wilson's *Sociobiology* in which he elaborates on altruism, selfishness, and spite illustrates the deliberate use of commonsense knowledge as an ally of sociobiological knowledge.

> The personal actions of one member toward another can be conveniently classified into three categories in a way that makes the analysis of kin selection more feasible. When a person (or animal) increases the fitness of another at the expense of his own fitness, he can be said to have performed an act of *altruism*. Self-sacrifice for the benefit of offspring is altruism in the conventional but not in the strictly genetic sense, because individual fitness is measured by the number of surviving offspring. But self-sacrifice on behalf of second cousins is true altruism at both levels; and when directed at total strangers such abnegating behavior is so surprising (that is, "noble") as to demand some kind of theoretical explanation. In contrast, a person who raises his own fitness by lowering that of others is engaged in *selfishness*. While we cannot publicly approve the selfish act we do understand it thoroughly and may even sympathize. Finally, a person who gains nothing or even reduces his own fitness in order to diminish that of another has committed an act of *spite*. The action may be sane, and the perpetrator may seem gratified, but we find it difficult to imagine his rational motivation. We refer to the commitment of a spiteful act as "all too human"—and then wonder what we meant. (1975: 117)

The elucidation of the sociobiological conceptions of selfishness, altruism, and spite is brilliantly interwoven with their commonsense counterparts in a way that advances the validity of their sociobiological meanings. Sociobiology is presented as fully equipped to account for the pretheoretical, commonplace understanding of altruism, selfishness, and spite. "Altruism," or self-sacrifice for the benefit of another, is indexed against degrees of relatedness. Commonsensically, we regard altruistic acts in defense of offspring as quite disparate from those in support of total strangers. Sociobiology confirms this mundane distinction, and then explains it by positing that altruism for offspring is expectable, for in actuality it is a form of genetic selfishness. Sociobiology predicts that genuine altruism should be rare. From the standpoint of common sense as well, a "noble" act of altruism calls for some kind of explanation—its rationale is not self-evident in the way that the motivation of a mother's sacrifice for her child, for example, is self-evident. The idea of "selfishness" is extended from a personality or action descriptor to the level of genes; the sociobiological extension is achieved in virtue of the implicit signification of something like "me always first." Given the sociobiological logic of maximizing genetic success, selfishness is expected: in ordinary reasoning also, Wilson writes, we sympathize with and understand selfish acts, even if we (publicly) disapprove. Finally, "spite" is to a large extent evolutionarily incoherent; it is not surprising, Wilson insinuates, that we intuitively say it is "all too human," although if we do not know that evolution works on an inexorable calculus of benefits and costs, we do not know why we say it.[12]

Wilson is not simply tying together biological and ordinary uses of concepts and playing one off another. Keeping a tense alignment between sociobiological and commonsense meanings, he gives sociobiology a tremendous boost by making it an ally of commonsense knowledge. He places these potent words—centrally, *selfishness* and *altruism*—in the context of the evolutionary story of gene proliferation. Under the auspices of this argumentative format, not only are ordinary intuitions about these ideas validated, they are entirely clarified. In other words, while the sociobiological concepts of selfishness and altruism are extended from vernacular use and reasoning and respecified in an evolutionary narrative, their respecifications swiftly loop around to form the very background against which their ordinary meanings originally emerged. By keeping the boundary between commonsense meanings and sociobiological conceptions of social categories fluid, sociobiologists simultaneously rely upon and explain widely shared intuitions. This is an ingenious argumentative strategy for strengthening scientific claims, as it makes them continuous with the widely shared stock of knowledge.

The extension of social-category terms to animals, therefore, does not so much anthropomorphize animals as it "zoomorphizes" humans. The applicability of those concepts to animals reflects back on human society, exposing the animal face of human norms and relations. The language reveals, or suggests, that social-category concepts have a field of legitimate and literal applicability wider than the confines of human society. While the original use of such terms involves naming human affairs, the sociobiological implication is that the origins of the conditions named by the words are older than the act of naming. This is the fear at the root of attacks on the naming of animal relations with social-category terms: that it transgresses the boundary between nature and culture not anthropomorphically, by giving animals a human mind, but zoomorphically, by indirectly disclosing the animal face of human society.

Applying a common language of society to humans and animals may be likened to a medium that is a window on one side and a mirror on the other. It is composed of an open-ended set of terms that allow a view into animal society such that human affairs reflect it. Concepts such as "desertion," "coyness," "altruism," and "selfishness," among many others, are naturalized by demonstrating their broad applicability. Sociobiology achieves this by invoking, either tacitly or overtly, what we already know, or at least what we think we know, about these concepts: not only their extant mundane meanings, but also how deeply anchored are the actions, attitudes, or sentiments that they crystallize. Common sense is not only the knowledge domain from which concepts such as these are borrowed, but also, according to sociobiological reasoning, the linguistic domain that echoes, incompletely and without reflexive awareness, an evolutionary heritage. The sociobiological respecification of social-category concepts as natural-kind terms can thus implicitly claim to complete and reflexivize the knowledge already embedded in common sense by revealing its evolutionary roots. Sociobiology gets a tremendous boost through these conceptual maneuvers, for not only does it make itself an ally of widely shared intuitions, it places itself as a knowledge domain at the very foundations of commonsense knowledge.

A standard reception of Wilson's 1975 work was to praise the first twenty-six chapters as a brilliant contribution to knowledge about animals, while rejecting the twenty-seventh, about *Homo sapiens,* as simpleminded, or outrageous, or politically offensive—in any case, as crossing a line that should not be crossed (see, e.g. Gould 1977). What I have argued, however, with respect to the use of social concepts is that in their respecification as natural kinds, the twenty-seventh chapter of Wilson's work is already largely contained in the first twenty-six. The sociobiological use of social-category concepts thus not only is a conceptual matrix for knowledge about animals, but profoundly affects the understanding of human affairs, tilling the soil for sociobiology to be transplanted into the human world.

Conclusion

In the investigation of sociobiological reasoning about animals, I have focused on the economic and social-category idioms. What makes the work of language in sociobiology especially consequential, and controversial, is that the idioms of representation chosen are extremely potent in their ramifications. With respect to the economic idiom, I have focused on the effects of the semantic heterozygosity created by the maintenance and transgression of a boundary between technical and ordinary language. This semantic mobility confers a great deal of argumentative force to sociobiology, making it both authoritative and evocative, or appealing in a way that is simultaneously cerebral and visceral. So while an economic idea such as "parental investment" may be given a special definition, its meaning does not remain confined to the technical level, but emerges more like a field blending the conceptual energies of technical definition and ordinary connotation. The notion of "parental investment," regardless of its genetic level of application, cannot be deployed without conceptually cutting across the pathway of the selfless affection that is supposed to mark parents' regard for their offspring. With respect to social-category concepts, I have argued that sociobiology transforms them into natural-kind concepts by showing their legitimate applicability in animal life, which in turn reflects back on how human affairs zoomorphize social relations. The application of these concepts thereby becomes a formidable vehicle for uniting the animal and human realms. The economic and social-category mediums of sociobiology jolt the reader in the way they transgress boundaries—of technical-ordinary semantics and human-animal worlds. The jolting effects of sociobiological language hook the imagination; it is no wonder that people respond so intensely to sociobiology, endorsing it or rejecting it with passion.

Sociobiology inherited from ethology, and from behavioral science more generally, the cautious ways of the skeptical stance. The inner life of animals is deemed unavailable to scientific scrutiny, and therefore inquiry should remain firmly rooted in the realm of what is observable in a way that can be measured. Sociobiology continues to espouse this injunction, and the economic idiom, methodological prescriptions, and frequency-laden descriptive style are outfitted to render intentionality and an everyday lifeworld pleonastic. In this way, sociobiology is directly continuous with ethology, which, as I argued in the previous chapter, elided mentality via generic description and a technical-causal framework.

In the analysis of the language of classical ethology, I argued that a mechanomorphic imagery of animals is supervenient to the depiction of their behavior as generated by an interface of mechanisms and stimuli beyond their pale of understanding and control. On one level, sociobiology follows an analogous pattern of representation. Animals emerge as pawns of genes that are pictured as having a nondeliberate agenda of their own—namely, to make copies of themselves. The realm of genes defines the hidden, core reality of life, while appearances can be illusory. Thus for example, Robert Trivers quips that "models that attempt to explain altruistic behavior in terms of natural selection are models designed to take the altruism out of altruism," for behavioral altruism is but veiled genetic selfishness (1978a: 187). "Caring for our own children or for others with whom we share genes," claims Barash, "is just a special case of those genes selfishly promoting themselves by watching out for others in whom they also reside" (1979: 133). Genes are paramount, and life is their game, for only they are immortal, while the individual organism is merely a chimera of their unique constellations. With respect to behavioral patterns and life histories, animals are "trapped by the exigencies of natural selection," as Hrdy puts it (1981); they are unwittingly subject to the whisperings of their genes, in Barash's words (1979). The elimination of meaning and authorship follows according to the same logic explicated in connection to ethological language. The calculus of genes is operative at a level entirely extrinsic to animals' phenomenal world: animals are subject to the impact of forces that are outside their epistemic boundaries and practical jurisdiction, coming across as marionettes executing the agenda of a genetic inheritance that they can neither know nor control. As in the case of ethology, the effect of this picture is to efface inner life or render it redundant. The existence of mind is silently pushed aside, rather than denied, by the operation of an economically described genetic infrastructure selected for in the course of evolution for its effects of maximizing fitness.[13]

While sociobiology and ethology have in common the application of a technical language to animals and its corollary effacement of inner life, with sociobiology the ardent adherence to a skeptical standpoint has been losing its tenacity. Thinking about the question of animal mind has begun to change radically; in certain ways sociobiology is caught up in these changes, and in other ways it is one of their central instigators. Within behavioral science, two (interconnected) events have begun to erode the stronghold of skepticism about animal mind: one is the establishment of the field of cognitive ethology—that is, the study of animal cognition and/or subjective mental experience—and the other is the enormous expansion of knowledge about primates, which has left little room for doubting the sophistication of their cognitive capacities and the richness of their conscious lives. If skepticism about animal mind has hinged on a secure, opaque barrier between human and animal worlds—such that no mirroring was officially permissible—then cognitive ethology and primate studies might be characterized as knocking down that barrier from the side of animal life. On the other hand, sociobiology might be said to be knocking down that barrier from the human side in applying evolutionary reasoning about animal social behavior to human affairs. The sociobiological predilection to encompass human and animal social behavior with a single biological-evolutionary framework is reflected not only in the direct application of sociobiological reasoning to human society, but also in the application of the language of human society to animal life. The move to unify the animal and human realms is an affirmation of the Darwinian idea of continuity, which extends, if only indirectly, to mental life. If the present time is marked by the dawning intent to bring down the human-animal barrier, or at least to make it more diaphanous and yielding, then sociobiology is not only squarely within, but at the very frontier of, our times.

5 Words as Icons
Comparative Images of Courtship

CENTRAL TO the question of animal mind, and the perplexities it presents to behavioral investigators, is that mental phenomena are not a homogeneous ensemble of "objects" united by a common essence. As the philosopher Stanley Cavell aptly puts it, "We don't know whether the mind is best represented by the phenomenon of pain, or by that of envy, or by working on a jigsaw puzzle, or by a ringing in the ears" (1976: 265). With respect to both their detection and ascription, mental phenomena tend to be heterogeneous and complex, and thus they can be neither off-handedly denied nor simply attributed to animals; their credible ascription or, obversely, their justified deletion requires solid grounds. Conceptual environments that support or block the witnessability of animal mind must be elaborated, and this is achieved in large measure through marshaling the resources of language: technical and ordinary vocabulary, conceptual inventory, verb usage, sentence construction, idiom implementation, argumentative style—all are brought into play.

The examination of Darwin's works, the naturalist genre, classical ethology, and sociobiology reveals that writings from various traditions and authors diverge markedly in their forms and their effects, entailing incongruous imagery of animal life and, often, conflicting forms of reasoning about the causation of behavior. They cultivate alternative conceptions of what it is like to be an animal and enclose different perceptual possibilities for the reader's imaginative participation. My interest has been to see how markedly different portrayals of animal life are created and to explore their divergent repercussions especially in connection to the theme of animal mind. In the discussion of Darwin and naturalists in the first two chapters, I examined features and methods of inscription that present animals as acting subjects, that is, as experiencing the world and authoring their actions. With the investigation of technical idioms, I explored the emergence of animals as natural objects—animated vessels compelled to emit behaviors via the triggering of mechanisms or the whispering of genes. In looking at ethology and sociobiology, however, I also emphasized the difference of effects on the portrayal of animals between constructing a technical language of *inner releasing mechanisms, stimuli,* and *fixed action patterns* and technically respecifying an already extant vocabulary of economic and social-category terms.

In this chapter I compare alternative portrayals of animal courtship to underline the theme that similar behaviors appear worlds apart within different interpretive frameworks. Images of subjectivity and objectification are intensely perspicuous in representations of courtship because courtship involves the design and presentation of gestures. Gestures, perhaps more so than any other type of action, can be apprehended as subjectively expressive, both loaded with import and intentionally addressed. The view of animals as natural objects also emerges most starkly in the portrayal of courtship displays, for their constitution through the medium of a technical terminology leads to what may be referred to as "the extinction of gesture."

The Courtship of the Male Stickleback Within Different Conceptions of Time

The differential affiliation of alternative uses of language with the representation of animals as subjects or objects reveals that modes of representation are intimately tied to the question of animal mind. This intimate link can be shown more clearly by comparing how identical behaviors are pictured in radically divergent ways through the use of different linguistic maps. Representations of courtship behaviors are unrivaled in this respect, because contrastive examples are so striking. Naturalist depictions of courtship are bursting with feeling and intensity; naturalists witness and render the surface forms of gesture and expression as the very home of inner life. Technical and causal conceptions, on the other hand, have the gestures of courtship arrive from exogenous locations—that is, from mechanisms or preconditions captured through technical constructs—to which only the observer in possession of specialized knowledge is privy. Within technical idioms, courtship activities cease to be sites of desire and intention, for inner life is rendered redundant as an explanatory or descriptive pathway. The surface forms of gesture and expression are lit from without by the neon light of theory, which outshines any glow emanating from within.

The mating behavior of the male stickleback is described by both Charles Darwin and Nikolaas Tinbergen, and it is interesting to compare their descriptions. Darwin conveys the courtship in terms of the male stickleback's ardor:

> Owing to the element that fishes inhabit, little is known about their courtship, and not much about their battles. The male stickleback *(Gasterosteus leiurus)* has been described as "mad with delight" when the female comes out of her hiding place and surveys the nest which he has made for her.

Darwin then proceeds to quote a description from the naturalist Warrington:

> "He darts around her in every direction, then to his accumulated materials for the nest, then back again in an instant; and as she does not advance, he endeavours to push her with his snout, and then tries to pull her by the tail and side-spine to the nest." (1981, 2: 2)

The darting back and forth of the male stickleback from the nest to the female and back again is a sequence of interconnected actions that aim at getting the female to the nest. The linked actions become assembled before the reader's eyes as phenomenally equivalent to how, for example, a dog anticipating a walk bounds from her owner to the door and back again, or how a child tugs the parent's hand and then runs forward, only to return and tug again. This attachment of reiterated actions, with its unstated play upon the reader's memory, allows the perception of expressiveness in the male stickleback: there is urgency and passion in his actions. With the darting back and forth, the pushing and the pulling, Warrington, and Darwin in his wake, find the grounds to speak of the male stickleback as being in a state of "madness from delight."

Tinbergen describes the male stickleback performing the same courtship behaviors in the same circumstances. In contrast to Darwin's account, however, technical terms such as *chain reaction* and *sign stimulus,* as well as idiomatic verbs such as *induce, stimulate,* and *release,* feature prominently in his account:

> One of the most complete analyses of chain reactions . . . has been carried out with the mating behaviour of the three-spined stickleback. Each reaction of either male or female is released by the preceding reaction of the partner. . . . The male's first reaction, the zigzag dance, is dependent on a visual stimulus from the female, in which, the sign stimuli "swollen abdomen" and the special movements play a part. The female reacts to the red

color of the male and to his zigzag dance by swimming right towards him.
This movement induces the male to turn round and to swim rapidly to
the nest. This in turn entices the female to follow him, thereby stimulating
the male to point his head into the entrance. His behaviour now releases the
female's reaction: she enters the nest . . . This again releases the quivering
reaction in the male which induces spawning. The presence of fresh eggs in
the nest makes the male fertilize them. (1989: 47–48)

Tinbergen depicts the events on a theoretical matrix of a series of stimuli
that release the corresponding appropriate reactions. The fishes' consecutive actions are assembled as exemplifying the technical notion of
"chain reaction"—taken from physics—which Tinbergen defines as "a
chain of separate reactions each dependent on a special set of sign stimuli"
(1989: 47).

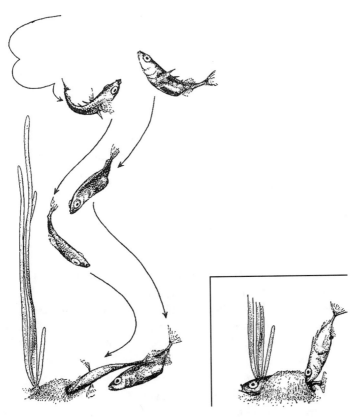

Figure 11   The mating behavior of the three-spined stickleback

A significant difference between the two accounts is that in Darwin the stickleback's actions are sequentially connected, while in Tinbergen the movements are serially placed. The difference between a sequence and a series has been described by the sociologist Harvey Sacks: "We can differentiate serial occurrence from sequential in that 'sequential' means roughly that the parts which are occurring one after the other . . . have some organization between them" (1987: 54). In Tinbergen's portrayal there is no connection between the consecutive responses of each fish; each behavioral pattern is a packaged reaction to an isolated sign stimulus. The sets of chain reactions culminate in the fulfillment of the biological function of reproduction.

Built into these stories of stickleback courtship are different conceptions of the experience of time. Darwin's male stickleback lives in a continuous stream of time—what Schutz, after Henri Bergson, calls the *durée*—in which actions merge seamlessly into one another (Schutz 1962: 85ff.). Within the stream of time no expression is isolated: each moment of action is meaningful in virtue of being part of the larger pattern and of a single feeling. The understanding of the cohesiveness and continuity of time *for* the stickleback allows the stickleback to emerge as an inhabitant of a meaningful world—a world in which fish can be mad with delight. With Tinbergen's sticklebacks each set of the chain reaction (a set being composed of one male behavioral pattern plus one female behavioral pattern) is complete as a stimulus-response unit, but discontinuous from the previous set and the next set. This discontinuity is equivalent to breaking the stream of time of each fish into separate, isolated segments. The sticklebacks, then, figure as inhabitants of a fragmented world, in which their actions cannot coherently focus on and be directed toward the events of courtship. The movements of Tinbergen's fish emerge as rigid, expressionless, and strictly functional. In contrast to Darwin's representation, Tinbergen's sticklebacks are utterly passionless.

The experience of an unbroken time continuum, of the never-ceasing *durée* of living, is incompatible—indeed, irreconcilable—with a stimulus-response conception of the relation between environment and behavior. Within a stimulus-response conception, time is sectioned into a series of moments in which a certain stimulus from the (internal or external) environment of the animal elicits a behavioral response. Every behavioral instance thus occurs within a pocket of time that is discontinuous from the previous pocket of time and the next. The unity of experience of the animal is obliterated, as its behavior is boot-strapped from one moment to the next by the stimuli at hand. The linkage between an animal's contiguous behaviors is undone, and along with this undoing the door is closed to a host of mental predicates, which for their intelligibility depend at least in part on the foundations of the temporal extension of experience residing in the ongoing flow of actions. To give a couple of obvious examples: the attribution of tropes of "intention" rests on the acknowledgment of a subject's ability to orient present activities toward, and in terms of, the future, while the ascription of "memory" depends on the recognition that the past remains seamlessly linked with the present. Given the fragmentation of the temporal continuum effected by the idea of "stimulus-response," it is not surprising that behaviorism never succeeded in getting a tight grip on human life, for its logic is incompatible with the irrefutable human experience of continuity. Behaviorism did get a temporary grip on animal life, however: not only is animal life sufficiently distant to allow for a stimulus-response respecification, but the conceptual road had already been prepared by Descartes with his proposition that animals have an automatonlike existence in a strictly physical world.

The close connection between the representation of time as continuous or fragmented and the affirmation or denial of animal mind speaks to one of the reasons that behaviorist thinking was so successful, for the better part of this century, in convincing behavioral scientists to either distrust or disregard the theme of animal mentality. By fragmenting time into a series of discrete moments, the stimulus-response matrix causally wedded behavior with stimuli, thereby almost unnoticeably obliterating agency in that agency becomes untenable once actions cease to flow from previous actions and dovetail into the next. Only through witnessing actions as sequentially continuous can the observer acknowledge an agent as the cohesive force in command. By disrupting the continuity of temporal experience, behaviorism effaced agency; it thus effectively built the negation of mind into its very logical structure. I argue, therefore, that the objectification of animals through lexical elements—such as technical constructs and particular grammatical patterns—precedes a suspicious or inimical stance toward animal mind. These elements create a conceptual milieu within which the negation of animal mind appears as a reasonable proposition. The conceptual edifice of behaviorism—especially with its effect of fragmenting time—made the nonexistence or superfluity of animal mentality plausible, as the foreclosure of mind was almost a side effect of its concepts and reasoning.

BIRD ANTICS: HUXLEY'S GREBES AND TINBERGEN'S GULLS

Julian Huxley's study of the courtship habits of the great crested grebes (1914) is regarded as a landmark of early field biology (Burkhardt 1992).[1] While it is considered among the early works of classical ethology, and the accounts of the grebes' displays are heavily laced with the theory of sexual selection, the language of Huxley's descriptions is rooted in the naturalist genre. He describes the birds' courtship displays in kinship with human tropes of conversational exchange, ceremonial gravity, and aesthetic expressiveness and appreciation. Indeed, his study might be regarded as transitional between the naturalist tradition and classical ethological studies. For example, in this study Huxley introduced the term *ritualization*, which later became a technical concept of ethology. His use of the term, however, especially in the context of describing the grebes' exchanges, remains semantically identical with the ordinary-language sense of *ritual*, for a sense of gravity, significance, and meticulous attention to form is pervasive in the description of the grebes' antics. Huxley narrates the courtship ceremonies that precede the birth and care of the young grebes. His lyrical descriptions are replete with human analogies, conveying the atmosphere of the birds' engagements. The names given to the ceremonies also impart the expressiveness of the grebes' displays. The form and atmosphere of each ceremony is disclosed consistently through episodic description. By narrating actual episodes of the ceremonies, Huxley engages the reader's imagistic participation, which is strengthened with the provision of beautiful drawings.

Huxley relates the ceremony he names the "weed-trick" and the "Penguin-dance." The male and female grebes come together after being separated for some time and, facing each other, begin their exchange with a "Bout of shaking": in a "peculiar and formal looking manner," they commence by shaking their heads in unison from side to side, alternating between intense and slow movements, "like a man nodding emphatic dissent" (1914: 496).

After the bout of shaking, the grebes keep their ruffs, ears, and heads erect and begin swimming side by side. Suddenly they dive, emerging separately a few seconds later holding weeds in their beaks. Next they begin to

Figure 12 Grebes' bout of shaking

swim toward each other with considerable speed, their heads lowered and necks parallel to the water. Huxley then describes their encounter.

> They did not slacken speed at all, and I wondered what would happen when they met. My wonder was justified: when about a yard apart they both sprang up from the water into an almost erect position. . . . Carrying on with the impetus of their motion, the two birds came actually to touch each other with their breasts. From the common fulcrum thus formed bodies and necks alike sloped slightly back—the birds would have fallen forwards had each not thus supported the other. Only the very tip of the body was in the water. . . . The appearance either bird presented to its mate had changed altogether in an instant of time. Before they had been black and dark mottled brown: they saw each other now all brilliant white, with chestnut and black surrounding the face in a circle.
>
> In this position they stayed for a few seconds rocking gently from side to side upon the point of their breasts; it was an ecstatic motion as if they were swaying to the music of a dance. Then, still rocking and still in contact, they settled very gradually down on the surface of the water. . . . After coming down from their erect attitude they ended the performance by what was simply an ordinary bout of rather excited shaking. (1914: 499–500)

Several features place this description within the naturalist genre. The scene is a unique episode, and its singularity, in combination with the illustrative picture, galvanizes the reader's visual attention. The portrayal of specific individuals performing activities together intimates a lifeworld of shared meaning and temporal continuity. An aesthetic sensibility is suggested in the observation that the birds present to each other an extraordinary view of their physique. The achieved grace of the "Penguin-dance" appresents the grebes as agents who appreciate ceremonial form and physical beauty. The naturalist's earnest involvement can be seen in the

Figure 13 Ceremony of the "weed-tick" and the "Penguin-dance"

way the author places himself in the writing ("my wonder was justified") as well as in the literary depiction of the grebes with a simile ("rocking gently from side to side as if to the music of a dance").

The characterization of the birds as "rocking gently" in an "ecstatic motion, as if they were swaying to the music of a dance" could be evaluated simply as a matter of poetic license on the author's part, rather than an attempt at realistic depiction. And yet regardless of whether such an expression is submitted as literary device, objective observation, or personal confession, it invokes an atmosphere of tenderness and sensuality in the birds' contact. This, in turn, communicates the condition of full engagement of the grebes with each other. The atmosphere of intimate engagement stems not only from the lyricism of description, but also from the active connectedness between the grebes' displays and the continuity between the different stages of their concerted actions, for the ceremony is pictured as composed of an opening, a middle section (with the climax of the Penguin-dance), and a closing.

The sense of full engagement pervades Huxley's monograph. A natural corollary to this ambiance is the incorporation of mental language. Regarding the "ceremony of discovery," for example, Huxley writes that it is performed when the grebes have been separated for a long time and "they *wish* to rejoin each other" (1914: 512, emphasis added). He relates one particular episode of this ceremony when the swimming female looks from side to side, giving a short barking call (1914: 497). Her mate "appears to notice her," for he stretches out his neck and dives. The hen then goes into what Huxley calls the "Cat-attitude."

> At this [the dive] she changed her whole demeanor. Up went her wings: back between them, with erected ruff and ears, went her head. . . . The wings were brought up, half spread on either side of the body, with their anterior border pointing downwards. . . .
> All this took but an instant; directly the cock had dived she was in this attitude. As she *waited* for his re-appearance she turned *eagerly* from side to side, swinging nearly to the right-about and back again as if *not to miss him*. (1914: 497–98, emphasis added)

All elements of the description contribute to presenting the grebes' actions as *gestures* that are addressed and received. Each grebe's action is witnessed by its mate; every action is performed with due respect to being witnessed. Like an invisible ether, a state of heightened alertness envelops the pair. The birds are present to each other as subjects because they interact in a common field of meanings, rather than merely in a shared physical space. Under the auspices of this picture, the use of mental language is not only permissible, it is *expedient*. As the female grebe's Cat-attitude is a gesture incited by her mate's dive, and designed for him to see when he reemerges, she can be apprehended as "waiting for him eagerly," manifesting the wish "not to miss him" in her attempts to anticipate where he will surface. Her entire bearing is shot through with what we call intention and desire.

The birds' actions are gestures offered to each other, and even beyond this, Huxley portrays their encounters as almost choreographed. The aesthetic appreciation of the extraordinary transforms the grebes' courtship into an exquisite performance. Commenting on the female grebe in Cat-

Figure 14   Female grebe's "Cat-attitude"

attitude, Huxley writes that "the bird's whole appearance was wonderfully striking, and as unlike as possible to that of its everyday self" (1914: 498). During the courtship season, the birds exit ordinary reality to live and act within an aesthetic, theatrical realm. Huxley also sees an aesthetic sensibility in the subsequent response of the male grebe to the female's Cat-attitude, which he calls the "Ghost-dive." As the female waits with eager movements in the Cat-attitude, the male makes an unhurried reappearance in a most extraordinary pose.

> Eventually he came up, three or four feet on the far side, and facing away from her in the most amazing attitude. I could scarcely believe my eyes. He seemed to grow out of the water. First his head, the ruff nearly circular, the beak pointing down along the neck in a stiff and peculiar manner; then the neck quite straight and vertical; then the body, straight and vertical too; until finally the whole bird, save for a few inches, was standing erect in the water, and reminding me of nothing so much as the hypnotized phantom of a rather slender Penguin.
>
> As I say, it grew out of the water, and as it grew it gradually revolved on its long axis until at its fullest height it came to face the hen. Though all this was done with an unhurried and uniform motion, yet of course it took very little time. Then from this stiff, erect position he sank slowly on to the surface; the hen meanwhile put down her wings and raised her neck; and the pair settled down to a bout of the head-shaking. (1914: 498)

Figure 15　Male grebe's "Ghost-dive"

The male grebe's remarkable ascent, in its "unhurried and uniform" execution, is captured as honoring the precision of proper form. The deliberate quality of the Ghost-dive is affirmed with the closure of his display, where the male revolves around the axis of his elongated body so as to face the female. This simple turning movement, while preserving the form, comes through as doubly intentional, for "facing" is an alignment that encloses both seeing and being seen.

The almost contrived style of these performances contributes a sense of ceremonial gravity. Where classical ethologists would later see "fixed action patterns" in the recurrence, rigidity, and invariance of certain behaviors—displays, in particular—Huxley grasps the repetition of expressive postures as signifying their ceremonial quality. He describes the bout of shaking, for instance, as "peculiar and formal looking" (1914: 496). Contrary to seeing the gestures' stiltedness as a symptom of their fixed or compulsory character, in their rigidity Huxley intuits the feeling of erotic rigor mortis. He writes that "before sinking down into the passive pairing attitude . . . the birds usually assume a curious fixed and rigid pose"; and, quoting the naturalist Edmund Selous, he continues, "there was no mistaking the entirely sexual character of this strange performance, the peculiar fixed rigidity full of import and expression" (1914: 502).

Huxley understands the grebes' exchange of gestures as a form of language. "All birds express their feelings partly by voice and very largely by motions of neck, wings, and tail; and the expression can be, and is, employed as a form of language" (1914: 516). He implicitly depicts their communication in affinity with human conversation. His representation of the grebes' courtship calls upon our tacit knowledge of the design of conversation in order to convey both how the grebes communicate and the meaning of their communication. To elaborate on this point, the sequencing of the different postures of the ceremony of the Cat-attitude and the Ghost-dive is concertedly achieved by the birds. The total composition of this ceremony is portrayed as a set of three paired actions: (1) the female calling, the male diving; (2) the female in Cat-attitude, the male in the Penguin-pose; and (3) the mutual bout of shaking at the close. By emphasizing the synchronization of the male and female grebes' actions, the smooth transition from one assumed pair of actions to the next pair, a picture is imparted of the grebes fully intending their gestures for each other and orchestrating their movements to comply with the particular sequencing of paired forms at each stage of the ceremony. The simultaneity of intentional addressing and compliance to the appropriate template suggests kinship with what conversation analysts call the "recipient design" of conversation.[2] The birds are depicted as addressing their postures to each other with the kind of orientation and attention to turn-taking manifest in human conversation. It is noteworthy how entirely at odds this image is with a stimulus-response explanation of the displays, or with their being regarded as a "chain reaction," to use Tinbergen's expression.

Another sense in which the birds possess a form of language for Huxley is in the symbolic use of their gestures. In the mating ceremony of the grebes, which Huxley calls the "passive and active pairing attitudes" (1914: 502), one bird appears to be floating on the water, with body slightly humped and neck extended. The bird's mate swims alongside, examining the body, and then climbs on the passive bird with its body upright and leaning forward. Almost immediately the active bird slips back into the water, the passive bird jumps up, and the two swim together for a while. This is how the grebes mate, and in order for mating to occur successfully the passive grebe must be lying on a half-built nest (a "mating platform") that barely breaks the surface of the water. However, at certain times either the male or the female may assume the "passive attitude" on open water. In this case, the posture is no longer functional, since mating cannot occur without a supporting platform. On Huxley's understanding, the posture is *symbolic*—"it looks as if it were a signal to the first bird that the second was ready and willing to proceed in the matter" (1914: 504). Huxley maintains that "the [passive] attitude now being sometimes a mere symbol can be, and is, employed by either the active or the passive bird. In fact when one bird thus employs it symbolically, the other usually responds by immediately repeating its symbolic use" (1914: 507).

There are, then, two aspects to the birds' communication as language. First, there is the mutual connection of the birds' paired gestures. Emphasis on the communicative link that the birds establish and maintain impli-

Figure 16   Grebes' passive mating attitude

cates that the gestures are meaningful from the grebes' point of view. Second, as the birds are cognizant of the meaning of their gestures, they sometimes deploy these as signs or symbols. On both counts, the gestures are not simply *of use* to the grebes, but *used by* them.

Huxley interprets the grebes' strange duets in terms of the transformation from "functional behavior" to "ritual action." In the ceremony of the weed-trick and the Penguin-dance, where the birds present the weeds to each other, Huxley remarks that "there is no reason for supposing even this elaborate ceremony to have any direct relation whatever with coition. It is an expression of excitement and enjoyment, seemingly as thrilling to the birds as it is to the watcher, but, like all the other courtship-actions, self-exhausting" (1914: 513–14). The regard for the birds' communication as "all in all mutual and self-exhausting" (1914: 514) is allied with the view of animals acting for the sake of pleasure, discussed in Darwin's portrayals, and contrasts with an overemphasis on utilitarian function. For Huxley, the grebes' duets are ends in themselves, having no direct use-value other than affording pleasure and excitement. So in another instance, regarding a recently paired couple of blue tits, Huxley writes that "although feeding [they] were perpetually calling to each other and at frequent intervals coming close up side by side; it was perfectly obvious that they simply took pleasure in each other's presence, like the engaged couple that they were" (1914: 517).

Huxley's lyrical language creates an atmosphere of romance that colors the grebes' antics and forms an empathic connection between the birds and their human observers. Their courtship, notes Huxley, appears "as thrilling to the birds as it is to the watcher." He ropes together human and grebe experience, writing that "by comparing the actions of the birds with our own in circumstances as similar as possible, we can deduce the bird's emotions with much more probability of accuracy than we can have about their nervous processes: we can interpret the facts psychologically better than we can physiologically" (1914: 510). The kinship between birds and humans is further strengthened, for the courtship rituals are like conversation in the tight, turn-by-turn connection of gestures, and they are like language in the occasional symbolic use of gestures. The readers' eyes are guided to see the rigidity of the grebes' movements express ceremonial form and sexual tension. The birds' intimate engagement is charged with a feeling of active surrender. And the courtship duets are performed as ends in themselves, being portrayed as celebrations of beauty and love.

In contrast to Huxley's assessment that "we can interpret the facts psychologically better than we can physiologically," in his study of gull communication Tinbergen is interested in a physiological explanation of gull displays. He interprets the actions of the gulls as outcomes of the interface between physiological states and impinging external stimuli. The unintended consequence of this interpretive register is that even as the gulls are interacting they appear disengaged. The paradox of disengaged interaction is an effect of what I call the "extinction of gesture." Gesture is extinguished when its origin is technically specified and thereby extrinsic to the actor's phenomenal world. As known almost by the definition of the word *gesture*, but, more important, from communicative experience, a gesture is immanently meaningful and intentional, designed and delivered by a subject. Therefore, if a "gesture" is constituted as originating in physiological mechanisms, or genetic programs, or even brain chemistry, it ceases to be a gesture, for it is no longer designed or delivered by anyone. To the mind's eye a gesture conceptualized in this way looks empty.

Nikolaas Tinbergen's depiction of gulls illustrates how displays can be portrayed in a manner that extinguishes their apperception as gestures. The invocation of human experience and use of lyrical language are all but completely absent in Tinbergen's work on gulls. Like Huxley, he names the gulls' displays, but the names are not evocative, like Huxley's "Phantom-penguin," "Cat-attitude," or "Ghost-dive." Tinbergen's names are functional and descriptively straightforward, as for example, "Forward," "Upright," "Choking," and the like (see 1972b: 35–44). The descriptions of the gulls' postures bear the stamp of the perspective of atomism, which seeks to understand the whole in terms of the assemblage of its component parts. Tinbergen's analyses work on the assumption that behavioral sequences can be broken down into elementary, physical units. For Tinbergen, the behavioral units are the displays, which are regarded as highly invariant and fixed. The gulls' displays are conceptualized as context-independent, packaged forms. Each display can be treated as an isolated unit in that (1) it can be described with minimal reference to the particular communicative setting, or specific circumstances, in which it occurs, and (2) it can be assigned a fixed interpretation, regardless of concrete episodes, or types of contexts, of its occasion.

In Huxley's study, because of the grebes' active synchronicity, the unit of analysis is the interacting pair. With Tinbergen the analytical unit is not the courting pair (nor the rival gulls in the case of agonistic displays) but instead the display as such. The display qua analytic unit is all the more abstract as it is rendered largely through generic depiction rather than through the verisimilitude of embodied instantiations. Tinbergen often casts the interaction between the birds in physical, theory-laden terms.

> A Grass-Pulling Herring Gull means business; it is intensely aroused, though at the same time inhibited by fear; if he attacks, he will do so more vigorously than after merely having adopted the Aggressive Upright; and again this is "understood" by its opponent. Thus we see that both partners in the encounter are nicely adapted to the interindividual function of spacing-out; the posturing bird has conspicuous, unambiguous effectors (the displays) and the other bird has the specific sensitivity, the "receptory correlate" which gives the postures their usual effects. (1972b: 62–63)

The interaction is first presented via the terms *fear* and *attack,* which make its antagonistic character clear. These terms of understanding are subsequently displaced by recasting the interaction at the level of physical machinery, with the "effectors" working as stimuli on the "receptory correlate"—in other words, on the IRM previously discussed (Chapter 3). The technical, quasi-mechanical terminology of effectors and receptors locates the causation of the birds' displays and responses in the body's physical equipment. The mental connotations of the concepts "fear" and "attack" are further suspended by the placement of quotation marks about the word *understood.*

As discussed in Chapter 3, the pattern here is to use and then immediately negate terms such as *fear* and *attack.* Such terms are absolutely required in behavioral accounts, for they enable the reader to attribute meaning to the actions depicted. Mental concepts can never be eradicated from the description and explanation of behavior, they can only be "translated": qualified with caveats, suspended with quotation marks, distrusted in begrudging use, or used and then displaced by technical artillery.[3] In the above example, the concepts "fear" and "attack" are swiftly resorbed by a technical idiom of effectors and receptors. In that translation, their mental implications, the field of subjective experience they connote, becomes submerged. Agency is effaced by transferring the interaction of animals onto the interface of technically identified and causally operative physical factors. Furthermore, reference to the displays' adaptive function of "spacing-out" identifies another causal nexus at an evolutionary level. This temporal dislocation of function from the here and now to the remote past underlines the loss of agency. With proximate (physiological) and ultimate (evolutionary) causes of behavioral patterns in place, there is neither logical space nor felt need to reference intention, understanding, or desire within the animals' world. The redundancy of aware presence is poignantly accentuated by scare-quoting the concept of "understanding." The work of the quotation marks is to deny, or express grave misgivings, that the gulls grasp the meaning of their displays or of the events that are transpiring. For Tinbergen, then, each display has a given and fairly invariant interpretation, even as it is questionable whether it has meaning from the gull's point of view.

Further, his causal analysis of the displays resolutely removes their meaning from the animals' purview. According to Tinbergen, displays originate in "the simultaneous arousal of two or more tendencies" within the gull (1972: 56). "Conflict" within the gull follows from the clash between discrepant, physiologically defined tendencies. Tinbergen interprets the rigid, contrived appearance of displays with the following explanation of their origin: in another gull's presence a gull may, at the same time, be driven to attack and to flee. The conflict of instincts takes place at a physical level, with the simultaneous activation of different "action-specific energies" within the bird resulting in the release of conflicting behaviors. The outcome is the display: a droll postural configuration or potpourri of derived movements. The displays are thereby further analyzed into their component parts, as mosaics of different tendencies. For example, the "Aggressive Upright" is, in origin, a mosaic of components of attack and escape behaviors (1972: 71). The derived movements "have undergone ritualisation . . . define[d] as adaptive evolutionary change in the direction of increased efficiency as a signal" (ibid.).

Tinbergen applies this theoretical model to the courtship displays of the gulls. In the case of the black-headed gull, for example, the exchange begins at the nesting site the male has chosen with the male's agonistic display of the "Oblique-cum-Long" posture. An unmated female alights near him. Both birds then adopt the "Forward," which, being a posture observed in boundary fights, is also agonistic, according to Tinbergen; there is a slight modification of the posture, however, in that the male and female point their bills a little more upward than in hostile encounters and there is a tendency for the pair to stand parallel. After a few seconds of this posture both birds come into the "Upright" posture, which is also agonistic, but with their faces turned away from each other. According to Tinbergen, they thus moderate the hostility of the Upright with a posture of appeasement. The explanation that Tinbergen provides for this series

Figure 17 Displays of the black-headed gull

of displays is that the birds find themselves in the thrall of three conflicting impulses—to attack, to escape, and to remain near each other. The postures of the gulls are the outcome of opposing impulses within each gull— an interpretation of the display forms on a model of internal-physiological causation.

The connectedness of the displays as addressed or mutually orchestrated gestures is deemphasized, if not severed. The severance is a result of the unit of analysis being the isolated display rather than the interacting couple. On Tinbergen's view, the meaning of each display is fixed. For example, the "Oblique-cum-Long" and the "Upright" are agonistic, while "Turning Away" is a display of appeasement; this is what they signify regardless of the context of their use. For Tinbergen, the meaning of a display is not achieved in use, in accordance to whom it is addressed or for what purposes it is intended, but has been formed and fixed in the course of evolution. The meaning of the isolated display is stable and context-independent. The melange that happens in courtship displays does not yield, as a whole, an expressive gesture, but reflects an underlying conflict between opposing drives (very often, for example, the simultaneously "released" impulses to escape and to attack). The function of displays is that they become effective as "signals." However, there is no communicative link between the birds on this analysis.

So, for example, the "Forward" posture of the male and female while standing in parallel is not an expressive mutual act of courtship. The displays are decomposed into their parts—"Forward" meaning aggression, with standing parallel (or looking away) signifying appeasement. The tension is not between the gulls, but between the conflicting impulses—conceived as physiological occurrences, not experiences. The contrast to Huxley's grebes is vivid, for with Tinbergen's gulls no feeling links the birds, no atmosphere envelops them. The gulls are not presenting their displays; rather, they appear as pawns in the irresistible grip of occurrences they can neither control nor comprehend. Again this contrasts with Huxley's grebes, which use the mating posture in a different context (other than the purely functional one of coition) in order to express their desire or, as Huxley unforgettably puts it, in order to "show their thoughts."

With the grebes Huxley conveyed a picture of each bird intentionally addressing its mate; a feeling of anticipation, excitement, and eroticism; a capacity of the grebes to use their gestures symbolically; and an ambiance of gravity, with the reciprocating gestures almost choreographed. With Tinbergen's gulls all these features are absent, because the element on which they turn, the communicative link, is severed. Tinbergen does not see the gulls as addressing each other. He instead apprehends each separate gull as going through an involuntary series of motions that are the fortuitous outcome of an inner conflict of physiologically defined tendencies. Of course, it is not Tinbergen's intention to sever the communicative link between the gulls, but rather to explain communication in physiological terms. The paradoxical effect, however, is that this form of explanation annihilates the exchange as communication by extinguishing the intimation of the birds' displays as gestures. The connection to the theme of animal mind is once again evident here. The very logic of explaining action as the outcome of extrinsic causation renders mind superfluous. If there were a mind there—that is, awareness, understanding, alertness, will, desire, or whatever—it would be utterly adventitious, something for which there are no identifiable pathways to track anything in the world. Having become redundant in this way, mind disappears from the described scenery. A technical-causal account of action can thus erase mentality without ever denying its existence.

At the turn of the century the biologist Jakob von Uexküll wrote that "when a dog runs, the animal moves its legs; when a sea urchin runs, the legs move the animal" (1957: 32). The difference that exists, according to von Uexküll, between the dog and the sea urchin is a useful gloss for describing the difference between Huxley's and Tinbergen's depictions of the birds' courtship. While Huxley's grebes *perform* their courtship rituals, the sequence of mating displays is something that *happens to* Tinbergen's gulls. Tinbergen's depiction of the exchanges between male and female gulls shares few of the apparently anthropomorphic qualities of Huxley's portrayals. Yet, as I have endeavored to show in my analyses, relinquishing an anthropomorphic idiom is no guarantee of achieving greater objectivity. Any linguistic avenue chosen has a perceptual and cognitive aftermath that is never impartial with respect to animal mentality. Whether poetic or pedantic, ordinary or technical, prolix or dry, language use partakes in advancing a perspective on the range and limits of awareness in the animal world. Unavoidable commitments find their way into the textual portraiture of animals even in the face of authors' peerless resolution to be neutral or agnostic about mentality. The question of mind is *always* relevant, and the words chosen are always answering that question—one way or the other. In behavioral studies there is no detour from the inner life of animals, no avoidance tactic that can succeed, perhaps because, like the inner life of human beings, there is very little that is "inner" about it.[4] Action either has a face or it does not—and its face is what we call mind.

TINBERGEN'S DISENGAGED BUTTERFLIES
AND FABRE'S OGLING SCORPIONS

The effect of the extinction of gesture consequent upon a technical-causal portrayal of animal communication in general, and courtship in particular, is explored more fully in the examination of Tinbergen's courtship of the Grayling butterfly (*Eumenis semele*). His study of the butterflies' courtship exemplifies many of the features of the ethological constitution of animals as objects. Tinbergen introduces his paper on the Grayling by setting forth his theoretical concerns:

> From the start, we directed our attention toward detailed analysis of an "innate releasing mechanism." An excellent possibility for this was provided by the most conspicuous response of the Grayling: when the male is ready to copulate he flies upwards towards a female passing overhead. It was evident from the beginning of the study that males fly not only towards females but also towards many other animals and objects, and from this it was deduced that the "approach flight response" requires, and must be controlled by, a very unselective stimulus pattern. The experimental study of this "releasing stimulus situation" . . . seemed worth pursuing. (1972a: 197)

From the outset, the theoretical interest guiding the study is paramount. The importance of the theoretical focus is seen in the identification of the object of study as the "innate releasing mechanism," rather than the animal's life and behavior. The stated goal is the analysis of the mechanism, and the observation of the animals becomes the vehicle for inferring the underlying mechanism. The introduction of the study as one of the "releasing stimulus situation" sets the framework and tone for the analyses of behavior that follow, especially of the male's "approach flight response." This response is defined as the outcome of an "innate releasing mechanism" triggered by a "releasing stimulus pattern." The male butterfly's flying toward many animals and objects, in addition to female butterflies, is understood in terms of his response "requiring and being controlled by a very unselective stimulus pattern." The reader is clearly forewarned that the technically outfitted account of the male Grayling's impetuous flights will be exempted from a language of action and desire.

Following the introduction of the study's theoretical motives, Tinbergen provides certain background facts about this species of butterfly, such as its physical appearance and geographical-ecological distribution. He also describes its basic behavior patterns in general terms under separate headings, titled "Feeding," "Defense Reaction," "Basking," "Courtship," "Antenna Spinning," and "Oviposition." His presentation of the behavior patterns is largely through generic description. For instance, in the section on feeding, Tinbergen writes:

> *Eumenis semele* detects the trees by smell. One can often observe flying animals become suddenly alerted when they pass a sap tree on the lee side; when flying past, they are often caught in the scent clouds wafted away from the tree by the wind. Here they change their behaviour abruptly, they brake, and fly slowly upwind, oscillating in a horizontal plane, until they reach the source of the scent.
>
> The animals also learn to orient visually towards a tree where they have previously fed. One can detect such "regular customers" since they fly directly towards the tree from any direction. (1972a: 202–3)

Tinbergen uses action verbs that present the butterflies as actors with particular orientations toward objects in their environment: they detect and become alerted to sap trees, they brake and then fly until they reach the scent. The purposeful and subjective orientation that action verbs can evoke, however, is offset by the mode of generic description, which presents the typical behavior of *Eumenis semele*—that is, of any member of the species, not of a specific individual butterfly.

In contrast to the focus of episodic description on the concretely real—effected through the depiction of the singular case, as will be seen again shortly in Fabre's courting scorpions—animals of generic description have an abstract and anonymous character. And as Alfred Schutz puts it (in connection always to human action), "an increase in anonymity involves a decrease in fullness of content" (1962: 18). In presenting the anonymous and typical case, generic description of behavior tends to be laconic and thin in content. At the same time, because such descriptions do not mark themselves as abstract constructs, they implicitly communicate the message that *this* is the form the behavior takes whenever encountered. With generic description the typified form thus becomes real, suggesting precisely what episodic description by its very nature repudiates, namely, uniformity and homogeneity of behavior patterns.

The use of vernacular action verbs in Tinbergen's passage on feeding may also intimate a phenomenal world, that is, the existence of a world as it appears to, and is experienced by, a butterfly interested in food. This intimation is partially deflected through the presentation of the butterflies' perceptual orientation in passive and abstract terms—"they are caught in the scent clouds" and they "orient visually." The avoidance of active terms in rendering perception averts the suggestion of the world as a place of experience.

The picture of perceptual passivity is further buttressed by the interpretation of certain experiments designed to isolate the features that attract butterflies to flowers. Tinbergen carried out these particular experiments by placing butterflies temporarily in cages. Actual flowers were replaced with compatibly sized pieces of paper, some colored and some gray. The substitution of pieces of paper for flowers enabled the ethologist to disjoin the stimuli of scent and color, naturally entangled in flowers. (This is the device of ethological experimentation of modeling the object and tinkering with its various features so as to isolate the "sign stimulus," discussed in Chapter 3.) The results of this experiment were so tidy that they corroborate ethological reasoning. The papers alone, whether colorful or gray, did not attract the butterflies. In the absence of scent the butterflies were indifferent to the paper flowers. The moment, however, that scent was experimentally released (using "a variety of flower oils"), "the animals reacted immediately, but by flying toward the colored papers" (1972a: 204). Disentangling the stimuli of scent and color revealed, for Tinbergen, that the butterfly's orientation to flowers is "activated by scent" and "directed by color." The behavior is thus conceived as the synthetic product of two stimuli, one "activating" and the other "directing." Neither of these mechanically conceptualized aspects is effective alone, but together they form the necessary and sufficient combination that causes the butterfly's flight to the flower. With the decomposition of the butterfly's flight to the flower into "activating" and "directing" facets, the allure of flowers for butterflies is transfigured into a mechanomorphic image.

The interest in the component parts of behaviors, in terms of activating (releasing) and directing (guiding) stimuli, is consilient with the overall atomistic approach of ethology, that is, its predilection for breaking down behaviors into fundamental units. In this vein, behaviors are generally not described as they occur in natural sequence on some particular occasion. Rather, they are named and described separately, usually with the method of generic description. This approach, then, extracts abstract units from the stream of activity that, at any *specific* time, encompasses a butterfly's behaviors in singular and variable order, with local modulations of circumstance, and manifesting the idiosyncratic expressions of the individual animal.

Behaviors are consistently described in terms of the stimuli releasing them. Behavioral patterns are portrayed as packaged possessions that are activated, released, and steered by elements of the environment. In the section on basking, for example, Tinbergen writes:

> The fact that this behavior occurs only in cool weather with sunshine indicates that temperature plays a part in its release. But in its orientation, light may well be important: with thick cloud cover it may happen that a relatively light patch of sky appears quite a distance from the sun, and then the butterflies turn their broad side toward this patch. . . . The possibility of other stimuli, e.g. temperature stimuli, having an orienting effect has not been investigated. (1972a: 209)

According to this representation, it is not the butterfly that orients to the sun, but rather light and temperature that orient the butterfly. The stimuli of light and temperature—with their objective, measurable qualities— release the behavior of basking. Any intimation, therefore, that the behavior may express an experiential perspective is carefully avoided. The idea that basking when the temperature is cool may originate in the butterfly's feeling cold is elided. Corollary to this elision, the butterfly's turning its wings toward the "light patch of sky" is not seen as a performed action; in contrast, for example, to Darwin's representation of the male golden pheasant tilting his wings so as to intercept the path of the female's gaze (discussed shortly), the butterfly does not turn its broad side toward the light in order to receive the fullest impact of the sun's rays. An authored, subjective dimension of the act is carefully evaded, or implicitly evaluated as irrelevant so far as the properly scientific explanation of basking is concerned. And yet evading a subjective viewpoint is not simply a matter of a gratuitous, additional aspect of the behavior being cautiously sidestepped. The inclusion of a subjective orientation would transform the basking into something the butterfly *does* when it is cold and sunny. The task of explanation in terms of causally effective stimuli would then be implicitly thwarted, coming into logical tension with the idea that "the butterfly basks in the sun when [/*because*] the butterfly feels cold." The [/*because*] of the latter statement does not indicate that the behavior is causally determined, but—in affinity with an analogous human action—is akin to the reason the butterfly basks: a reason that is seen to be embodied in the butterfly's action and put into words by the witness.

Darwin's description of the bird courtship illustrates the alternative rendition of actions as performed rather than caused. He notes that, in general, "ornaments of all kinds, whether permanently or temporarily gained, are sedulously displayed by the males, and apparently serve to excite, or attract, or charm the females" (1981, 2: 86). More specifically, Darwin portrays the courtship displays of the male golden pheasant and Polypectron as gestures that are fully delivered with the intent to be received:

> The gold-pheasant *(Thaumalea picta)* during his courtship not only expands and raises his splendid frill, but turns it, as I myself have seen, obliquely towards the female on whichever side she may be standing, obviously in order that a large surface may be displayed before her. Mr. Bartlett has observed a male Polypectron in the act of courtship, and has shewn me a specimen stuffed in the attitude then assumed. The tail and wing-feathers of this bird are ornamented with beautiful ocelli, like those on the peacock's train. Now when the peacock displays himself, he expands and erects his tail transversely to his body, for he stands in front of the female, and has to shew off, at the same time, his rich blue throat and breast. But the breast of the Polypectron is obscurely coloured, and the ocelli are not confined to the tail-feathers. Consequently the Polypectron does not stand in front of the female; but he erects and expands his tail-feathers a little obliquely, lowering

Figure 18 Ornamental feathers of the male Polypectron

the expanded wing on the same side, and raising that on the opposite side. In this attitude the ocelli over the whole body are exposed before the eyes of the admiring female in one grand bespangled expanse. To whichever side she may turn, the expanded wings and the obliquely-held tail are turned towards her. (1981, 2: 89–91)

Darwin calls attention to how the angle of the postures of different birds is specifically designed to reveal the most beautiful parts of their bodies. The Polypectron's presentation of his wings on an oblique plane not only shows the "bespangled expanse" of their designs, but is appropriately placed with due respect to intercepting the gaze of the admiring female. The image Darwin conjures is infused with self-consciousness, intention, and aesthetic rapture. On his description, the displays emerge as voluntary addresses, for in a field of action where the appreciation of beauty is paramount, gestures are willfully, even ostentatiously, proffered.

Regarding voluntary action, Alan White writes that "to do x voluntarily is to do x with the awareness that one has an alternative course open to one" (1968: 6). In the case of Darwin's golden pheasant and Polypectron, the witnessing of their gestures as voluntary does not entail the positing of such a self-conscious choice between alternative courses of action. Instead, the voluntary nature of the courtship display is a compounded effect of the following elements: (1) seeing the gesture as an active doing ("I am *doing* this for you"); (2) presenting the gesture as bearing conspicuously, on its surface configurations, the mark of intention ("I am doing this *for* you"); and (3) intimating an active reaching out of the gesture as a means of forming a bridge between two subjects ("*I* am doing this for *you*"). The intentionality of the gesture is deciphered in the contrivances of the gesture itself, especially in the care that is taken by the males to position their displays in such a way that their beauty is fully presented and in clear view of the female.

On the other hand, when displays are portrayed as caused by physiological or environmental stimuli (or their combination), they emerge as involuntary. As a consequence, when behavioral patterns are conceptualized as determined and their causes are sought, then an animal's interactional conduct cannot, on pain of irresolvable logical tensions within a text, be pictured in the form of gestures that are performed, addressed, anticipated, or greeted by co-participants. Gestures are thus discursively elided, and their elision is in turn itself effaced as the gestures become respecified as physical movements. The inevitable corollary, therefore, of representing animal displays in a technical idiom is the extinction of gesture. The extinction of gesture is an unavoidable consequence of the logical tension between the gesture as an instigating, meaningful action and its portrayal as a movement that is caused by external stimuli impinging upon internal states. The tension is between the voluntary quality of the gesture—a quality that is logically and perceptually part and parcel of the initiative and intentionality of a gesture—and the involuntary character of behavior represented as an outcome of physical movements or motions that are caused.

The contrast between the depiction of voluntary action and caused response can be seen in yet another aspect of Tinbergen's account of the Grayling butterflies. The sexual flight of the male is recognized in virtue of its directness and speed, yet these features are not overtly portrayed as expressing desire and urgency; while betraying to the observer the sexual nature of the flight, they are not taken as adequate grounds to acknowledge an experiential dimension in the male butterfly's orientation.

> A male moves in an unmistakable manner toward a female flying overhead. The movement of the wings is more hurried, the flight is faster and the trajectory is straighter than in other types of directional flight, as for instance in the approach to a flower. Thus one can recognize the sexual flight by its movements alone. (1972a: 214)

The unmistakable manner of the flight is not regarded as resting on the urgency it might be seen to express, but instead discloses the type of underlying mechanism at work. So after noting that the male flies not only toward the female butterfly but toward other animals, Tinbergen continues:

> Apart from these [other species], the male often responds to falling yellow, green or brown birch leaves, to fluttering leaves on trees, to pine cones lobbed overhead or even to patches of shade that such objects throw on the ground. Sometimes a male will even fly toward its own shadow. From these observations alone, one can infer that the approach flight response must be dependent on a very simple stimulus pattern. (1972a: 215)

The male butterfly's impetuosity only exposes that the "approach flight response" is released by a "very simple stimulus pattern." The wide range of objects that ignite the male's sexual flight is not taken as a symptom of the male's eagerness. Rather, it stands as evidence that the mechanism holding the behavior in check can be easily tripped. Hence Tinbergen's assessment:

> We realised that here was an excellent opportunity to study, in detail, a "releasing response situation." Through a systematic recording of the re-

sponses of males to a variety of dummies differing in one characteristic after another, and comparing those responses to those elicited by an optimal dummy we could hope to characterize accurately the relative stimulating value of each of these characteristics. (1972a: 215)

When Tinbergen turns to the courtship rituals of the butterflies, he relies again on generic description, presenting what is done typically by any male and any female of the species. The atomistic approach of decomposing behaviors into their elementary units is once more evident in the distinction and naming of the components of the courtship. Along with these regular features of ethological thought, the use of the passive voice of verbs also becomes pronounced. The effect of these elements on the reader's reception is that, while the male and female butterflies are interacting, they appear curiously disengaged. The abstract quality of the description results in the behaviors appearing empty. This sense of emptiness is corollary to the "extinction of gesture."

> When a male flies toward a receptive female, she will sooner or later, sometimes immediately, settle on the ground. The male settles near, and usually behind her, and then proceeds by short jerky movements around her until he is facing her. [//] This "circling" involves a series of rapid sideways steps interspersed with pauses, and takes about 3 sec. Then the actual courtship begins with "wing quivering." The male's forewings are slowly raised several times with slightly spread frontal margins, then quickly closed and lowered. Usually two such movements occur per second. Each movement is a little more pronounced than the previous one and the forewing margins are spread a little further each time. By the time of the last occurrence, approximately half the forewings protrude from the hindwings. A bout of wing quivering is usually followed by two other movements, which occur simultaneously: "fanning" and "spinning."
> In fanning the forewings are kept in a raised position. Their leading edges are separated from each other and closed again rhythmically and at a fast tempo. Only the frontal one-third of the wings are opened and they separate no more than approximately 1 mm. (1972a: 210)

I interpolate the marker [//] in Tinbergen's text to indicate where in the passage the male butterfly ceases to be the subject of the sentences. The location is noteworthy, since the last action reported as something the male butterfly does (*he is facing her*) marks the beginning of the courtship between the two butterflies, that is, the beginning of their interaction.

The idea of *facing*, as the prelude of courtship, suggests intimate encounter. The moment the butterflies' engagement commences, however, the writing itself becomes disengaged and abstract. A sense of interaction is further undermined as the female butterfly disappears—her comportment being presumably relatively inactive and thus not worthy of report. Additionally, the verbs now have as their subject the movement ("'circling' involves" or "each movement is pronounced") or the act ("the actual courtship begins"). The courtship movements are described in the passive voice: "wing quivering is followed," "the forewings are kept," "are separated," "are closed, " and "are opened." An authoring force of action is grammatically screened out from the surface of the writing. The butterfly's movements appear expressionless, carrying no signification of agency, of aesthetic form, or of feeling.

This lack of meaning of the butterfly's movements is not a semantic blankness intrinsic to them, but a consequence of wording that cautiously shuns rendering the butterflies' movements as gestures that are addressed to another participant. In the observation of interaction, only as gesture can movement appear meaningful. The descriptive language here carefully avoids casting movements as expressive. In this courtship story no gestures are offered and none are received. The extinction of gesture persists throughout the depiction of the butterflies.

> During quivering, the antennae of the males are spread horizontally and at right angles to the longitudinal axis of the body. As soon as quivering develops into fanning, the antennae begin to perform a remarkable movement. Held completely stiff, they make a conical sweep so that the tips describe a circle. Both antennae move synchronously and in the same direction, that is, back-upwards-forwards-down. Gradually this circle becomes an ellipse with its longitudinal axis inclined forwards and upwards, making an angle of 45 with the ground. The downward movement is clearly faster than the upward one. Also the antennae are gradually directed forwards. We observed one male in which the antennae rubbed against the legs of the female, but this is by no means the rule. Each complete circling lasts about ¾ sec. A bout of wing fanning and antenna spinning can last from 1 sec to several minutes. Fanning is the first to cease when courtship lapses, e.g. when a cloud covers the sun; its tempo becomes slower and finally antenna spinning is also completely suspended. (1972a: 210–11)

The movements are not performed by the male butterfly, but by parts of his body. The antennae "begin to perform a remarkable movement . . . they make a conical sweep . . . [and] describe a circle." The passive voice is used to describe the antennae's positioning—they are "held completely stiff." The presence of the male butterfly as an agent is not so much suppressed as sidestepped—other aspects are promoted as central. The physical mechanics of the antennae's movements are described minutely, and the timing (in seconds) of the movements of the wings and antennae is also given. Accuracy of description corresponds to detailing the spatiotemporal measurements of the movement of body parts.

There is little intimation of expressiveness. This does not look like an omission or an occlusion. Rather, the narrative suggests that there is not sufficient information or evidence for registering the circling of antennae and the quivering of wings as expressive. In one case, the antennae of the male were observed "to rub against the legs of the female," but a possible understanding of this as a gesture is rescinded in that "this is by no means the rule." As a singular instance, diverging from the average case, it cannot be seen to possess any significance, general or particular. The antennae rubbing against the female cannot be seen as "touching," in any case, because the movement as such is never even assembled as an action.

Overall, given its impersonal qualities of the use of the passive voice and the presentation of mathematicized spatiotemporal dimensions, the modality of description discloses an inability, or a demurral, to render the butterfly's movements as expressive actions. This descriptive mode, in turn, disallows the reader to visualize the butterfly's movements as expressive actions. In this sense, not only does the text voice skepticism, it also, so to speak, brings skepticism to life, in cajoling the reader to participate in its plausibility. The reader must make a deliberate effort to picture the motions of the antennae by thinking through the calibrations provided. Thus, while the description is impeccably precise, it is not the type of description to evoke an image; while it is mathematically exact, it is not visually intimate.

The courtship ritual of the butterflies ends in the following way:

The last component of the actual courtship is "bowing." In this spectacular display the male spreads both pairs of wings and brings the forewings very far forward so that they are completely separated from the (likewise somewhat raised) hindwings. Once in this forward inclined position, the male closes the wings again extremely slowly—as it were, "with emphasis." In most cases, this catches the antennae of the female between the male's forewings. As soon as the male has shut the wings, they are drawn backwards. The whole movement lasts about a second and is a perfect and elegant finale. (1972a: 211)

In this final component of the butterflies' courtship, the extinction of gesture comes through fully. In "bowing," the forewings of the male catch the female's antennae. The actual physical contact—which is significant for

Figure 19   The bowing ceremony of the Grayling butterflies

Tinbergen, as it occurs "in most cases"—could suggest that the movement is an oriented gesture—a touch. This implication is actively averted, however, as Tinbergen writes that "*this* catches the antennae of the female between the male's forewings." The alternative locution of "*the male butterfly* catches the antennae of the female between his forewings" would deliver the action as a deliberate gesture. In its active avoidance of implicating that the male butterfly intends to catch the female's antennae in his wings, the wording inevitably nullifies the butterfly's move as an oriented gesture.

At the same time that gestures are extinguished, replaced by mathematically described movements, Tinbergen also characterizes the movement of the antennae as "remarkable" and "bowing" as a "spectacular display" and "a perfect and elegant finale"; he observes that the male butterfly "closes the wings extremely slowly—as it were, 'with emphasis.'" What is it that makes the antennae's movements remarkable or bowing spectacular? And how can the closing of wings be emphatic without implying that their closing is meaningful in some way? These exclamatory remarks point toward some enigmatic quality of the display that, while present to the viewing, is actively kept outside the writing.

In Tinbergen's portrayal the engagement between the butterflies cannot be seen as communication. John Searle (1978) notes that communication embeds a double level of intentionality: the sender performs an action with the intention not only of conveying a sign, but also of producing in the receiver the recognition that the action was performed precisely with such an intention (see also Grice 1957; Bennett 1976). Simply put, this double level of intentionality means that the gesture not only reaches out to the other, but marks itself as reaching out to the other; its full success depends on the other's acknowledgment of this mark. So, for example, an ordinary requirement in human conversation is that the speaker direct her or his gaze to the addressee, expecting the addressee to return that gaze in a full display of recipiency. Indeed, detailed analyses of conversations show that speakers who lose the gaze of their recipients will often pause, or stall by drawing out their words, until they reengage eye contact (Goodwin 1979; Heath 1984). While eye contact is not necessary for clarifying who the participants in conversation are (especially in two-party conversations), the work of the eyes underscores and can be used to intensify the intentionality of the utterance—that is, a common field of understanding that the utterance is both directed and received.

Tinbergen writes that during the bowing ceremony the "female bends the antennal knobs outwards in such a manner that the terminal surface of the knobs lie almost parallel to the upper surface of the male's wings" (1972a: 245). The significance of the female's positioning of her antennae is not apprehended as participation in a communicative setting, as the way of receiving the male's closing wings. Instead, it is rendered in its physiological-stimulating function: "The movements of the male's wings and the female's antennae during courtship are such that the male's scent stimulus has the greatest opportunity of being carried to the female's che-moreceptors" (1972a: 248). The coordinated movements of the male's wings and the female's antennae are in the service of the underlying phys-iological, reproductive mechanisms. The movements are vehicles for the work of these mechanisms; they are never portrayed as actions, and so, a fortiori, they cannot become assembled as intended gestures. Therefore the butterflies' interaction cannot be seen as communication.

The character and effects of Tinbergen's presentation of butterfly court-ship comes into stark relief when contrasted with Fabre's portrayal of scorpion courtship.

25th April, 1904.—Hullo! What is this, something I have not yet seen? My eyes, ever on the watch, look upon the affair for the first time. Two Scor-pions face each other, with claws outstretched and fingers clasped. It is a question of a friendly grasp of the hand and not the prelude to a battle, for the two partners are behaving to each other in the most peaceful way. There is one of either sex. One is paunchy and browner than the other: this is the female; the other is comparatively slim and pale: this is the male. With their tails prettily curved, the couple stroll with measured steps along the pane. The male is ahead and walks backwards, without jolt or jerk, without any resistance to overcome. The female follows obediently, clasped by her fingertips and face-to-face with her leader.

The stroll is interrupted by halts that do not affect the method of conjunction; it is resumed, now here, now there, from end to end of the enclosure. Nothing shows the object which the strollers have in view. They loiter, they dawdle, they most certainly exchange ogling glances. Even so in my village, on Sundays, after vespers, do the youth of both sexes saunter along the hedges, every Jack with his Jill.

Often they tack about. It is always the male who decides which fresh direction the pair shall take. Without releasing her hands, he turns gracefully to the left or right about and places himself side by side with his companion. Then, for a moment, with tail laid flat, he strokes her spine. The other stands motionless, impassive. . . .

At last, about ten o'clock something happens. The male has hit upon a potsherd whose shelter seems to suit him. He releases his companion with one hand, with one alone, and continuing to hold her with the other, he scratches with his legs and sweeps with his tail. A grotto opens. He enters and, slowly, without violence, drags the patient Scorpioness after him. Soon both have disappeared. A plug of sand closes the dwelling. The couple are at home. (1991: 227–28)

The differences between Fabre's depiction of insect courtship and Tinbergen's are striking. Fabre describes a singular episode, in contrast to Tinbergen's largely generic descriptions of the Grayling displays. The different stages in the scorpions' concerted actions are portrayed in continuity, almost seamlessly linked, not analytically separated and distinctly named, as in the case of Tinbergen's butterflies.

In Fabre's account the animals are, more often than not, the subjects of action verbs. The effect of this is twofold. First, it implicates that the subject is the authoring force from which action radiates. Second, the use of active verbs allows, and even demands, a proliferation of the pronouns *she* and *he*. It is worth indicating the necessity of the use of these terms even in Tinbergen's courtship account:

When a male flies toward a receptive female, she will sooner or later, sometimes immediately, settle on the ground. The male settles near, and usually behind her, and then proceeds by short jerky movements around her until he is facing her.[//]

While the pronoun *it* can generally be used in descriptions of animal activity, in describing a female and a male interacting in courtship *it* suddenly becomes awkward; *he* and *she* can hardly be avoided, as they become indexically necessary. These vernacular name substitutes, being omnirelevant in human everyday life, carry connotations of subjectivity and individuality. So when Tinbergen switches to the passive voice (after the marker [//], and through the remainder of the account previously cited) he is able to arrest the proliferation of *she*'s and *he*'s. Such a proliferation has a cumulative perlocutionary effect on the reader in that, if sustained through the entirety of an account, she or he (i.e., the reader) begins to lose the picture of anonymous and generic animals.[5] This is precisely what happens in Fabre's account, where the emergence of the two scorpions as actual individuals is in part an effect of the recurrent use of the personal pronouns *he* and *she*, as well as *her* and *him*.

Both Fabre and Tinbergen understood their behavioral projects as scientific. Both provide descriptions of what "really happened." But their visions of what is real, and of what counts as an accurate description, are as different as can be. Fabre draws the picture of two scorpions courting by rendering how their actions are expressive. Tinbergen draws the picture of two butterflies courting by calibrating the spatial and temporal parameters of their movements. Fabre's portrayal is imagistically available, while Tinbergen's is available only in striving, mathematically, to picture it.

The reason that Fabre's depiction is available to the imagination so readily is that the scorpions' engagement is portrayed as communication. Their uncanny communion emerges holistically, that is, their linked movements come through on a level of the whole being greater than the sum of the parts: the scorpions are not simply linked physically, they are linked as subjects—"they hold hands." The scorpions' linked movements are equivalent to a couple's stroll or dance. This image is reinforced by the male being described as the leader, who is followed "obediently" and who turns "gracefully" from side to side. On the other hand, Tinbergen's spatial mechanics and temporal dimensions of physical movements leave the butterflies not only imagistically distant from the reader, but curiously disengaged and remote from each other.

Fabre's account is different on both counts, for not only are these scorpions fully engaged, but their engagement is very human. Fabre's imagination is nothing if not audacious.

> Nothing shows the object which the strollers have in view. They loiter, they dawdle, they most certainly exchange ogling glances. Even so in my village,

on Sundays, after vespers, do the youth of both sexes saunter along the hedges, every Jack with his Jill.

In his *Philosophical Investigations,* Wittgenstein writes that "there is a lack of clarity about the role of *imaginability* in our investigation. Namely about the extent to which it ensures that a proposition makes sense" (1953: para. 395). This comment addresses some of the perplexities that arise with respect to this particular moment (and similar moments) of Fabre's depiction of the scorpions. Clearly the idea of scorpions exchanging "ogling glances" has only imaginable sense; nothing can evidence the realism of such an assessment. "Ogling glances" between scorpions can hardly stand as a literal proposition, for it cannot be attached to anything that is witnessable. It makes sense not as something actual in the world, but as something possible in the world as Fabre sees it (and his readers with him).

"Ogling scorpions" is the sort of proposition that can provoke derisive hostility against the excesses of anthropomorphism. Yet this kind of anthropomorphism cannot be seen as leading to error—in its conflation of the glances exchanged between Jack and Jill, on one hand, and scorpions, on the other—unless it is assumed that Fabre is so naive as to offer "ogling glances" as a literal proposition. Rather, this type of expression, often encountered in naturalist writing, is an excursion of the imagination into a potentially real yet unwitnessable world: the first move is into the realm of the plausible, often engaging the stance of "seeing as" (for instance, seeing physical contact as touching, when Fabre writes that "then, for a moment, with tail laid flat, he strokes her spine"); the next move is into the realm of the possible ("they loiter, they dawdle"); and finally into the realm of the imaginable ("they exchange ogling glances"). Each of these moves is a step further away from the boundaries of what counts as real, that is, of what can be, in some convincing way, witnessed. What fastens the reality of the unknowable to the familiar world is a common universe of significations. If the scorpions can be seen to "hold hands," then the male's touch can be seen as "stroking her back," it might be sensed that "they loiter, they dawdle," and perhaps it could be imagined that they "exchange ogling glances." These scorpions inhabit a single universe of meaning, even though the author—along with the reader he has engaged—cannot witness all they do on the same ontological plane, nor convey all their actions with equal credibility.

The ethological technical language of behavior partially succeeded in preempting the conceptual territory of mental terminology. Classical ethology aligned itself with a skeptical stance and its presupposition that mind is invisible and hence unverifiable. Yet, as I have argued in the preceding analyses, the replacement of the ordinary language of action with technical terminology does not yield a more objective view—only a different one. Even if ethological writing does not wander into the realm of what is imaginable, in the way that Fabre and other naturalists do, this is no guarantee that it has escaped metaphysics, for the demurral to see, for instance, butterflies' movements as expressive and communicative gestures is not only a precaution against the pitfalls of anthropomorphism, but simultaneously the ticket to mechanomorphism. And the image of disengaged yet courting butterflies may belie what is real as much as what is real is stretched with the ascription of ogling to scorpions.

6   Unraveling the Distinction Between Action and Behavior

MY AIM in this work has been to show the powerful role of language in the portrayal of animals. Beginning with the observation that animal life is represented in profoundly divergent ways by different authors and schools of thought within behavioral science, I have explored the formative import of all aspects of language use in the portrayal of animals. My project has been comparative in elucidating how knowledge about animals is differently construed through the use of alternative linguistic maps. The distinction between technical and ordinary language has served as a springboard to consider the effects of various linguistic features: ordinary and technical concepts; active, passive, or idiomatic verbs; descriptive styles; and qualifying devices. In their obvious or subtle effects, different words and their combinations guide the reader's imagination to disparate landscapes of animal life. In what follows, I briefly recapitulate certain features of those landscapes as they have been discussed in this work.

- The language of the lifeworld—with its emphasis on the ceaseless cascade of actions and a world where meanings are shared—is, prototypically, the everyday language of human affairs. In transferring this language to animal life, its qualities as they pertain to the human context are assembled in the case of animals as well. There are three seminal dimensions of this language: authorship, or the deliverance of action as initiated and directed by an actor; meaningfulness, or the understanding of action and its surrounding context as subjectively experienced by the actor; and temporal continuity, or the idea that actions are seamlessly connected in the stream of living. These dimensions assemble a representation of animals as subjects: in turn, this results in the supervenience of inner life, that is, of witnessing the animal world as a place of knowledge, emotion, intention, thinking, and memory. As I have emphasized, these tropes of mentality need not be explicitly attributed, but may be effects that surface indirectly.

- Technical languages of behavior are built on the basis of ordinary language. This continuity is required in order to preserve the fundamental intelligibility of the behaviors and events described. Such languages are characterized by specialized vocabularies, which are either constructed (for example, the ethological concept of the IRM) or appropriated from another disciplinary domain or from ordinary language and given special definitions (for example, the sociobiological notion of "parental investment"). Technical terms acquire meaning from their place within particular theories and from their connections to other terms. In short, a technical idiom is a nexus of technical and quasi-technical terms held in coherent constellation by a theoretical framework. For the most part, on the model of a received conception of the task of science, such theories are designed to provide causal explanations of animal behavior. Emphasis can be on "proximate" causes, as in the case of classical ethology, or on "ultimate" causes, as in the case of the neo-Darwinian evolutionary angle of sociobiology. The implementation of such languages may rest on a skeptical stance with respect to animal mind, or it may be spurred by the ambition to provide theoretical explanations of behavior. In any case, a most significant consequence of technical-causal linguistic mediums is the partial, if not complete, displacement of mind. Concepts of mentality effectively present an agent as the cause of action. Through the use of technical terminology, on the other hand, the causation of action becomes coupled to the referents of technical constructs. As a consequence, a technical-causal language of behavior extinguishes authorship from the animal world, or alternatively translocates it onto causes that are theoretically identified—for example, neurophysiological mechanisms, environmental stimuli, or genetic programs. An experiential outlook upon the world is swept aside, for its existence has no role to play in the production of action. Animals become portrayed as vessels steered by forces they neither control nor comprehend, and as a consequence, behaviors emerge as events that happen to animals, rather than as active achievements.

- I have endeavored to elucidate the character of anthropomorphism and mechanomorphism in writings about animals. In contrast to a taken-for-granted pejorative connotation of "anthropomorphism" as mere metaphor or category mistake, by investigating the writings of sterling naturalists I argued that their ostensibly anthropomorphic depictions make a realist bid that deserves serious attention: it advances a powerful view of animal life as experientially meaningful, authored, and temporally cohesive and articulates a compelling argument for human-animal evolutionary continuity. Anthropomorphism cannot be offhandedly dismissed, for the understanding of animal life in semantic kinship with the human world yields an imposing and cogent perspective in the hands of outstanding observers and masterful writers, like Charles Darwin, Jean Henri Fabre, and George and Elizabeth Peckham. A mechanomorphic description of animals, on the other hand, need not involve either the overt denial of mentality or the explicit likening of animals to machines. As I argued in the investigation of classical ethology, mechanomorphism is an unintended effect of a technical-causal language.

Such a language delivers animals as puppets: they are portrayed as compelled to behave and react by a technically defined grid of forces that is extrinsic to all possible lived forms of experience. As a consequence, animals appear mindless; put otherwise, the conceptual space for a tacit or explicit attribution of mentality drastically shrinks.

• Respecifying, via the provision of special definitions, a vocabulary that is already familiar to the reader can invoke, and argumentatively exploit, its extant meanings and connotations. I argued that such is the case with the use of economic language in sociobiology. The capacity of economic language to expand beyond the core of specially defined terms into its ordinary-language extensions, as well as its propensity to appear in multiple grammatical positions of a sentence, is precisely what makes it an idiom. Given its semantic and syntactic expansiveness, the economic idiom utterly consumes the representation of animal life, creating a worldview of behavioral-purposive rationality, namely, of animals as unwitting or Machiavellian agents that pursue the maximization of self-interest. Such a view implicitly sidesteps an alternative understanding of animal sociality as a lifeworld. Once selfishness is given such ground-level status, an alternative understanding of sociality as a lifeworld where animals share significations—even when their interests on occasion conflict—is excluded. The sociobiological transformation of economic vocabulary into an all-consuming idiom might be interpreted as a form of rhetoric, a surreptitious means of persuasion, for it is a move that harnesses two powerful dimensions of language use: the authority of technical definition and operationalization, as well as the familiarity and evocative quality of ordinary meaning. If this is "rhetoric," however, it is not to be understood in logical opposition to, or necessary tension with, "objective" representation. Recent scholarship addressing the role of rhetoric in science recognizes that there is no such thing as "rhetoric-free" science. As Philip Kitcher puts it, "The notion of a plain idiom in which logical structures are presented naked is as illusory as that of a language of pure observation in which the deliverances of the senses stand bare" (1995: 52; see also Toulmin 1995).

• Throughout this work, I have reiterated the idea of "portrayals" of animals so as to highlight that a supervenient effect of the consistent use of particular linguistic mediums is the creation of alternative visions of animals. My aim has been to elucidate how diverse linguistic tropes impart significantly discrepant messages. Complete and coherent visions of animal life take form gradually in the reader's imagination. So, for example, in arguing that naturalists portray animals as inhabitants of a "lifeworld," I do not mean that it is possible to point to where, specifically, this lifeworld can be found in the writing. Instead, the image of a lifeworld—of ceaseless action, immanent meaning, and temporal continuity—gradually takes perceivable shape in the reader's imagination after immersion in naturalists' works. My methodology of the analysis of language use thus does not implicate a commitment to the idea that "everything is text": even as words are the medium of the reader's travel in the animal world, the profound ramifications of behavioral writings happen beyond the words themselves. A whole view of animal life, a portrayal, is created through compounded conceptual and imagistic effects. Jürgen Habermas' notion of "portrait"—which he uses to clarify the meaning of "worldview"—may be useful to approximate the idea I have in mind in connection to the creation of divergent "portrayals of animals." "Inasmuch as worldviews refer to totalities," writes Habermas, "we cannot get behind them as articulations of an understanding of the world, even if they can be revised. In this respect they are like a portrait that claims to represent a person as a whole. A portrait is neither a *mapping* that can be exact or inexact, nor a *rendering of facts* in the sense of a proposition that can be true or false. A portrait offers rather an angle of vision from which the person represented appears in a certain way. . . . Similarly, worldviews lay down the framework of fundamental concepts within which we interpret everything that appears in the world in a specific way as something" (1981: 58). Borrowing Habermas' formulation, different portrayals of animals offer alternative angles of vision. A portrait is responsive to how the world really is, so that it *is* a "mapping" and a "rendering of facts." At the same time, a portrait is a conceptual and perceptual composition that can make incursions upon "independent reality," delivering how things are from its particular angle of vision; a portrait, then, can render the world, or specific instances of the world, in its own image. For example, in the analysis of sociobiological language, I argued that the description of female deer feeding close together in terms of "tolerating" one another is an interpretive incursion upon an observed activity. It is a description that configures a specific behavioral instance in accordance with the sociobiological overall portrait of animal life as competitively oriented toward the maximization of self-interest.

- In behavioral works, styles of description matter. Descriptions constitute a significant component of knowledge about animals, having intrinsic ramifications as well as forming the basis of subsequent explanations, comparisons, and generalizations. The descriptive style, then, is constitutive of the nature of knowledge about animals. Episodic description delivers behaviors in their concrete here-and-now instantiations. The focus on the stream of living of a specific episode sustains the sequential integrity of actions. The unified character of the act as a whole is preserved in this focus on a sequence of events and actions that constitute one cohesive episode. Episodic description cultivates an image of a world of meaning and agency; it upholds the subjective dimension of action by attending to the idiosyncrasies of the unique and singular event; and it presents actions as achievements by focusing on specific individuals. Generic description, on the other hand, generalizes from many different here-and-now instantiations of a behavioral pattern to deliver its typified form. The focus on typified behavior, separating it out of the stream of lived events, is consilient with an atomistic perspective; indeed, classical ethologists often provide lists of the behavioral patterns of a species (referred to as "ethograms"), describing them as isolated units. Generic description discourages the perception of subjectivity in animal life by implicitly projecting the typified behavior as the essential form of any concrete instantiation. In conjunction with a causal language, generic description can convey the message that behaviors are unwittingly emitted by animals. Generic description may thus bolster a mechanomorphic image of animals by displacing individuality with typification, and by representing behaviors as fixed packages of conduct that are determined by forces utterly extrinsic to animals' experiential possibilities. Finally, frequency-laden description presents the mathematical average of the occurrence of behaviors in delivering information about animal life via quantitative markers. The description of the individual's behavior disappears—in its concrete manifestation and often in its typified form as well. A world of experience is not refuted, but tacitly proclaimed irrelevant next to the generalizations, extracted from statistical operations, that frequency-laden description emphasizes. This descriptive style submits that what is important is the generalizations that can be drawn and the predictions that can be articulated on the basis of statistical operations on the data. The lives of animals become vehicles for the articulation of models that apply across taxonomic boundaries.

• In the documentation of animal life, the ways that activities and expressions of animals are engraved in the writing lead to a strong link between reading and seeing. Scenic qualities emerge differentially with divergent linguistic mediums. A central interest in this work has been to show how mental phenomena are either made viewable in the behavioral scenery or blocked from surfacing. Language use is thus integrally linked to the theme of animal mind not only conceptually—through applying or withholding mental concepts—but also perceptually via visualization effects. The influence of language is powerful because it is operative not only at the level of abstract thought, but also, perhaps even more consequentially, at the level of direct perception. To the extent that descriptions of animal behavior open up visual fields upon scenes, we *see* animals as aware and intentional, or conversely we see them as unconscious and meaning-blind. Language can make inner life sensually present by assembling an image in the reader's mind. For example, Julian Huxley's female grebe in "Cat-attitude," turning eagerly from side to side so as not to miss the resurfacing of her mate, is an image infused with tropes of awareness and feeling. Conversely, language can draw readers into compliance with a skeptical stance toward animal mentality by inviting them to bear witness to behaviors as physical movements rather than expressive gestures. Tinbergen's example of providing the mathematical coordinates of the courtship movements of Grayling butterflies is a case in point.

A central question of this investigation has been "How do different uses of language guide the reader's imagination to divergent images of animals and disjunctured ways of understanding the nature of their lives?" Language affects the understanding not only directly, through its specific substantive messages, but also indirectly, through perlocutionary effects. Different uses of language involve asymmetrical perlocutionary effects. Whether deliberate or implicit, a perlocution is a signification that, while absent from or cloaked within the surface of the words, reverberates through their use. A perlocutionary effect, then, may be likened to the energetic counterpart of a field of words. Austin identifies the meaning of a perlocutionary effect in connection to spoken language: "Saying something will often, or even normally, produce certain consequential effects upon feelings, thoughts or actions of the audience . . . ; and we may then say, thinking of this, that the speaker has performed an act in the nomenclature of which reference is made either . . . only obliquely, or even . . . not at all" (1962: 101). In behavioral writing, perlocutionary effects occur beyond the components of propositional content and performative work of statements (see also Habermas 1981: 288–90). To clarify these levels of language use with an example, when Fabre writes of the *Sphex* wasp that "she held the Mantis rooted with her eyes," the propositional content is simply what is stated about the proximity of the two insects and the crisscrossing of their eye contact; the performative force is what this description does, which is to present the wasp as the active agent operating within a meaningful situation; and finally, the perlocutionary effect is the atmosphere conveyed, which is that of "awareness" as a viewable dimension of the insects' engagement. There is, no doubt, something artificial about taking apart language in terms of these distinct levels of propositional content, performative force, and perlocutionary effect. The exercise is useful, however, in calling attention to the rich and variegated effects of language, its reverberations beyond the one-dimensional space of the print on a page.

In explicating perlocutions, Austin refers to the effect of words on the feelings, thoughts, or actions of the hearer. In the representation of animal behavior, perlocutionary effects work much more pronouncedly at the level of the reader's imagination, for words operate as vehicles for *seeing*.

The powerful impact of language is not, therefore, manifest only at the level of abstract ideas, but also at that of the reader's perceptual and affective experience. The overall view of animal life is educed through the interlacing of understanding and seeing, which is the experience of reading. The visual dimension of this experience may be further clarified with a couple of brief examples. Describing the hunting behavior of the wasp *Ammophila,* Fabre submits the following image:

> The Ammophila scratched the ground at the foot of the plant, at the junction of root and stem, pulled up slender grass rootlets and poked her head under the little clods which she had lifted. She ran hurriedly this way and that around the thyme, inspecting every crevice that could give access to what lay below. She was not digging herself a home but hunting some game hidden underground; this was evident from her behavior, which resembled that of a Dog trying to dig a Rabbit out of his hole. (1915: 269–70)

He deploys the availability to the mind's eye of the ways of a dog at a rabbit's hole as a method of communicating the wasp's comportment more lucidly—more visually. Fabre relies upon the availability of the dog's excitement around a rabbit hole not only to support his understanding that the wasp is engaged in hunting, but also as an image for the reader to superimpose upon the wasp's conduct "at the foot of a tuft of thyme." The perlocutionary effect of transposing the image of "a Dog trying to dig a Rabbit out" on the wasp's actions amounts to a transference of the intelligibility of the dog's actions to the wasp's digging, hurrying, poking her head under, and inspecting. It is, in part, this effect of seeing the wasp "like a dog" that creates a visual-interpretive barrier to the possibility of seeing the wasp in accordance with a mechanistic model, for example, as a "well-programmed robot," "on automatic pilot" (see Gould and Gould 1982: 293, 276). The effect of superimposing the familiar image of a dog digging for a rabbit is to deliver the wasp's activities as irreducibly intentional. Her intentionality is not conveyed as an inference about some esoteric "inner state," but rather as the visible conformation of the pressing and methodical nature of her actions.

Another example that elucidates the visual import of behavioral descriptions is from Darwin, who cites Audubon's depiction of the male heron "walking with great dignity before the female and bidding defiance to rivals" (1981, 2: 68). "Walking with dignity" and "bidding defiance" are interpretive statements about the heron's bearings, yet their perlocutionary effect is also descriptive, soliciting ways to imagine the bird's bearing. Another illustration of the connection between reading and seeing is Darwin's writing that the male smooth-tailed stickleback "is continually employed in gently leading back the young to the nest when they stray too far" (1981, 2: 20). "Leading back the young to the nest" is an action that has a face—it is done *gently*. How much is delivered with the inclusion of this one simple word: a description, a relationship, and an atmosphere—an entire image.

Descriptions of "defiant herons" and "gentle sticklebacks" have been, and sometimes continue to be, dismissed as anthropomorphic. As I have argued, however, the notion of anthropomorphism, etymologically denoting "human-likening," not only is indefinable, but actually lacks substantive content. The term is evaluative, deployed to disparage certain accounts of animals as flawed, metaphorical, unscientific, amateur, or erroneous. Anthropomorphism is looked upon with trepidation, as a naive approach to animal life, replete with the potential for unrestrained comparisons between humans and animals. Vernon Reynolds, for example, warns against the danger of anthropomorphism when he states that "it is all too easy for us, with our well-developed linguistic ways of thought, to attribute meanings and motives to animals which arise from our own experience of life in human society" (1986: 55). As a demoting label, "anthropomorphism" is intended to undermine the credibility of any language use that, in some way or another, allows a flow of common meanings between animal and human life.

In this work I have set aside the evaluative connotations of the term in order to examine its constituent conceptual features, forms of reasoning, and grammatical patterns. Yet beyond rejecting the negative implications of anthropomorphism for the purposes of unbiased examination, I have advanced a stronger claim. The underlying assumption of the repudiation of anthropomorphism as erroneous or figurative linguistic usage is that a neutral language exists, or can be constructed, and that this will yield incontestably objective accounts of animal behavior. This is an untenable assumption and aspiration from the comparative standpoint of this work. The analyses of the conceptual structures, patterns of reasoning, and descriptive methods of classical ethology and contemporary sociobiology disclose that even if technical idioms succeed in quelling so-called anthropomorphism, they produce their own perspectival effects. Language is not a neutral instrument in the depiction of animals, and, in particular, it is never impartial with respect to the question of animal mind. Different uses of language create alternative, and sometimes incompatible, conceptual and imagistic effects, and what words are used and how they are used entail consequences with respect to the deliverance, foreclosure, or elision of the inner life of animals. In this concluding chapter, I want to bring this argument to bear on a final topic: the distinction between "action" and "behavior."

The opposition between action and behavior has been elaborated within the social and behavioral sciences. Briefly put, "action" is identified as conduct accompanied and/or preceded by mental states, while "behavior" is conceived as physical conduct, the output of the body, or a mere physical response stemming from environmental or inner-physiological stimuli without any corollary states of knowing, understanding, intending, or feeling. The social theorist Max Weber defined action as "all human behaviour when and in so far the acting individual attaches a subjective meaning to it" (1964: 88). Alfred Schutz viewed action as "human conduct devised by the actor in advance, that is, conduct based upon a preconceived project" (1962: 19). Both these definitions advocate an understanding of action as "behaviour plus a mental component" (Rubinstein 1977: 214). In this way, human actions are conceived as bodily expressions with certain necessary or contingent mental antecedents (White 1968: 7). In the literature on the naturally occurring behavior of animals, at least since the contributions of classical ethology, behavior is conceived as the physical outcome of external, steering influences on a body, given certain initial conditions of physiological states, internal makeup, and genetic predispositions (Thorpe 1973). The goal of the behavioral sciences has been the explanation of animal behavior on the basis of "the constitution of organs," as René Descartes first articulated it.

Action is ostensibly the prerogative of human beings, while behavior is produced by animals. In contrast to behavior, action is intrinsically mindful; according to a recent explication by the sociologist Harry Collins, action is "what humans do when they intend to do something, whereas behavior is unintended" (1990: 30). The distinction between behavior and action is a definitional superimposition, as these concepts are largely interchangeable in ordinary usage. Their essentialist bifurcation guarantees that animal and human affairs remain qualitatively separate, thereby calling for discrepant frameworks of description and explanation. The division between action and behavior is often presented as though it were a natural-kind classification that reflects the regular, stable, available-to-all arrangement of things in the world. The implicit advocacy of behavior-versus-action as a natural-kind classification is accomplished by condensing an essential and momentous difference into these two words. The artifice of this conceptual synopsis is to impart the impression that an act of naming—and hence of *reference*—has been accomplished.

However, while the terms *action* and *behavior* are presented as naming two species of conduct, their distinction enjoys neither the implicit consensus associated with natural-kind classifications nor the explicit consensus achieved through intellectual or scientific agreement. The distinction between action and behavior is, quite literally, constructed: it is elaborately built up through the deployment of various linguistic resources and techniques. The crowning touch of this discursive construction is to ignore all the work required for its elaboration, and present the ideas of action and behavior as a self-evident or settled classification typology of conduct. What I have endeavored to show throughout this work is that erecting and defending the border between action and behavior requires intricate and sustained conceptual work.[1] In this concluding chapter, I enjoin abandoning the chimera that two species of conduct exist, one stemming from the mind, the other from the body. I unravel the distinction between action and behavior, first by locating its conceptual invention in Descartes' views on animals and next by discussing the impossibility of stabilizing it in the language of representing animals. With these critical approaches—of revealing the origins and showing the instability of the action-behavior distinction—I intend to disrupt the idea that there is such a thing as a natural typology of conduct.

René Descartes was pivotal in elaborating the foundations of a view of radical discontinuity between animals and humans. As he developed the idea, particularly in his *Philosophical Letters,* mind or soul is strictly a possession of human beings. Descartes' specific conceptualization of animal-human discontinuity is kept alive in the contemporary antithesis between behavior and action.

> But there is no prejudice to which we are all more accustomed from our earliest years than the belief that dumb animals think. Our only reason for this belief is the fact that we see that many of the organs of animals are not very different from ours in shape and movement. Since we believe that there is a single principle within us which causes these movements—namely the soul, which both moves the body and thinks—we do not doubt that some

such soul is to be found in animals also. I came to realize, however, that there are two different principles causing our motions: one is purely mechanical and corporeal and depends solely on the forces of the spirits and the construction of our organs, and can be called the corporeal soul; the other is the incorporeal mind, the soul which I have defined as a thinking substance. Thereupon I investigated more carefully whether the motions of animals originated from both these principles or from one only. I soon saw clearly that they could all originate from the corporeal and mechanical principle, and I thenceforward regarded it as certain and established that we cannot at all prove the presence of a thinking soul in animals. I am not disturbed by the astuteness and cunning of dogs and foxes, or all the things that animals do for the sake of food, sex, and fear; I claim that I can easily explain the origin of all of them from the constitution of their organs. (1970: 243)

Several argumentative moves are interwoven here to lead to the defense of an essential and final saltus separating humans and animals. Descartes begins by flagging "accustomed belief," or the widely shared "prejudice" acquired "from our earliest years" that "animals think." At the same time that he destabilizes commonplace ideas by implicating their illusory, nonrational nature, Descartes actively constructs an alternative conception. He begins by casting conduct as "motion," and then introduces a dichotomy between two "principles of motion": (1) the soul, the "incorporeal mind" or "thinking substance," and (2) the body, the "purely mechanical and corporeal" or the "corporeal soul." The categorical classification of the causes of motion as "incorporeal mind" and "pure corporeality" is set up as beyond, and even in opposition to, the arena of experience: this classification is turned into a pure index that is far more real than how things ordinarily merely appear. Therefore, once Descartes has ascertained that he can explain all animal motion on the basis of "the forces of the spirits" and "the construction of organs," he remains utterly unperturbed in the face of the counterevidence of "the astuteness and cunning of dogs and foxes" and "all the things animals do for the sake of food, sex, and fear."

For Descartes nothing real-worldly disturbs the truth of the finality of the difference between the two principles of motion—of the corporeal and of the incorporeal. Animal movements are entirely explainable by the constitution of their bodies:

The souls of animals are nothing but their blood, the blood which is turned into spirits by the warmth of the heart and travels through the arteries to the brain and from it to the nerves and muscles. This theory involves such an enormous difference between the souls of animals and our own that it provides a better argument than any yet thought of to refute the atheists and establish that human minds cannot be drawn out of the potentiality of matter. (1970: 36)

In this passage, Descartes portrays motion as a consequence of physically identified "spirits" traveling to the brain, the nerves, and then the muscles. The subtext of this portrayal is a view of conduct that is subjectively empty. Descartes' idea of "motion caused from pure corporeality" is the prototype—the original blueprint—of what is presently called "behavior"; authorship and experience have disappeared, or been rendered redundant, by a nexus of interacting physical mechanisms that result in animal movement. Descartes' language of "spirits" is of course archaic, but the same form of reasoning, and the identical effect of the extinction of agency, underpins the contemporary idea of behavior as conduct minus a mental component. Moreover, the conceptual cousins of "behavior"—for example, the notions of stimulus-response, genetic programming, and even neural nets—exhibit an isomorphic configuration to Descartes' "spirits": they describe physical states and processes that produce behavior, displacing any need for awareness, knowledge, or intention in the animal world.

Descartes' invocation of theological arguments reveals that in establishing a saltus between humans and animals, "an enormous difference," he wants to safeguard the uniqueness of the human soul and secure its immortality. The implication is that if humans and animals equally possessed "incorporeal souls," then this would present Christian theological doctrine with the problem of the resurrection or immortality of an unwieldy number of creatures. The theological motive, then, of the division between corporeal principle and thinking soul is to avoid this embarrassing problem and simultaneously to guarantee that immortality is gratis for human beings. While the theological affiliations of Descartes' views have come undone, the essentially identical distinction between "two principles of motion" has persisted in secular and scientific arenas of thought. Descartes' conception of a "purely mechanical" body and an "incorporeal" soul composes the ancestral form of the distinction between behavior and action. Action originates in thought, while behavior is the output of the body; behavior is something that happens to an organism or an object, while action is performed by an agent or a subject.

Descartes' idea that the souls of animals are "nothing but their blood" goes hand in hand with the conception of human action as emerging from "thought." The two juxtaposed constructs—bodily spirits and thought—are elaborated and purified in conjunction.

> It does not seem to me a fiction, but a truth which nobody should deny, that there is nothing entirely in our power except our thoughts; at least if you take the word "thought" as I do, to cover all the operations of the soul, so that not only meditations and acts of the will, but the activities of seeing and hearing and deciding on one movement rather than another, so far as depends on the soul, are all thoughts. In philosophical language there is nothing strictly attributable to a man apart from what is covered by the word "thought"; for the activities which belong to the body alone are said to take place in a man rather than to be performed by him. (1970: 51)

Activities are performative strictly in the human realm, for they do not come from the "body alone" but from "thoughts." Not only are thoughts human possessions, stemming as they do from the soul, but for Descartes thoughts cover the entire gamut of mentality. This collapse of all mental phenomena into the single realm of "thought," leaving to animals only the purely corporeal principle, is a prerequisite for erecting the opposition between humans and animals in terms of the presence or absence of "consciousness." Indeed, Descartes' philosophical formulations were pivotal in the creation of a series of familiar antithetical characterizations of conduct: involuntary versus performed; automatic versus aware; unintended versus intended; unconscious versus conscious. As these polarities have proliferated, the image of an unbridgeable saltus between humans and animals has deepened its conceptual hold on the Western imagination.

Having built the antithesis between his two principles of motion, Descartes, referring to an interlocutor, makes the following extraordinary claim:

> He supposes that I think that animals see just as we do, i.e. feeling or thinking they see, which is said to have been Epicurus's view and is still almost universal. But . . . I explain quite explicitly that my view is that *animals do not see as we do when we are aware we see, but only as we do when our mind is elsewhere*. In such a case the images of external objects are depicted on our retinas, and perhaps the impression they leave in the optic nerves cause our limbs to make various movements, although we are quite unaware of this. In such a case we too move like automata. (1970: 36, emphasis added)

The digital, unrealistic distinction between how we see "when we are aware" and "when our mind is elsewhere" is founded on Descartes' idea of the soul as a substance that may be present in a body (humans) or absent (animals). Descartes' specific word, *soul,* is no longer in use, but the identical concept with all its grammatical, constructed ramifications persists in the conception of "consciousness" as an internal mental state that accompanies human action, but—being divorceable from mere sentient physical motion—does not (necessarily) accompany animal behavior (see Kennedy 1992 and Carruthers 1989 for extreme expressions of this view). Descartes thus originated a most captivating conception, with both interpretive and perceptual dimensions: that there are two kinds of conduct, "mindful" and "mindless." The behavioral sciences, as well as Western philosophy, sustain and honor this conception in the present-day opposition between behavior and action. This conceptual pair forms an elaborate interpretive-perceptual scheme that configures an oppositional conception of the human and animal nature.

As Descartes himself admits, his opposition between purely mechanical and thoughtful motion clashes with ordinary reasoning about sentient conduct, where there is no equivalent to the purified categories of action versus behavior, or to that extraordinary reification of the states of "seeing when we are aware" and "seeing when our minds are elsewhere." His ideas come up against ordinary reasoning about animals, which is highly variable, heterogeneous, and replete with informal, nonsystematized notions of continuities and discontinuities with human life. So in order to draw the sharp qualitative line between animal and human conduct, Descartes must discredit the commonplace idea that animals think and feel. He repeatedly disparages it as "childlike" and "prejudiced." The passage that follows is an example of this rhetorical incursion:

> Most of the actions of animals resemble ours, and throughout our lives this has given us many occasions to judge that they act by an interior principle like the one within ourselves, that is to say, by means of a soul which has feelings and passions like ours. All of us are deeply imbued with this opinion by nature. Whatever reasons there may be for denying it, it is hard to say publicly how the case stands without exposing oneself to the ridicule of children and feeble minds. But those who want to discover truth must distrust opinions rashly acquired in childhood. (1970: 53)

Descartes endeavors to make light of the fact that ordinary language and common beliefs do not support a human-animal hiatus. The idea that animals think, or that they have feelings and passions, is the stuff of child-hood and feeble minds.

In short, Descartes constructed a clear-cut theoretical index to distin-guish essentially different forms of conduct. He created a captivating and anthropocentric picture of mindful and mindless action by means of highly abstract arguments, supported by rhetorical moves and theological appeals. His inventory of two types of conduct, and his conceptions of awareness and thinking as properties of the soul, rest pivotally on the idea that mind (or soul) is a realm of pure interiority, often entirely inaccessible and always incompletely available. As Descartes put it, "We base our judgment [about animals] solely on the resemblance between some exte-rior actions of animals and our own; but this is not at all a sufficient basis to prove that there is any resemblance between the corresponding interior actions" (1970: 54).

The assumption that mind is an insular and private domain leads to an intractable problem of evidence, or lack of certainty, regarding either the very existence or the possibility of knowing the nature of other minds. Skepticism is an inveterate refusal to bridge behavioral evidence and the affirmation of the inner life of animals. The impasse of the skeptical stance with respect to the mentality of animals is expressed poignantly in the words of its founder, Descartes: "But though I regard it as established that we cannot prove there is any thought in animals, I do not think it is thereby proved that there is not, since the human mind does not reach into their hearts" (1970: 244). T. H. Huxley voiced the identical sentiment in his qualified defense of the Cartesian thesis of "animal automatism," writ-ing that "it must be premised, that it is wholly impossible absolutely to prove the presence or absence of consciousness in anything but one's own brain, though by analogy, we are justified in assuming its existence in other men" (1874: 219). Skepticism, or doubting the existence or acces-sibility of other minds, is a corollary of certain entrenched assumptions: the view that the "mind" is something essentially separate from the "body"; the conception of the realms of mind and body on the spatial metaphor of "inner" and "outer," respectively; and the idea that mind, whether human or animal, is invisible, elusive, and hence always at best indirectly knowable. Descartes' idea of the incapacity of the "human mind to reach into the hearts of animals" and Huxley's cognate idea that it is "impossible absolutely to prove" consciousness in another reveal the in-dispensable premise of skepticism, namely, the privacy of mind. Animal mind has inherited the perplexities of what Cavell calls the "philosophical problem of privacy" (1976: 265) with redoubled force, for the relative privacy of another person's mind becomes absolute inscrutability in the case of animal mind.

The skeptical position is affiliated with philosophical solipsism, that is, the view that "my own mind is the only mind I have indubitable access to and certain knowledge about." Solipsism is the logical—if extreme—consequence of a strict adherence to a skeptical stance. Solipsism is the idea that, strictly speaking, no evidence is capable of disproving, beyond all doubt, that "I" am not the sole conscious being in existence. Every other human and sentient creature might well lead an automatonlike existence, even if contrived skillfully enough to appear mindful. The immediate problem that solipsism encounters is its spuriousness in the face of the de facto intersubjectivity of human social life. In the *Verstehen* attitude of everyday life we encounter and deal with the subjectivity of others with the same sort of inexorable existential palpability with which we handle physical objects. Wittgenstein pointed out the incoherence of doubting another's mental experience by confronting the solipsistic stance with the pragmatic and sensual knowledge of everyday life: "Just try—in a real case—to doubt someone else's fear or pain" (1953, para. 303).

Solipsism is belied by the knowledge exhibited in the pragmatic stance of everyday life. It is exceedingly vacuous when set in contrastive relief with the availability of the mental life of others in the world of daily affairs. The "problem of other minds" evanesces rapidly when brought to bear upon how people routinely present, express, and display their *inner* lives—whether they do so deliberately, unintentionally, or unselfconsciously. The stark and unavoidable availability of the minds of others is profoundly constitutive of the social landscapes we inhabit. We do not see others as physical bodies, institutional bodies, or bodies enacting roles. Rather, we relate to others as "embodied minds," witnessing and comprehending their actions by way of a largely direct grasp of their intentions, plans, beliefs, thoughts, sensibilities, feelings, tastes, and judgments. The mental life of others is not something that, for the most part, we come to know by *inference*—as though there were the general option of refraining from our deductions in favor of merely experiencing the surface forms of others' being. The inner life of others is more like something we are obliged to engage, to tread through, to handle, and to live by. In the face of the transparency of others' minds in everyday life, philosophical solipsism is a house of cards.

While the view that "I" might be the only mindful human is absurd enough not to merit serious attention, what Vicki Hearne calls "species solipsism" has, by contrast, been far more readily palatable. There is sufficient existential and ontological distance between humans and other animals that doubt about the existence, nature, or scope of animal mind can be sustained as long as it is not consistently invalidated by experience.[2] Species solipsism gets a grip with the idea that there is an unbridgeable gap setting conscious human life apart from animal existence. Humans are unique, special—and alone. This saltational view is reconfirmed in the behavioral and human sciences with the distinction between mindful action and mindless behavior. The specialized meanings of these concepts stand in contrast to the nonessential differences in their usage in ordinary language. The respecification of these words into referents of two distinct species of conduct is wedded to Descartes' doctrine of a sharp division between human and animal life. At the same time that the distinction and its doctrinaire context are established, the antithesis between action and behavior is neither self-evident nor widely agreed upon but, on the contrary, both unstable and constantly disputed. An implicit argument linking the exegeses of this work is that making the distinction between action and behavior credible calls for elaborate textual strategies, demanding particular uses of language, the inclusion of background assumptions, and the consistent application of patterns of reasoning. Behavioral discourse has to be streamlined along linguistic paths that are differentially conducive to the emergence of conduct-as-action and conduct-as-behavior, respectively.

One of the greatest theoreticians of animal behavior in the twentieth century, Konrad Lorenz, implicitly admits the difficulty of maintaining a watershed between "action" and "behavior," in acknowledging the impossibility of purging animal behavior writings of what he calls "the terms of human psychology." The problem and proposed solution are stated in a most telling passage:

> The most "objective" observer cannot escape drawing analogies with his own psychological processes. Language itself forces us to use terms borrowed from our own experience. We speak of postures of "fright," expressions of "rage" and the like. It is easier to avoid such analogies in lower animals who are farther from us in the system. Surely no objective observer has ever associated the attacking reaction of a termite warrior with fury, or the defense pattern of a sea-urchin with fright.
>
> But it would be idle quibbling to throw out the whole terminology of human psychology when describing animal behavior. However, these terms

should always be used in the same sense. Biology has had to coin words to describe the psychological behavior of lower animals, since there were none in the vocabulary. These words are used consistently in the same strictly limited sense that their initial user gave them. . . .

In using observations that others have made, we meet with another difficulty. Some people use terms of human psychology only where they see true homologies, others apply them even where the analogy is only an apparent one. When a shrimp's antennae touch the tentacles of a sea-anemone, we may describe its escape reaction by saying, "Now it is scared." Or, when a young male bird cannot quite utter his courting call yet, we may say, "Now he wants to say something and can't yet." But these remarks are made in quotes, whereas many observers (even psychologically trained ones) often put such statements on paper without making it clear whether they are meant with or without quotes. (1957a: 92–93)

Lorenz's remedy against the infiltration of psychological terms in accounts of animal behavior is the regulation of language. The most seminal facet of this regulation is the recommendation to deploy a technical vocabulary, to be used in a uniform and undeviating manner. A corollary device to the establishment of a technical vocabulary is the textual qualification of mental language that cannot be impeached; he thus writes that certain remarks should be "made in quotes." Lorenz accedes to the skeptical premise that psychological processes are invisible and unverifiable; he deems terms such as *fright, rage,* and *fury* to be problematic and locates their origin in mere analogies with human psychological processes. Lorenz thus takes language to battle, for it must be molded to comply to the watershed between psychology and behavior if it does not do so of its own accord.

Lorenz's struggle with language is representative of a problematic that has been ongoing in the behavioral sciences. He does not consider that the natural intrusion of mental terms implicates the unavoidable entanglement of mind in the observation of behavior. Far from being resources for understanding animal behavior, for Lorenz the "terms of human psychology" are more like obstacles to objective knowledge that have to be managed. The appearance of these terms, however, is also admitted as a perennial problem in that "language itself forces us to use terms borrowed from our own experience." This situation is rectified with the avoidance of mental terms or their specially defined use, the introduction of technical terms ("coining words"), and the use of quotation marks as a deflective device against the implications of mental vocabulary. At the same time, Lorenz effectively confesses that the encounter and inscription of animal life derails the successful purification of the language of conduct from psychological terminology. Otherwise put, the dam between action and behavior leaks perennially and frequently collapses. Descriptions of "pure" behavior are unavoidably contaminated by unobtrusive or conspicuous mental language. Lorenz's linguistic rectification of this problem precisely reflects that sustaining the distinction between action and behavior requires proactive and elaborate intervention, from the introduction of technical concepts, to the redefinition and qualification of defiant mental terms.

Ironically, Lorenz divulges the recalcitrance of mental language when he writes that "no objective observer has ever associated the attacking reaction of a termite warrior with *fury,* or the defense pattern of a sea-urchin with *fright*" (emphasis added). In barring the terms *fury* and *fright* as nonobjective with respect to termites and sea urchins, he is, paradoxically, also asserting that their application is possible and intelligible. Indeed, the exclusion of these terms can make sense only against the tacit backdrop of their possible application. The intelligibility of their use stems from the fact that the notion of "fury" may well be constituently associated with an "attacking reaction" of a termite "warrior," and "fright" can be part and parcel of a "defense pattern." Mental experiences like "fury" and "fright" are embedded in the sorts of states of affairs described, and thereby arise spontaneously, "forcing" their use on the writer or observer.

While censoring the use of the terms *fury* and *fright* as problematic, Lorenz does not hesitate to speak of the expressions *attacking reaction* and *defense pattern.* Yet the ideas of "attack" and "defend" do not conform to the polarization between behavior and action or, on Lorenz's terminology, to a division between behavioral and psychological. They belong to the vast class of conceptual hybrids: words—psychological terms and action verbs, in particular—with fields of meaning that encapsulate, simultaneously and indivisibly, physical form and mental attitude. *Attack* and *defend* do not simply refer to certain patterns of physical motion towards objects in the world, but also incorporate intentionality and emotions. The intentionality involved in the words is evident in their referring to "activities [that] are identified by dual criteria, the one as to their immediate characteristics, and the other as to their upshot" (Harré 1984: 99). *Attack* and *defend* implicate a directedness of action beyond their immediate contour of form, and involve affective experience by their regular association with feelings such as, for example, fury and fright. In containing facets of activity, intention, and affect, the concepts "attack" and "defend" are "impure," noncompliant with a counterfeit classification in terms of mindful action and physical movement.

The erection of the border between action and behavior is seen in Lorenz's masterful manipulation of the language. He was a leading figure in terms of setting an example and providing writing strategies for at least two generations of ethologists. In this passage, he parries the intimations of intentionality and emotion that are *built into* the concepts of "attack" and "defense": he writes of an "attacking *reaction*" and a "defense *pattern*." The attached notions of "reaction" and "pattern" alter the effect of the concepts of "attack" and "defense" by dislodging intention in two ways: (1) by cultivating the impression that the resulting total concepts are technical, rather than ordinary, and (2) by suggesting that the activities of an attacking termite and defensive sea urchin are generic behavioral packages and therefore stereotyped, as opposed to deliberately intentional and attentive.

The intimations of emotion and intention, affiliated semantically and observably with "attack" and "defense," are also neutralized ideologically with Lorenz's appeal to a hierarchy of organisms, a "system" within which certain animals are "higher" and others are "lower." The invocation of a diffusely shared conviction that fury and fright are beyond the pale of termites and sea urchins is an a priori move that has been quite widespread in the behavioral literature. "Surely no objective observer," Lorenz offhandedly remarks, "has ever associated the attacking reaction of a termite warrior with fury, or the defense pattern of a sea-urchin with fright." Lorenz here invokes the "deep-seated reluctance to grant anything remotely comparable to human mentality to 'lower' animals" (Griffin 1992: 243). Descartes, the originator of the action-behavior distinction, also called upon the example of "lower" animals—specifically inverte-brates—to argue for the improbability of the existence of an animal think-ing soul (1970: 208). "It is more probable," Descartes wagers, "that worms and flies and caterpillars move mechanically than that they all have immortal souls" (1970: 244).

The purpose of citing Lorenz's struggle with language, and revisiting Descartes as the progenitor of the modern distinction between action and behavior, is to underscore the argument—advanced throughout this book—that the distinction between two species of conduct, one originat-ing in mind (for example, Weber's "subjective meaning," Schutz's "pre-conceived purpose," or Collins' "intention") and the other deriving from physical operations upon and/or states of the body is neither a natural classification nor an unproblematic one. It is not a distinction that people settle into as self-evident or indisputable with respect to either human or animal conduct. Instead, the distinction between action and behavior calls for painstaking construction, requiring, as I have shown, particular uses of language, proactive interventions, the inclusion of background assumptions, and the systematic application of grammatical patterns, rhetorical tropes, and forms of reasoning.

As the hierarchical reasoning of Descartes and Lorenz indicates, a crucial facet of the discursive construction of the action-behavior distinction is that it is nested within a powerful paradigm of Western thought, namely, the positioning of animals according to the linear, altitudinal metaphor of higher-to-lower. This view is a ready-made register that Wittgenstein characterizes in the following terms:

> The evolution of the higher animals and of man, and the awakening of consciousness at a particular level. The picture is something like this: though the ether is filled with vibrations the world is dark. But one day man opens his seeing eye, and there is light.
>
> What this language primarily describes is a picture. What is to be done with the picture, how it is to be used, is still obscure. Quite clearly, however, it must be explored if we want to understand the sense of what we are saying. But the picture seems to spare us this work: it already points to a particular use. This is how it takes us in. (1958: 184)

The idea of a system of organisms pictured as a vertical scale with insects (and invertebrates, in general) at the lower end and the so-called higher animals and man at the upper end is entangled with, and reflected in, the division between behavior and action. Somewhere along the vertical continuum of animal forms a line is drawn; beneath that line there is behavior, where "the world is dark," and above that line there is action, where the "seeing eye is open and there is light." Mental phenomena are the prerogatives of "higher" animals—epitomized, of course, by man—while being either absent or barely nascent in the "lower" animals.

In thinking about the marvelous world of animals, this picture is an impediment to the imagination: it spares us the work and takes us in, for it is readily available, familiar, and self-serving. The hierarchical regime of higher-to-lower is ready-made and often unquestioned, and, in setting humans apart from the animals, it has fueled our self-importance and propped our thoughtless and destructive relationship with the natural world.

Notes

Introduction

1. This study does not examine works of comparative psychology. In this latter tradition, animal behavior has been studied in laboratory settings, with an interest in the range of behavior modification and learning. I focus on field studies, which investigate the behavior of animals in their natural environments.

Chapter One

1. See Descartes's *Philosophical Letters* (1981) for his explicit denouncements of the existence of animal mind.

2. For the purposes of flow, citations have been omitted. Citations can be found in Crist 1996, which is a separately published version of this chapter.

3. See, for example, Gould and Gould 1982. On the a priori regard of insects, and invertebrates generally, as "mindless automata," see Donald Griffin's critical comments (1992).

4. The ethologist Colin Beer also criticizes Ghiselin's view that Darwin's anthropomorphism was merely metaphorical. Beer states that "this reading cannot be sustained when Darwin was expressly seeking to establish continuities between animal and human mental faculties" (1992: 72).

5. Darwin defines sexual selection as "depend[ing] on the advantage which certain individuals have over other individuals of the same sex and species in exclusive relation to reproduction" (1981, 1: 256). Traits perpetuated and amplified through sexual selection do not contribute to survival, but appear solely in connection to reproductive advantage; examples are antlers or horns used in fighting contests during the breeding season, or ornamental structures that attract mates, like the elaborate plumage of certain birds.

6. Griffin (1984: 41; 1992: 254) observes that behavioral scientists often assume that if a behavior is instinctual (or, in contemporary terminology, "genetically programmed"), then it cannot also be conscious. Criticizing this view, he maintains that "the customary assumption that if some behavior has been genetically programmed, it cannot be guided by conscious thinking, is not supported by any solid evidence" (1992: 254).

7. Darwin did not reserve the concepts of love, fear, desire, and so on for mammals alone.

8. While Darwin himself rarely uses terms like *marriage*, which denote specifically human institutions, he sometimes cites such expressions from other natural-

ists and informants. Elsewhere he writes of a "wife" among crustaceans (1981, 1: 334) and of a "concubine" among canaries (1981, 1: 270).

9. Adaptationism is a superfunctionalist tendency to seek to identify adaptive functions for whatever traits or behaviors are examined. The adaptationist proclivity of much neo-Darwinian thinking has been criticized by Stephen Jay Gould and Richard Lewontin for its one-sidedness as explanatory strategy and for its story-inventing, speculative status (1986).

10. Romanes' 1882 work *Animal Intelligence* essentially consists of a collection of anecdotes—stories documenting animals' (sometimes astounding) abilities. In compiling this type of document of intelligence in the animal world, Romanes apparently did not carefully sort through the anecdotes he gathered from various sources. The attack and subsequent disparagement of the anecdotal method were in large part a backlash to Romanes' work (see Boakes 1984).

11. The naturalist Len Howard explicitly makes this connection, which is also reflected in the titles of her wonderful works *Birds as Individuals* (1953) and *Living with Birds* (1956). She describes the behaviors of individual birds and narrates many anecdotes, repeatedly emphasizing and demonstrating how markedly individuals of the same species differ in their behaviors, capacities, and temperament. Her approach is a biographical description of individual wild birds that lived in her garden and house.

12. This is not to suggest that Darwin accepted *any* anecdote as reliable. It appears that he regarded the story of the birds feeding their blind companions as truthful, since he had three different anecdotal sources—about pelicans, crows, and a cock—corroborating this particular behavior.

13. Skeptics have invoked this type of thinking—which is both reflective and language-bound—to justify their doubts regarding the existence of animal mind. The influential social psychologist George Herbert Mead submitted this argument in defending the view that "mind" exists only as a consequence of language, which only human beings possess. Mead maintained that "only in terms of gestures as significant symbols is the existence of mind or intelligence possible; for only in terms of gestures which are significant symbols can thinking—which is simply an internalized or implicit conversation of the individual with himself by means of such gestures—take place" (1962: 47).

14. In a similar vein, the philosopher Ludwig Wittgenstein writes of "the expression, the behavior, of considering. Of what do we say: It is considering something? Of a human being, sometimes of a beast. . . . One sign of considering is hesitating in what you do" (1980: para. 561). Of course, pausing before action is neither a necessary nor a sufficient condition of thinking, reasoning, considering, and so forth.

Chapter Two

1. See Schutz 1962: 312–26. For a systematic and incisive critique of the idea of "subjective meaning as private," see the work of Jeff Coulter (1979, 1983a, 1987, 1989).

2. This conception of the lifeworld follows ideas developed in the phenome-nological and ethnomethodological traditions of sociology, in particular, the works of Schutz (1962, 1967), Garfinkel (1967), and Sacks (1984). See also Button 1991.

3. "Indexicality" means that the precise sense of a word becomes clarified or determinate only through consideration of its context of application or reference (see Garfinkel and Sacks 1970: 348 and passim). This is the sense in which the "doorway" of a human house and the "doorway" of a wasp nest are indexically distinct expressions.

4. Charles Taylor maintains that this antithesis reflects different conceptions of knowledge, linked with different worldviews: one is the Aristotelian model, ac-cording to which the knower "participates in the being of the known object" (1987: 467), and the other is the Cartesian-representational model, which fosters a picture of the knower as "ideally disengaged" (1987: 471).

5. See the edited collection of Hollis and Lukes (1986) for an introduction into the debate between the two perspectives. Briefly put, constructivists argue that knowledge is thoroughly "man-made"—culturally relative, interest-dependent or interest-enhancing, always perspectival, and socially created. For realists knowl-edge is, or ought to be, a faithful mirror of independently existing phenomena, thereby compelling assent regardless of the intervention or influence of contingent social variables. Increasingly, scholars in the field of science and technology studies are pointing out the spurious character of this opposition (see, for example, Har-away 1988; Latour 1993; Jasanoff 1996).

6. The Peckhams' cautious approach to the question of animal mind through-out their work is underscored in the humorous quip with which they close their book. They write: "'It hath been an opinion,' says Lord Bacon, 'that the French are wiser than they seem, while the Spaniards seem wiser than they are.' We leave it to our readers to determine whether the wasps are wiser than they seem or seem wiser than they are" (1905: 306).

7. This distinction is made by Merleau-Ponty, quoted in Lynch 1993: 128.

8. See Donald Griffin, who, in advancing evidence for animal mentality, dedi-cates two chapters of his latest work to the construction of artifacts and the use of tools and special devices by animals (1992: 67–114). He refers, in fact, to this use of a pebble as a tool by the wasps of the genera *Ammophila* and *Sphex* (1992: 102–3). See also J. L. Gould and C. G. Gould's *The Animal Mind* (1994), chapter 6: "Animals as Architects."

9. On the organizational connection of sequential actions, see the conversa-tion-analytic work of Sacks (1987), Schegloff (1972), and Coulter (1983b). The empirically rigorous appreciation of the sequential, intersubjective generation of meaning in conversational interaction is a central contribution of the sociological field of conversation analysis. For an introductory discussion of conversation anal-ysis, see Heritage 1984. The edited volumes of Atkinson and Heritage (1984) and Button and Lee (1987) are collections of excellent papers in this field.

10. The analogy is borrowed from Wittgenstein 1980: para. 437.

11. Donald Culross Peattie titles his chapter on Fabre "The Epic of the Com-

monplace" (1938). On Jean Henri Fabre's work and life, as well as his original contributions to knowledge about insect life and his pioneering use of experimentation in behavioral studies, see also Legros 1913; Teale 1991.

CHAPTER THREE

1. Other influential naturalists predating the classical ethologists are Maurice Maeterlinck (1901), Julian Huxley (1914), Henry Eliot Howard (1964), and Edmund Selous (1931). On the early history of behavioral science and the emergence of classical ethology, see the work of the historian of science Richard W. Burkhardt Jr. (1981, 1983, 1988, 1990).

2. Thus while a mechanomorphic language does not *entail* a commitment to a mechanistic philosophy of animal behavior, there is certainly an affinity between the two. Importantly, mechanomorphic representations can work as rhetorical support and confirmation of a mechanistic perspective.

3. In the past two decades or so, with the writings of Donald Griffin and the subsequent development of the field of cognitive ethology, behavioral researchers have begun to question the philosophical and empirical sensibility of defending an a priori denial of animal mind and eschewing mental language even when it naturally or compellingly suggests itself. See Griffin 1976, 1981, 1984, 1992; Walker 1983; Ristau 1991; Bekoff 1993, 1995; Bekoff and Allen 1992; Bekoff and Jamieson 1990.

4. Though behaviorists are thought of as emphasizing environmental influences on organisms, J. B. Watson also conceived of stimuli as both external and internal; by internal stimuli he meant "physiological." Thus he writes that "the whole mass of visceral, temperature, muscular and glandular stimuli, both conditioned and unconditioned, present inside the body, are just as truly objects of stimulation as are chairs and tables. They constitute . . . man's . . . internal environment" (1970: 198).

5. The idea of "meaning-blind" is borrowed from Wittgenstein (e.g., 1980: paras. 198, 344).

6. For the connection between verbs and the imputation of agency, see Davidson 1980, especially essay 6.

7. This causal efficacy does not make ethological accounts equivalent to the behaviorist view, since ethologists additionally presuppose a minimal inner physiological, energetic action-specific readiness for the behavior.

8. This expression is from Martin Heidegger, who writes: "We ponder the question, 'What about language itself?' . . . We ask, 'In what way does language occur as language?' We answer: '*Language speaks*'" (1971: 190).

CHAPTER FOUR

1. The term is inspired by Harold Garfinkel's analysis of how "models of men" theories—namely, grand-scale sociological or psychological accounts of human action—tend to portray human beings as "judgmental dopes" who blindly enact

roles, pursue interests, or follow standardized courses of action as a consequence of social causal factors of which they are ostensibly unaware (1967: 66ff.). There is, arguably, a strong relationship between how animal life is conceptualized in Western discourses and how animals are treated or used in Western societies (see Noske 1989). With the idea that animals are "disempowered," I allude to this connection. In this work, however, I do not look at the political issues regarding the status of animals. I refer to the "objectification" of animals in an epistemological sense and not a political one, although the two are obviously not disconnected.

2. While I focus on sociobiology, much of the analysis also applies to the contemporary field of behavioral ecology. Behavioral ecology and sociobiology are sister disciplines, being in agreement on central theoretical tenets and methodological approaches to animal life. Indeed, certain authors refer to the two disciplines interchangeably (for example, Barlow 1989; Krebs 1985). Both are part of the contemporary neo-Darwinian synthesis sharing the assumption that, insofar as behaviors have a genetic component, then, given their prior subjection to the shaping force of natural selection, they are expected to maximize the individual organism's fitness (see Krebs and Davies 1991).

3. The transition from an ethological conception of behavior to a contemporary sociobiological and behavioral-ecological approach has occurred smoothly and almost unnoticeably. The transition was mediated especially by work in the mid-1960s and early 1970s on "inclusive fitness" and evolutionary theory (Hamilton 1964; Williams 1992; Trivers 1978; Maynard-Smith 1975). Contemporary behavioral thinking gives prominent place to the concept of the gene and its corollary theoretical context of ultimate causation. "Ethology" continues to be the field of biological inquiry into animal behavior, but many of the theoretical concepts developed by classical ethologists are largely absent or deemphasized in contemporary works. The leading journal *Ethology and Sociobiology* is a genuine reflection of the present-day assimilation and nonantagonistic relation of the two fields. In a paper titled "Has Sociobiology Killed Ethology or Revitalized It?" George Barlow discusses certain of the differences between the fields, but argues that ultimately there is no sharp distinction between ethology and sociobiology and "the [scientific] articles one sees today reflect this blurring of boundaries" (1989: 35, 21).

4. The relationship between sociobiology and anthropomorphism is more complicated, however. As will be discussed, one recurrently encountered critique of animal sociobiology, coming from those who object to human sociobiology in particular, is its "anthropomorphic" language.

5. The idea that the rhetorical use of language is an "underhanded" means of persuasion in science is increasingly recognized as indefensible by philosophers, sociologists, and historians of science. On the contrary, the artful use of language is an integral component of scientific argumentation, and rhetoric and objectivity are not, necessarily, in tension. See Latour 1987; Nelson, Megill, and McCloskey 1987; Myers 1990; Dear 1991; Locke 1992; Krips, McGuire, and Melia 1995; Gross 1996.

6. See Habermas 1981, especially Part II, "Max Weber's Theory of Rationalization."

7. The open-endedness of the economic idiom is perhaps most vividly revealed in the informal discourse of sociobiologists. To give an example, in a sociobiological class lecture on bird song that I attended, the lecturer spoke of female birds choosing their mates on the basis of "real estate" considerations—that is, the quality of territory defended by the male—generally preferring "high-rent" districts. The limits of economic talk are the limits of any behavioral investigator's imagination.

8. With respect to human life, Habermas has described the analogous effect as the form of life promoted by purposive-rationality—oriented toward the acquisition of status and wealth—colonizing the lifeworld of communicative action. See Habermas 1987, especially Part VI, "System and Lifeworld."

9. Kennedy is particularly set against developments in the field of cognitive ethology. See Crist 1994 for a review of Kennedy's *The New Anthropomorphism.*

10. Behavioral scientists themselves often justify their use of language in precisely this way. An example from Robert Trivers illustrates this. He writes that "to discuss the problems that confront paired individuals ostensibly cooperating in a joint parental effort, I choose the language of strategy and decision, as if each individual contemplated in strategic terms the decisions it ought to make at each instant in order to maximize its reproductive success. This language is chosen purely for convenience to explore the adaptations one might expect natural selection to favor" (1978b: 64).

11. The idea of "commonsense knowledge" is based on discussions from Garfinkel (1967, especially chapter 2) and Schutz (1962). Commonsense knowledge is neither a clearly circumscribed body of knowledge nor an explicitly articulated one, but rather comprises diffuse, culturally available, and heterogeneously yet widely distributed beliefs, practices, interpretations, and expectancies that are routinely alluded to, deployed, and relied upon in everyday life.

12. Although Wilson also presents scenarios according to which spite might have evolved (1975: 119).

13. On this level sociobiology is conducive to the sort of elision of mentality referred to as "methodological behaviorism" in philosophical terminology (Sober 1993: chap. 7). Mental tropes are not explicitly denied—by ideology or mechanistic frameworks—but simply assigned no work in the production of behavior. What this means is that the analysis does not call upon "inner states" as sources of behavioral patterns, but accounts for the latter in theoretical terms. Methodological behaviorism does not deny the possible operation of mental forces, but purports to remain agnostic toward their existence.

CHAPTER FIVE

1. See also Tinbergen 1960: 113; Grier 1984: 282; Wilson 1975: 225–26.

2. "By 'recipient design,'" write conversation analysts Sacks, Schegloff, and Jefferson, "we refer to a multitude of respects in which the talk by a party in a

conversation is constructed or designed in ways which display an orientation and sensitivity to the particular other(s) who are the co-participants" (1974: 727). See Crist 1997 for a detailed discussion on how interaction on the model of conversational recipient design can illuminate animal expression. Among conversation-analytic writings that show the interactional finesse of human conversation are Jefferson 1987; Schegloff 1984; Schegloff and Sacks 1974. For a cognate view of animals as mutually negotiating their relations and interactions, see Strum and Latour 1987.

3. The term *translation* is borrowed from Callon 1986.

4. See Coulter 1991; Rubinstein 1977.

5. The idea of the perlocutionary effect of descriptions of animal life is discussed in the next chapter.

CHAPTER SIX

1. See also the critique of the action-behavior division in the analysis of Oskar Pfungst's construction of Clever Hans (Crist 1997).

2. Thus, people who live or work with animals find "species solipsism" untenable. See Arluke and Sanders 1996; Serpell 1986.

Bibliography

Arluke, Arnold, and Clint Sanders
1996 *Regarding animals.* Philadelphia: Temple University Press.

Asquith, Pamela J.
1984 The inevitability and utility of anthropomorphism in description of primate behaviour. In R. Harré and V. Reynolds, eds., *The meaning of primate signals.* Cambridge: Cambridge University Press.

Atkinson, J. M., and John Heritage, eds.
1984 *Structures of social action: Studies in conversation analysis.* Cambridge: Cambridge University Press.

Austin, J. L.
1962 *How to do things with words.* Cambridge: Harvard University Press.

Barash, David
1979 *The whisperings within.* New York: Harper and Row.

Barlow, George W.
1989 Has sociobiology killed ethology or revitalized it? In P.P.G. Bateson and P. H. Klopfer, eds., *Whither ethology.* Perspectives in ethology, vol. 8. New York: Plenum.

Barnett, Samuel A.
1958 The "expression of emotions." In S. A. Barnett, ed., *A century of Darwin.* New York: Books for Libraries Press.
1963 *The rat: A study in behaviour.* Chicago: Aldine.

Beer, Colin
1992 Conceptual issues in cognitive ethology. In P.J.B. Slater, ed., *Advances in the study of behavior.* San Diego: Academic Press.

Bekoff, Marc
1993 Common sense, cognitive ethology and evolution. In P. Cavalieri and P. Singer, eds., *The great ape project.* London: Fourth Estate.
1995 Cognitive ethology and the explanation of nonhuman animal behavior. In H. Roitblat and J. A. Meyer, eds., *Comparative approaches to cognitive science.* Cambridge: MIT Press.

Bekoff, Marc, and Colin Allen
1992 Intentional icons: Towards an evolutionary cognitive ethology. *Ethology* 91: 31–16.

Bekoff, Marc, and Dale Jamieson, eds.
1990 *Interpretation and explanation in the study of animal behavior.* Boulder: Westview.

231

Bennett, J.
1976 *Linguistic behaviour.* London: Cambridge University Press.
Bleier, Ruth
1985 Biology and women's policy: A view from the biological sciences. In V. Sapiro, ed., *Women, biology, and public policy.* Beverly Hills: Sage Publications.
Boakes, Robert
1984 *From Darwin to behaviorism: Psychology and the minds of animals.* Cambridge: Cambridge University Press.
Burkhardt, Richard W. Jr.
1981 On the emergence of ethology as a scientific discipline. *Conspectus of History* 1(7): 62–81.
1983 The development of an evolutionary ethology. In D. S. Bendall, ed., *Evolution from molecules to men.* Cambridge: Cambridge University Press.
1985 Darwin on animal behavior and evolution. In D. Kohn, ed., *The Darwinian heritage.* Princeton: Princeton University Press.
1988 Charles Ottis Whitman, Wallace Craig, and the biological study of animal behavior in the United States, 1898–1925. In R. Rainger et al., eds., *The American development of biology.* Philadelphia: University of Pennsylvania Press.
1990 Theory and practice in naturalistic studies of behavior prior to ethology's establishment as a scientific discipline. In M. Bekoff and D. Jamieson, eds., *Interpretation and explanation in the study of animal behavior.* Boulder: Westview.
1992 Huxley and the rise of ethology. In C. K. Waters and A. Van Helden, eds., *Julian Huxley: Biologist and statesman of science.* Houston: Rice University Press.
Button, Graham, ed.
1991 *Ethnomethodology and the human sciences.* Cambridge: Cambridge University Press.
Button, Graham, and John R. E. Lee, eds.
1987 *Talk and social organization.* Clevedon: Multilingual Matters.
Byrne, R. W., and A. Whiten
1988 *Machiavellian intelligence: Social expertise and the evolution of intellect in monkeys, apes, and humans.* Oxford: Oxford University Press.
Callon, Michel
1986 Some elements of a sociology of translation: Domestication of the scallops and the fishermen of St Brieuc Bay. In J. Law, ed., *Power, action, and belief.* London: Routledge and Kegan.
Carruthers, Peter
1989 Brute experience. *Journal of Philosophy* 86: 258–269.
Cavell, Stanley
1976 *Must we mean what we say?* Cambridge: Cambridge University Press.

Clutton-Brock, T. H., F. E. Guinness, and S. D. Albon
1982 *Red deer: Behavior and ecology of two sexes.* Chicago: University of Chicago Press.
Clutton-Brock, T. H., and Paul H. Harvey, eds.
1978 *Readings in sociobiology.* San Francisco: W. H. Freeman and Company.
Collins, Harry
1990 *Artificial experts: Social knowledge and intelligent machines.* Cambridge: MIT Press.
Coulter, Jeff
1979 *The social construction of mind: Studies in ethnomethodology and linguistic philosophy.* London: Macmillan.
1983a *Rethinking cognitive theory.* London: Macmillan.
1983b Contingent and a priori structures in sequential analysis. *Human Studies* 6: 361–76.
1987 Wittgenstein and ethnomethodology. Transcripts from course lectures, Boston University.
1989 *Mind in action.* Atlantic Highlands, NJ: Humanities Press International.
1991 Cognition: "Cognition" in an ethnomethodological mode. In G. Button, ed., *Ethnomethodology and the human sciences.* Cambridge: Cambridge University Press.
Crist, Eileen
1994 Review essay: Donald Griffin's *Animal minds,* John S. Kennedy's *The new anthropomorphism,* and Barbara Noske's *Humans and other animals. Society and Animals* 2(1): 77–88.
1996 Darwin's anthropomorphism: An argument for animal-human continuity. *Advances in Human Ecology* 5: 33–83.
1997 From questions to stimuli, from answers to reactions: Case of Clever Hans. *Semiotica* 113(1–2): 1–42.
Darwin, Charles
1958 [1892] *The autobiography of Charles Darwin and selected letters,* ed. Francis Darwin. New York: Dover Publications Inc.
1964 [1859] *On the origin of species.* Cambridge: Harvard University Press.
1965 [1872] *The expression of emotions in man and animals.* Chicago: University of Chicago Press.
1981 [1871] *The descent of man and selection in relation to sex.* 2 vols. Princeton: Princeton University Press.
1985 [1881] *The formation of vegetable mould through the action of worms, with observations on their habits.* Chicago: University of Chicago Press.
Davidson, Donald
1980 *Essays on actions and events.* Oxford: Clarendon Press.
Dawkins, Richard, and John R. Krebs
1978 Animal signals: Information or manipulation? In J. R. Krebs and N. B. Davies, eds., *Behavioural ecology: An evolutionary approach.* Oxford: Blackwell Scientific Publications.

Dear, Peter, ed.
1991   *The literary structure of scientific argument.* Philadelphia: University of Pennsylvania Press.

Degler, Carl N.
1991   *In search of human nature: Decline and revival of Darwinism in American social thought.* Oxford: Oxford University Press.

Dennett, Daniel C.
1987   *The intentional stance.* Cambridge: MIT Press.

Descartes, René
1981   *Descartes: Philosophical letters* [1629–1649], trans. and ed. A. Kenny. Minneapolis: University of Minnesota Press.

Dewsbury, Donald A.
1984   *Comparative psychology in the twentieth century.* Stroudsburg, PA: Hutchinson Ross.

Fabre, Jean Henri
1915   *The hunting wasps.* New York: Dodd, Mead and Company.
1918   *The wonders of instinct.* New York: Century.
1991   *The insect world of J. Henri Fabre.* Boston: Beacon.

Fisher, John A.
1990   The myth of anthropomorphism. In M. Bekoff and D. Jamieson, eds., *Interpretation and explanation in the study of animal behavior.* Boulder: Westview.
1991   Disambiguating anthropomorphism: An interdisciplinary review. In P.P.G. Bateson and P. H Klopfer, eds., *Human understanding and animal awareness.* Perspectives in ethology, vol. 9. New York: Plenum.

Garfinkel, Harold
1967   *Studies in ethnomethodology.* Cambridge: Polity.

Garfinkel, Harold, and Harvey Sacks
1970   On formal structures of practical action. In J. C. McKinney and E. A. Tiryakian, eds., *Theoretical sociology: Perspectives and developments.* New York: Appleton Century Crofts.

Ghiselin, Michael T.
1969   *The triumph of the Darwinian method.* Berkeley: University of California Press.

Goodwin, Charles
1979   The interactive construction of a sentence in natural conversation. In G. Psathas, ed., *Everyday language: Studies in ethnomethodology.* New York: Irvington.

Gould, James L.
1982   *Ethology: Mechanisms and evolution of behavior.* New York: Norton.

Gould, James L., and Carol G. Gould
1982   The insect mind: Physics or metaphysics? In D. R. Griffin, ed., *Animal mind—human mind.* Berlin: Springer-Verlag.

Gould, Stephen J. Biological potentiality vs. Biological determinism. In *Ever Since Darwin.* New York: W. W. Norton and Company.

Gould, Stephen J., and Richard Lewontin
1986 [1979] The spandrels of San Marco and the Panglossian paradigm: A critique of the adaptationist programme. In J.F.A. Tranniello, M. P. Scott, and F. Wasserman, eds., *Readings in animal behavior.* Lexington, MA: Ginn.

Grice, H. P.
1957 Meaning. *Philosophical Review* 66: 377–88.

Grier, James W.
1984 *Biology of animal behavior.* St. Louis: Times Mirror/Mosby College.

Griffin, Donald
1976 *The question of animal awareness.* New York: Rockefeller University Press.
1984 *Animal thinking.* Cambridge: Harvard University Press.
1992 *Animal minds.* Chicago: University of Chicago Press.

Griffin, Donald, ed.
1981 *Animal mind—human mind.* Berlin: Springer-Verlag.

Gross, Alan G.
1996 [1990] *The rhetoric of science.* Cambridge: Harvard University Press.

Habermas, Jürgen
1981 *The theory of communicative action,* vol. 1: *Reason and the rationalization of society.* Boston: Beacon.
1987 *The theory of communicative action,* vol. 2: *Lifeworld and system: A critique of functionalist reason.* Boston: Beacon.

Hacking, Ian
1991 A tradition of natural kinds. *Philosophical Studies* 61: 109–26.

Hamilton, W. D.
1964 The genetical evolution of social behaviour, I and II. *Journal of Theoretical Biology* 7: 1–52.

Hamlyn, D. W.
1981 Behavior. In V. C. Chappell, ed., *The philosophy of mind.* New York: Dover.

Haraway, Donna
1988 Situated knowledges: The science question in feminism and the privilege of partial perspective. *Feminist Studies* 14: 575–99.

Harré, Rom
1984 Vocabularies and theories. In R. Harré and V. Reynolds, eds., *The meaning of primate signals.* Cambridge: Cambridge University Press.

Hearne, Vicki
1982 *Adam's task: Calling animals by name.* New York: Vintage.

Heath, Christian
1984 Talk and recipiency: Sequential organization in speech and body movement. In J. M. Atkinson and J. Heritage, eds., *Structures of social action: Studies in conversation analysis.* Cambridge: Cambridge University Press.

Heidegger, Martin
1971 *Poetry, language, thought.* New York: Harper Colophon.

Heritage, John
  1984 *Garfinkel and ethnomethodology.* Cambridge: Polity.
Hollis, Martin, and Steven Lukes
  1986 [1982] *Rationality and relativism.* Cambridge: MIT Press.
Howard, Henry Eliot
  1964 [1920] *Territory in bird life.* New York: Atheneum.
Howard, Len
  1953 *Birds as individuals.* New York: Doubleday
  1956 *Living with birds.* London: Collins.
Hrdy, Sarah Blaffer
  1981 *The woman that never evolved.* Cambridge: Harvard University Press.
Huxley, Julian
  1914 The courtship habits of the Great Crested Grebe (Podiceps cristatus);
        with an addition to the theory of sexual selection. *Proceedings of the
        Zoological Society of London* 35: 491–562.
Huxley, Thomas H.
  1874 On the hypothesis that animals are automata, and its history. In *Col-
        lected essays,* vol. 1. London: Macmillan.
Jasanoff, Sheila
  1996 Beyond epistemology: Relativism and engagement in the politics of sci-
        ence. *Social Studies of Science* 26: 393–418.
Jefferson, Gail
  1987 On exposed and embedded correction in conversation. In G. Button and
        J.R.E. Lee, eds., *Talk and social organization.* Clevedon: Multilingual
        Matters.
Keller, Evelyn Fox
  1983 *A feeling for the organism: Life and work of Barbara McClintock.* New
        York: W. H. Freeman.
Kennedy, John S.
  1992 *The new anthropomorphism.* Cambridge: Cambridge University Press.
Kitcher, Philip
  1987 *Vaulting ambition: Sociobiology and the quest for human nature.* Cam-
        bridge: MIT Press.
  1995 The cognitive functions of scientific rhetoric. In H. Kripps, J. E. Mc-
        Guire, and T. Melia, eds., *Science, reason, and rhetoric.* Pittsburgh: Uni-
        versity of Pittsburgh Press.
Krebs, John R.
  1985 Sociobiology ten years on. *New Scientist* 1476: 40–43.
Krebs, John R., and Nicholas B. Davies, eds.
  1991 *Behavioural ecology. An evolutionary approach,* 3rd ed. Oxford: Black-
        well Scientific Publications.
Krebs, John R., and Richard Dawkins
  1984 Animal signals: Mind-reading and manipulation. In J. R. Krebs and
        N. B. Davies, eds., *Behavioural ecology: An evolutionary approach,*
        2nd ed. Oxford: Blackwell Scientific Publications.

Kripps, Henry, J. E. McGuire, and Trevor Melia, eds.
1995 *Science, reason, and rhetoric.* Pittsburgh: University of Pittsburgh Press.

Latour, Bruno
1987 *Science in action.* Milton Keynes: Open University Press.
1993 *We have never been modern.* Cambridge: Harvard University Press.

Legros, George V.
1913 *Fabre: Poet of science.* New York: Century.

Locke, David
1992 *Science as writing.* New Haven: Yale University Press.

Lorenz, Konrad
1950 The comparative method in studying innate behaviour patterns. *Symposia of the Society of Experimental Biology* 4: 221–68.
1957a [1935] Companionship in bird life. In C. H. Schiller and K. S. Lashley, eds., *Instinctive behavior.* New York: International University Press.
1957b [1937] The nature of instinct. In C. H. Schiller and K. S. Lashley, eds., *Instinctive behavior.* New York: International University Press.
1965 Preface. In Charles Darwin, *The expression of emotion in man and animals.* Chicago: University of Chicago Press.
1971 [1963] Do animals undergo subjective experience? In *Studies in animal and human behaviour,* vol. 1. Cambridge: Harvard University Press.

Lorenz, Konrad, and Nikolaas Tinbergen
1957 Taxis and instinctive action in the egg-retrieving behaviour of the Greylag goose. In C. H. Schiller and K. S. Lashley, eds., *Instinctive behavior.* New York: International University Press.

Lynch, Michael
1993 *Scientific practice and ordinary action: Ethnomethodology and social studies of science.* Cambridge: Cambridge University Press.

Maynard-Smith, John
1975 *The theory of evolution.* Harmondsworth: Penguin Books

Maeterlinck, Maurice
1901 *The life of the bee.* New York: Dodd.

Mayr, Ernst
1982 *The growth of biological thought: Diversity, evolution and inheritance.* Cambridge: Belknap Press.
1984 Typological versus population thinking. In E. Sober, ed., *Conceptual issues in evolutionary biology.* Cambridge: MIT Press.

Mead, George Herbert
1962 [1934] *Mind, self, and society: From the standpoint of a social behaviorist.* Chicago: University of Chicago Press.

Morgan, Lewis H.
1965 [1868] *The American beaver: A classic of natural history and ecology.* [Original title: *American beaver and his works.*] New York: Dover.

Myers, Greg
1990 *Writing biology: Texts in the social construction of scientific knowledge.* Madison: University of Wisconsin Press.

Nagel, Thomas
1981 [1974] What is it like to be a bat? In D. R. Hofstadter and D. C. Dennett, eds., *The mind's I*. New York: Basic Books.
1986 *The view from nowhere*. New York: Oxford University Press.
Nelson, John S., A. Megill, and Donald McCloskey, eds.
1987 *The rhetoric of the human sciences: Language and argument in scholarship and public affairs*. Madison: University of Wisconsin Press.
Noske, Barbara
1989 *Humans and other animals*. London: Pluto.
Peattie, Donald C.
1938 Fabre and the epic commonplace. In *Green laurels: Lives and achievements of the great naturalists*. New York: Garden City Publishing Company.
Peckham, George, and Elizabeth Peckham
1905 *Wasps: Solitary and social*. Westminster: Archibald Constable and Company.
Pfungst, Oskar
1911 *Clever Hans (the horse of Mr. von Osten): A contribution to experimental animal and human psychology*. New York: Henry Holt.
Polanyi, Michael
1962 [1958] *Personal knowledge: Towards a post-critical philosophy*. Chicago: University of Chicago Press.
Reynolds, Vernon
1986 Primate social thinking. In J. G. Else and P. C. Lee, eds., *Primate ontogeny, cognition and social behavior*. Cambridge: Cambridge University Press.
Richards, Robert J.
1987 *Darwin and the emergence of evolutionary theories of mind and behavior*. Chicago: University of Chicago Press.
Ristau, Carolyn A., ed.
1991 *Cognitive ethology*. Hillsdale, NJ: Lawrence Erlbaum Associates.
Romanes, George J.
1882 *Animal intelligence*. London: Kegan Paul, Trench.
Rubinstein, David
1977 The concept of action in the social sciences. *Journal of the Theory of Social Behaviour* 7(2): 209–36.
Sacks, Harvey
1972 On the analysability of stories by children. In J. J. Gumperz and D. Hymes, eds., *Directions in sociolinguistics: The ethnography of communication*. New York: Holt, Rinehart and Winston.
1984 Notes on methodology. In J. M. Atkinson and John Heritage, eds., *Structures of social action: Studies in conversation analysis*. Cambridge: Cambridge University Press.
1987 On the preferences for agreement and contiguity in sequences in conver-

sation. In G. Button and J.R.E. Lee, eds., *Talk and social organization*. Clevedon: Multilingual Matters.

1992   [1966] The baby cried. The mommy picked it up. Lectures 1 and 2. In *Lectures on conversation*, ed. G. Jefferson, 236–66. Cambridge: Cambridge University Press.

Sacks, Harvey, Emmanuel Schegloff, and Gail Jefferson
1974   A simplest systematics for the organization of turn-taking for conversation. *Language* 50(4): 696–735.

Sahlins, Marshall
1976   *The use and abuse of biology. An anthropological critique of sociobiology*. Ann Arbor: University of Michigan Press.

Schegloff, Emmanuel A.
1972   Sequencing in conversational openings. In J. J. Gumperz and D. Hymes, eds., *Directions in sociolinguistics: The ethnography of communication*. New York: Holt, Rinehart and Winston.

1984   On some questions and ambiguities in conversation. In J. M. Atkinson and J. Heritage, eds., *Structures of social action: Studies in conversation analysis*. Cambridge: Cambridge University Press.

Schegloff, Emmanuel A., and Harvey Sacks
1974   Opening up closings. In R. Turner, ed., *Ethnomethodology: Selected readings*. Harmondsworth: Penguin.

Schutz, Alfred
1962   *Collected papers: Problem of social reality*, vol. 1. The Hague: Martinus Nijhoff.

1967   *The phenomenology of the social world*. Chicago: Northwestern University Press.

Searle, John R.
1978   Sociobiology and the explanation of behavior. In M. Gregory and A. Silvers, eds., *Sociobiology and human nature*. San Francisco: Jossey-Bass.

Selous, Edmund
1931   *Thought transference (or what?) in birds*. London: Constable and Company.

Serpell, James
1986   *In the company of animals: A study of human-animal relationships*. Oxford: Basil Blackwell.

Shapin, Steven, and Simon Schaffer
1985   *Leviathan and the air-pump: Hobbes, Boyle, and the experimental life*. Princeton: Princeton University Press.

Silk, Joan B.
1987   Social behavior in evolutionary perspective. In B. B. Smuts et al., eds., *Primate societies*. Chicago: University of Chicago Press.

Smith, Roger
1990   Behaviourism. In R. C. Olby et al., eds., *Companion to the history of modern science*. London: Routledge.

Sober, Elliott
1993 *Philosophy of biology.* Boulder: Westview.
Strum, Shirley S., and Bruno Latour
1987 Redefining the social link: From baboons to humans. *Social Science Information* 26(4): 783–802.
Taylor, Charles
1987 Overcoming epistemology. In K. Baynes, J. Bohman and T. McCarthy, eds., *After philosophy: End or transformation?* Cambridge: MIT Press.
Teale, Edwin W.
1991 Introduction. In J. Henri Fabre, *The insect world of J. Henri Fabre.* Boston: Beacon.
Thorpe, W. H.
1973 Ethology as a new branch of biology. In M. W. Fox, ed., *Readings in ethology and comparative psychology.* Monterey: Brooks/Cole.
Tinbergen, Nikolaas
1950 The hierarchical organization of nervous mechanisms underlying instinctive behaviour. *Symposia of the Society for Experimental Biology* 4: 305–12.
1960 *The herring gull's world: A study of the social behaviour of birds.* New York: Harper Torchbooks.
1972a [1942] The courtship of the Grayling *Eumenis* (=*Satyrus*) *semele* (L.). In *The animal and its world: Explorations of an ethologist (1932–1972),* vol. 1. Cambridge: Harvard University Press.
1972b [1959] Comparative studies of the behaviour of gulls (Laridae). In *The animal and its world: Explorations of an ethologist (1932–1972),* vol. 1. Cambridge: Harvard University Press.
1989 [1951] *The study of instinct.* Oxford: Clarendon.
Trivers, Robert
1978a [1971] The evolution of reciprocal altruism. In T. H. Clutton-Brock and P. H. Harvey, eds., *Readings in sociobiology.* Reading: W. H. Freeman.
1978b [1972] Parental investment and sexual selection. In T. H. Clutton-Brock and P. H. Harvey, eds., *Readings in sociobiology.* Reading: W. H. Freeman.
Toulmin, Stephen
1995 Science and the many faces of rhetoric. In Henry Kripps, J. E. McGuire, and Trevor Melia, eds., *Science, reason, and rhetoric.* Pittsburgh: University of Pittsburgh Press.
Turner, Roy, ed.
1975 *Ethnomethodology: Selected readings.* Harmondsworth: Penguin.
Von Uexkull, Jacob
1957 [1934] A stroll through the worlds of animals and men. In C. H. Schiller and K. S. Lashley, eds., *Instinctive behavior.* New York: International University Press.
Walker, Stephen
1983 *Animal thought.* London: Routledge and Kegan Paul.

Watson, John B.
1970 [1924] *Behaviorism.* New York: Norton.
Weber, Max
1964 [1947] *Max Weber: Theory of social and economic organization,* ed.
T. Parsons. New York: Free Press.
White, Alan R.
1968 Introduction. In A. R. White, ed., *The philosophy of action.* Oxford:
Oxford University Press.
Williams, George C.
1992 [1966] *Adaptation and natural selection: A critique of some current
evolutionary thought.* Princeton: Princeton University Press.
Wilson, Edward, O.
1975 *Sociobiology: New synthesis.* Cambridge: Belknap Press.
Winch, Peter
1958 *The idea of a social science.* London: Routledge and Kegan Paul.
Wittgenstein, Ludwig
1953 *Philosophical investigations.* Oxford: Basil Blackwell.
1980 *Remarks on the philosophy of psychology,* vol. 1. Chicago: University of
Chicago Press.

Index

action: authored versus caused, 38, 164,
170–72, 203; and authorship, 4, 35, 40,
74, 82–83, 87, 92–94, 98, 104, 114,
181, 189, 202; and awareness, 84; and
causation, 5, 85, 109, 112, 189, 191,
212; for the sake of pleasure, 35–36,
179; purposive-rational, 139; series versus sequence, 102, 104, 170; undecidability of meaning of, 61–71; voluntary
versus involuntary, 38, 120–21, 191.
See also lifeworld; subjectivity; time;
Verstehen
action versus behavior, 10, 202–22
adaptationism, 36, 224
altruism, 160, 161–62, 164
anecdotes, 12, 40–49, 224
animal mind: agnosticism about, 139; and
anecdotal evidence, 41, 43–49; availability of, 28; avoidance of, 12, 95, 116–18,
134, 139, 150, 164, 181–82, 185, 201,
228; body-mind dualism, 23, 28, 35, 50;
complexity of, 166; and experience, 36;
implicit attribution of, 67; and language
use, 6–7, 28, 33, 100, 116, 118, 123,
149, 166, 175, 185, 202–22; and limits
of evidence, 43, 46; Machiavellian intelligence, 138–39, 151, 159; observability
and unobservability of, 22, 33–34, 35,
95, 206; open-mindedness about, 149,
164–65; reasoning, 44–46; and sexual
selection, 18; and states of being, 32–36,
142. *See also* awareness; emotion; intentionality; skepticism; subjectivity
animals. *See* animal mind; behavioral
science
anthropomorphism: avoidance of, 12, 36,
134, 149, 156; Darwin's, 11–50; definition of, 7, 29, 83; and lifeworld, 83–86;
literal versus metaphorical, 12–13, 33,

53, 203; mock anthropomorphism, 150;
new anthropomorphism, 149–50; pejorative connotations of, 7, 14, 53–54,
133, 149–62, 200–1, 203, 209; and
sociobiology, 133–34, 149–62, 227; and
subjectivity, 29, 49, 53, 76, 90, 185; as
supervenient effect, 31–32, 83; and technical idioms, 86, 185, 201
Arluke, Arnold, 229
Asquith, Pamela, 29, 32, 157
atomism, 96, 109, 188
Austin, J. L., 207
authorship. *See* action; *see also* animal
mind
awareness, 20, 77, 84–85, 93, 104, 114,
121, 123. *See also* animal mind

Barash, David, 126–28, 133, 164
Barlow, George W., 126, 227
Barnett, Samuel, 11, 22, 24, 28–29, 84
Beer, Colin, 223
behavior. *See* action; action versus behavior; behavioral science; vacuum behavior
behavioral ecology, 227. *See also* sociobiology
behavioral science: comparative approach
to, 2, 9, 38, 89, 143–49, 153–54, 166–
201; and experimentation, 106–16;
methodology of, 89, 143–49; and objectivity, 2, 145–46, 201, 204; and statis-
tics, 134, 147, 149; theory and theory-
laden, 88, 90–95, 107, 114, 123, 181,
203. *See also* language use; realism
behaviorism. *See* comparative psychology;
stimulus-response; Watson, J. B.
Bekoff, Marc, 226
Bennett, Jonathan, 197
Bleier, Ruth, 151
Boakes, Robert, 89, 224

242